Nahma: A Gulf Polyphony

Credits

Editorial Concept:
Olivier Duport , Alan Marzo, Carl Åhnebrink (FLEE Project)

Contributors Book:
Toufic Kerbage, Marc Hobbs, Charles Stang, Talal Mattar, Abdulla al Suwaidi, Major Ali (Ali Saqar Al Suweidi), Paul Mattar, Abou Saleh, Noura Al Sayeh Holtrop, Hasan Hujairi, Talin Hazbar, Monira Al-Qadiri, Alan Marzo, Olivier Duport

Contributors Record:
Tomaga, YPY, Hieroglyphic Being, Tarek Yamani, Alan Strani, Ben Bertrand, Conny Frischauf, Aya Metwalli, Joakim, Poul Rovsing Olsen

Photographs:
Olivier Duport , Hassan Habib Touma, Henri Hänni, Arnold Heim, Georges Lusneau, Alan Marzo, Paul Mattar, Bas Princen, Moesgaard Museum

Artistic Direction:
Möbius Design Studio

Content Development:
Bureau Sepän

Translation & Proofreading:
Muhammad El-Hajj, Gabriella Seeman, Hasan Hujairi, Ruairi Collins, Daniel Lovrinov, Pierre-Eliott Rozan

Partners:
Pro-Helvetia, Institut Français, Moesgaard Museum , Musée d Ethnographie de Genève, Ambassade de France au Bahreïn, SSIF

Special thanks to:
Lene Halskov Hansen (Royal Danish Library), Neil Van Der Linden, Aisha Bilkhair (National Archives U.A.E), Chirine El Messiri (IMA), Georges Lusneau, Louise Lerche-Lerchenborg, Elizabeth Faier, Léonard Pouy, Fadi Yeni Turk, Andrea Zomboulis, Zahed Sultan, Madeleine Leclair (MEG), Océane Sailly, Umer Butt, Faissal El-Malak, Laurent Cartier, Layal Bushehri, Carl Wozniczka, Hala Mohammad al Khalifa, Mohammed Shameel, Arnaud Morand, Ghassan Chemali, Ayah al Zayat, Rahul Gudipi, Tulip Hazbar, Maurizio Salvatori, Ahmed bin Shabib, Rashid bin Shabib, Feras Mustafa, Hadeyeh Badri, Hala Al-Ani, Riem Hassan, Jaakko Viitalähde.

Typefaces:
Lyon Text, Lyon Arabic Slanted Text, 29LT Adir

ISBN:
978-2-9569677-1-2

Editorial - Shallow Waters

Alan Marzo
Olivier Duport

The sun is painting the horizon a pale yellowish tone on this afternoon of December, as several damaged dhows[1] moor on the shores of Muharraq. Stationary remnants of a different time, when the Arabian Gulf was bustling with agitation come the pearling season. Today, they provoke nothing but the indifference of the passing cars on the busy highway section leading to Manama's Airport. A perfect symbol of two worlds within a single regional reality that never fully coexisted: Oil and Pearls.

Yet, a hundred meters further, a majestic dhow is dry-docked and awaits repairs as the pearling legacy expects its long overdue return. Wounded by the invention of cultured pearls by Kokichi Mikimoto and wrecked by the discovery of oil in the region, pearling, despite retaining its prestige, never fully recovered from those blows.

On the other side of the road, a narrow path leads into the tortuous old streets of the ancient pearling hub that once was Muharraq. At night, those streets echo with polyphonic chanting and distinctive percussion. In a renovated Dar[2], one of the last few ensembles of pearl diving music gathers to celebrate the musical legacy of their ancestors.

Everybody around the Gulf knows about those sounds. An integral part of the region's identity, the music and chants of the pearl divers are the legacy of a vibrant population faced with a life of hardship on this capricious sea. Referred to as Fann al-Bahar or Fijiri, these specific musical practices greatly contributed to the local pearling heritage.

After centuries of torpor, pearls are now steadily rising in popularity, driven by advanced diving and scanning technologies, and the much-needed diversification of a monolithic economic model.

"Nahma: A Gulf Polyphony" aims to trace this legacy to its origins, to understand its contemporary evolution and challenges, in a transdisciplinary work that cross-references a plethora of figures and perspectives, explaining, describing and shaping the complex social and cultural phenomenon of pearling.

Guiding this journey, acclaimed composer and pearl diver music expert Toufic Kerbage tells us the stories and myths that paved the way for Fijiri as we know it today. By deconstructing the beliefs that led to their emergence while analyzing the structure they follow, he offers us a real dive into the essence of those chants. And who better than a Naham to give his first-hand perception of what this music means? Abou Saleh worked as lead singer on a dhow in mid-20th century Kuwait and Bahrain. In a conversation dating back to 1979, inspired by his own experience as a singer on many expeditions, he shares with researcher Paul Mattar his point of view on the vanquished era.

A major crossing point for numerous travelers and merchants, the Gulf sea quickly bore witness to an international appetite for its natural resources, pearls in particular. From a complex relationship with British rule, to the question of raising influxes of migrants, Dr. Marc Hobbs depicts how a globalized economy around pearling structured itself and prospered in dazzling proportions to the benefit of some, and to the misfortune of others. Through the scrutiny and rediscovery of numerous archives from the former regional Persian Gulf Residency[3], Hobbs deciphers a global trade between actors from the Global East and West, all uniting in the Gulf. At the crossroads of these exchanges, the Mattar family, one of the most prominent pearl merchant families in Bahrain, has been cherishing and trading natural pearls for centuries. Talal Mattar, a passionate pearl diving music player who runs the family business, shares his thoughts on local music culture while reflecting on the breakdown of the entire local pearling industry during the 20th century.

Further East, on the outskirts of the former pearl trading hub of Ras Al Khaimah, Abdullah al-Suwaidi watches over his pearl farm in the mangrove-crowned bay of Al-Rams at the very foot of the majestic Hajar Mountains. He has been the only one to break the symbolic threshold of cultivating pearls in the Gulf, which incarnates the demise of a once glorious industry. A traditional pearl diver himself, his most singular journey between scientific discoveries and innovative approaches towards the pearl industry offers an alternative perspective on the future of pearl diving.

Beyond their divergences, the strong commitment to transmit this heritage and legacy to the next generation unanimously bonds the various experts, artists and actors who took part in this project. Central to this endeavor, "Major Ali" is a former military man whose life was shaken by the first Gulf War and its terrible impact on the fragile ecosystem of the region. After this traumatic experience, the Major became the head of the Emirates Marine Environmental Group, a role through which he seeks to sensitize the new generations to their own culture while reminding them of the fragility of the environment - the oyster beds in particular. In an immersive conversation, this spiritual son of Jacques Cousteau focuses on what he perceives as challenges lying ahead to the safeguarding of oysters and their ecosystem in the region.

Cultural heritage safeguarding and preservations are difficult subjects, often leading to polarized positions. In Bahrain, Noura Al-Sayeh, director of the Pearling Path Program, speaks about her vision and strategy to honor and promote the legacy of pearl diving through the urban engineering and re-activation of Muharraq: an urban path, once at he heart of the Gulf's pearling industry. Tasked with a complex mission, the talented architect explains how she tries to fulfill her task while navigating through various challenges, among which the risk of disrupting the organic balance of communities living in the area in cities and countries more focused on modernity and technology.

While this initiative documents pearl diving and its associated culture through a psychological, sociohistorical and economic perspective, it also aims to give the floor to transmedia and conceptual artists involved in and with the Gulf region. In this context, Talin Hazbar, in her work "Leaking Pearls", explores the bottom of the sea and its evolution. Through the structure she created, plunged into the water, mimicking the journey of an oyster, she seeks to take the poll of seabeds, while using time as a central shaping tool for her marine sculptures.

The sculptures of Monira Al Qadiri are similarly shaped by time, at least, in a symbolic manner. In fact, the sophisticated and fragile pieces she created for the project seem to represent a chronologically interstitial space, between two major economically paradigmatic periods that have affected the Gulf countries: the pearl trade and the oil boom. Half pearl, half oil drills, using very hybrid and innovative colored materials, the Kuwaiti artist appears to suggest the region will have to reconcile its past and modern history to move forward.

It is this same history or, at least, the discourses on it, that Hasan Hujairi questions in both his transmedia essay and the music software he develops to transcend what he refers to as "failures". His work invites us to challenge the often too ludic approaches towards the celebration of Fijiri and the narrative on pearl diving. Inviting the reader to avoid a romantic and naive understanding of the subject, he reminds us that "the entire pearling industry and its associated cultures were built on exploitation and slavery, and yet they are publicly celebrated without acknowledgment of its darker histories".

Naturally, it is one thing to speak about a subject from various perspectives and disciplines, it is another to experience it first-hand. In order to be able to appreciate the subject in its entirety, this project includes a compiled work on the music of pearl divers consisting of undisclosed recordings by ethnomusicologist Poul Rovsing Olsen – the first person to ever record this genre. Willingly unedited, this takes inclusion on the compilation re-transcribes the intensity and meaning of the music performed by men who left their lives on shore for months on end while seeking those rare and precious pearls at sea. Influenced by cultures from around the world, the rhythms and chants were subsequently submitted to carefully selected artists who had to imagine new compositions in the form of a new sonic pearling expedition.

It is the belief of this project that the current polarized historical zeitgeist requires the establishment of inclusive, critical, cross-cultural and intergenerational dialogues. Moreover, this approach and philosophy captures the spirit of the Gulf region, and its history as a meeting point. In the words of theologist Charles Stang, analyzing what he perceives as a historical religious pluralism in the region, "this history would be to see the monks and mystics of the Gulf as part of a broader history of diversity and pluralism in the region, not surprising in fact, given that the Gulf is, among other things, a series of ports, where not only goods but ideas were traded...". In this regard, with various, and sometimes conflicting ideas and points of view, this project also questions the dynamics at stake around cultural heritage, its safeguard and promotion as well as the various patrimonialization processes at stake. "Nahma: a Gulf Polyphony" seeks to paint a large picture of the phenomenon, its history, its culture and, foremost, its music. It does this by navigating between various disciplines and mediums and avoiding a frozen approach towards this multifaceted culture.

"Did they really all risk their lives, day and night, for a glimpse of a tiny, shiny ornament? So that someday some faraway monarchs can sport them on their person, never knowing how people had literally lived and died for them to be extracted from the sea? Was it true that they were all slaves to one master - the Pearl?" The questions raised by artist Monira Al Qadiri are crucial, as they ultimately explore the notion of beauty; its ability to inspire deep, enchanted and enchanting rituals and practices; its capacity to be at the center of sometimes exploitative power dynamics; its commodification, and its place at the core of a global economic system. There, at the bottom of the sea, the shiny pearl becomes a very clear mirror, one which reflects human nature, its determinisms and addictions:

"Poor Fishermen! Dupes at first, cripples later, such is their lot. As for Ya Māl... (O, Fortune!), they sing it while others take it". (Albert Londres, Pearl Fishers, 1931)

[1] The generic name of traditional sailing vessels used in the Red Sea and Indian Ocean region.

[2] Small hut along the beach where sailors met to chat, drink tea and coffee, and foremost to make music and sing.

[3] British protectorate that allowed for varying degrees of political and economic control over several states in the Persian Gulf until 1947, including what is today known as the United Arab Emirates and at various times southern portions of Persia, Bahrain, Kuwait, Oman, and Qatar.

FLEE

Founded by Alan Marzo, Olivier Duport and Carl Åhnebrink, FLEE is an independent cultural engineering platform dedicated to the documentation and enhancement of hybrid cultures. As an interdisciplinary practice, the entity functions as a record label, publishing house and exhibition producer. Creatively exploring and emphasizing the outlines of globalization from a historical and critical perspective, FLEE focuses on shedding the light on subjectively selected cultural phenomena, while making them interact with contemporary artistic approaches.

Stories & Legends of the Pearl Divers Chants

Toufic Kerbage

The story of the pearl divers in the Gulf is as old as time. It seems almost a fantastic and marvellous fairytale, spun of both natural and supernatural elements, like a pearlescent excerpt from One Thousand and One Nights. The reality, though, is more arduous than that, with stories of endless expeditions and endurance across long months sailing along the coast of the Arabian Sea.

The journey would start with the appearance of the Taurus sign in the sky, around the end of May, and lasted until the end of September, when the Libra constellation is visible on the horizon at dawn. Sometimes the pearling season would also be extended to October – or even November – depending on the weather and whether or not the wind kept blowing.

This regular diving season was called "Ghaws Al Kabir", or "The Great Fishing", with its extensions into the fall referred to as "Al Ghaws al Saghir", "The Small Fishing".

The myth of the abandoned house : The genesis of pearl diver music

Once upon a time, as three friends were wandering together, far from their own neighbourhood, they were struck by strange noises and chanting emanating from one of the many abandoned houses in the region. The fear they felt at first soon disappeared as they approached the house and were captivated by the evermore distinct music. The three friends would return several times to this place to listen to the strange songs. One day, they decided to enter the abandoned house. It is hard to discern the reality from the fiction in this tale, with some believing that the three young men encountered Djinns[1] in this house. They took part in the dancing and festivities

image 1

several times until they had mastered a large part of the songs and rhythms that had first lured them into the house. However, they were never to reproduce this music for any other person in their lifetimes or they would be struck blind, the Djinns warned them.

The three friends grew old but continued to meet with one another to chant and perform the songs they had learned from the mystical beings. As time went by, one of the friends died, followed by the second one, leaving the third man by himself. Stranded by his friends, the old man thought about sharing the songs of the Djinns with his family as he was already losing his sight and hearing.

Convinced he had nothing left to lose, he decided to share the tales and musical secrets with his loved ones. Promptly upon breaking his promise, he went completely blind and died of his unfulfilled promise to the Djinns. Yet he had unwittingly given birth to the music that would come to be referred to as pearl diver music.

Throughout Mashreq[2] history, chronicles of Arab musicians tell of songs which melodies were borrowed from monasteries and transformed into secular songs. While most tales of the pearl divers' songs and music may be closer to myth than reality, most of their details are true and verifiable, at least in the musical sense.

In addition to diving and fishing, the pearl diving tradition rests on a very specific and demanding skill set of navigation and endurance, contradicting the belief that the fishing season owes its continuity to luck alone. At the time, tradition and well-established processes set the rhythm for the pearl diving crews's lives. The divers and other workers from the pearling crews were recruited on a yearly basis, depending on the debts they owed the Nakhuda[3]. By

image 2

withholding payment from the poorest divers at the beginning of the season when the pearls had not yet been sold, the divers would automatically accumulate debt with the owner of the ship to keep their families provided for while they were at sea. These debts would be pushed back from month to month so by the end of the season, the divers and other crew members would still be months of payments short. This cycle would be repeated from year to year in order to keep the crew shackled to the ship owner for life in a form of serfdom.

In the event that one of the crew members died during the expedition, the Nakhuda would enlist a boy from the dead man's family – only nine or ten years of age – who would take over the basic chores on the boat before becoming, in time, a complete member of the crew and, in some cases, a diver himself. This plucking from deceased crew members' families was the preferred recruitment method for divers. The men doing the work on the boat and pulling the divers out of the water were mostly strongly built and tall African slaves bought from the Zanzibar market or brought back from the East African shores that were controlled by the Arabs at the time.

While forced into a contract of life-long debt to the captain and their crew, the men were married in order to lead a more comfortable life considering their low pay, which allowed for a relatively peaceful work organization between the crew members and the ship-owners responsible for the expeditions. The opening of the season was a feast for the eyes, with an enormous number of embarkations[4] on display, from the larger, caravel-like "Boom"[5] boats, to a fleet of regular-sized "Jalboot"[6].

At least one professional singer was hired per boat. The Arabs, like the ancient Greeks, shared a strong belief in sea monsters, sirens and other mythical creatures that dwelt in the sea's murky depths. It is in direct reference to the "Nahm" – sea monster in Arabic – that the singers were called "Nahhām", those responsible for drowning out all other sounds during the voyage with their voices. Given that the entire expedition crew would sing in unison, it took a "monstrous" effort for the soloist to make himself heard over the constant loud choir, frenetic, off-beat percussion and clapping characteristic of this beautiful music. Some larger embarkations enlisted as many as four soloist singers for their expeditions but Nahhāms would never sing over each other, instead always taking turns.

They would take shifts setting the rhythm for the crew's daily lives, and performing the different subgenres of music, such as Bahri which was linked to work, and Fijiri for relaxation periods at sea.

The different expedition chores were always accompanied by singing, percussion and accented by the crew's strong vocal exaltations after actions like the release of heavy oars while at sea. A major difference between the music linked to labour and that linked to leisure, is that, as the men were busy rowing, hauling or engaged in other physically demanding chores, Bahri[7] had very little instrumentation while Fijiri[8] utilised the whole battery of percussions within the pearl divers' repertoire as

several crew members were available to play the instruments. The one exception in this dichotomy occured at the very end of the pearling expeditions, when the men returned the boat to be dry-docked[9]. On this occasion, all instruments would be brought back to land and some of the crew members would use them in a musical subgenre referred to as "Sanghiní".
Every subgenre's singing style, melody and rhythm differ enormously from one to the other. But, while musically distinct, the songs sometimes overlap according to the intended purpose and context, such as setting the sail. Over time, a multitude of exceptions meant some Bahri work songs used instruments and some Fijiri songs didn't, making the categories harder to discern for the uneducated ear. Commonly, a song is classified according to its rhythm, chanting and chanting style.

Due to the importance of music in this maritime context, the rhythmic cycle accompanying the unfolding of the "Jib"[10] sail will be sometimes granted the full battery of percussions, while some other times being interpreted only with a single great drum called "Tabl Al'Ôd"[11] and the cymbalettes, illustrating the variations possible within the same pearl diving songs subgenre.

The musical repertoire of the pearl divers is a rich one. From the work songs "khatfat Al shira" referring to the folding of the great sails, to the mesmerizing "Dawwāri" music that accompanies the ever-changing work around the anchor, borrowing some elements of the flamboyant "Fijiri" suite, the musical range is broad and subtle at the same time, leaving the possibility to crew members to either clap their hands or to play on the water jugs when not needed for a chore.

The Arab vocal tradition, dialectical and classical, reveals a very strong link between poetry and non-rhythmic melodies, called "Mawwāl"[12]. A short sonnet in contrast to the classical "ode", is the "Zouheyri"[13], with seven verses and two rhymes used majoritarily in the Gulf region. It is a strictly structured poetic form with full rhymes, each one a whole word, which has a different meaning at each verse-line. This poetic form is one of the dearest to the Arab mind and soul. The thousand-year-old Mawwāl became the dominant form of chanted music in the region. During pearling expeditions, the crew would sometimes have to wait longer periods of time for the wind to return to their sails and move them from one fishing location to the other. In order to distract themselves, the Nahham would deploy all their improvisation expertise for incredibly sad songs and poetry that brought more than one stoical sailor to tears.

"Ya Māl" (O, Fortune!)[14] would be repeated many times by the soloist, echoed by deep sounds from the choir that evoked the depths of the sea. As soon as the rowers resumed their hard labour, the chorus of violent, rhythmic expirations would once again become the sole accompaniment, echoing forever in the Arabian Gulf with the songs of its sailors.

image 3

[1] Jinn, also Romanized as djinn or Anglicized as genies (with the broader meaning of spirits or demons, depending on source), are supernatural beings in early pre-Islamic Arabian and later Islamic mythology and theology.

[2] Sometimes spelled Mashreq or Mashrek, is the eastern part of the Arab world, located in Western Asia and Northeastern Africa. This comprises the Arab states of Bahrain, Egypt, Iraq, Jordan, Kuwait, Lebanon, Oman, Palestine, Qatar, Saudi Arabia, Sudan, Syria, the United Arab Emirates and Yemen.

[3] Name derived from the Persian language describing the captain of the pearl diving boats and also sometimes the owner of the ship.

[4] In 1928, after the recent invention of culture pearls in Japan and as the fleet of pearling boats in the Gulf slowly started to decrease, the official estimations evaluated the fleet in Bahrain alone to be constituted of 400 boats.

[5] Literally "Owl".

[6] Phonetically, the word "Jalboot" sounds to an Arab like "Here-comes-the-boat".

[7] Generic term used to describe the sea songs and chants which can also be used specifically to refer to the work songs depending on the Arab formulation.

[8] Generic term used to refer to the leisure songs performed during resting periods and to all the music learned from the Djinns (in reference to the Myth described earlier).

[9] Dry docking is a term used for repairs or when a ship is taken to the service yard. During dry docking, the whole ship is brought to dry land so that the submerged portions of the hull can be cleaned or inspected.

[10] A small sail in the shape of a triangle, positioned in front of the main sail on a boat.

[11] A great double-sided cylindrical drum bound with animal skin. Each end is linked to cords out of animal intestines. It is played by drumming one side with a stick and the other one with the left hand. It is worn on the neck with a rope around 60cm long.

[12] In Arabic music, the Mawwāl is a traditional, poetic and popular Arabic genre of vocal music that is very slow in beat and sentimental in nature, and is characterised by prolonging vowel syllables, emotional vocals, and is usually presented before the actual song begins.

[13] Zouheyri is a sonnet with seven verses and two rhymes. This type of poetry is very strictly composed and represents one of the most venerated and respected poetic structures in the Arab Gulf.

[14] Same meaning in the material and figurative sense.

TOUFIC KERBAGE

Born in Beirut, Lebanon, Toufic Kerbage holds a PHD in Musicology from the University of Copenhagen, where he wrote a thesis entitled "The Rhythms of Pearl Diver Music. He also lectured in musicology and film music at the Kaslik University Lebanon from 1988 to 2006. Chairperson at the Higher Lebanese Conservatory department of Middle Eastern Music Theory and History since 1988, Professor Kerbage has been active teaching Western and Middle eastern Music Theory and History, as well as Analysis, Composition and Opera singing. A stakholder in many International Seminars and Colloquiums focusing on modern composed or traditional music from Europe and the Middle East, he has written several textbooks for various institutions. Author of the acclaimed book "Music in Bahrain: traditional music of the Arabian Gulf ", the teacher has written and edited many theory and history books on the music of the Middle East. As a musician and composer, he led prominent Middle-eastern singers and musician-ensembles around the world.

image 4

Singing Pearls: Paul Mattar talks with Abou Saleh in Kuwait (1978)

Paul Mattar

PAUL MATTAR: What is your name?

ABOU SALEH:
Rached Ibn Saleh Al Jimmaz.

PM: How old are you?

A.S: *70 years old.*

PM: What do you do?

A.S: *I am responsible for guarding a warehouse for the Ministry of Information.*

PM: What did you father do?

A.S: *My father had no job. He was a sailor.*

PM: Was he a diver?

A.S: *Yes, he spent his life at sea and dived. Once he had a fight with the Noukhaza (ship captain) and got injured in the process. He had chest pain and was coughing blood. The Noukhaza told him that he had to dive despite this as he had given him money to do so. He ended up diving but his soul left him. He was buried in the "Safaniya"*[1].

PM: Do you have children?

A.S: *Yes, I had seven children. One works at the municipality and the other one is a teacher of gymnastics. They never think about becoming sailors or about living at sea. Children are not supposed to be interested in the sea or pearl diving. It is me that had this life and then I raised them as much as possible for them to end up where they are now.*

PM: When did your life at sea start?

A.S: *I was eight years old when I went to sea for the first time. I was enrolled on a pearling boat and learned by doing as the years went by on the ship. I was then hired as a Tabab (cabin boy) because they considered my voice to be beautiful. Older people sang before me on the ship and I would follow them and sing after them.*

image 5

I then climbed the ladder and finally earned a share from the ones being distributed according to the systems in place on pearling ships – then equivalent to half of that of a diver. I am a Nahham.

PM: You never considered becoming a diver?

A.S: *Sure I did, but the captain refused and told me that if I dived, my sensibility would change. He told me that he had sacrificed thousands in money for my beautiful voice, not for diving. The salted water leaves unwashable stains and wounds on the diver's body. On his head, ears, eyes, chest, and even fingers.*

PM: How long did you spend pearling?

A.S: *More or less 20 years.*

PM: When was your last pearl expedition?

A.S: *The last time I departed on a pearling expedition, I was with Tahous Bin Chdayed[2], roughly 22 years ago. After that I dedicated myself to travels (commercial ones).*

PM: When you were on commercial trips, were you also hired as a Nahham?

A.S: *Absolutely, there too.*

PM: Do you remember what the pearling expeditions were like when you first started at eight years old and how they were at the end of your career?

A.S:*During my first trip I was only a cabin boy, and as such, the captain only gave my eight to ten rupees*[3]*. The pearling trip lasted four months and ten days. There were a couple of kids like me on board and I slowly progressed and moved up the hierarchy aboard, becoming a "Razif"*[4] *and earning a quarter of a share. Slowly but surely I ended up winning half a share as people started to recognize I had a nice voice. My function aboard was double. I was "sib"*[5]*, pulling the ropes for the divers, and I would sing.*

PM: You would always go out on sea with the same crew?

A.S: *Yes, always with the same crew. It was my community, my family. At the end of my career, and during my last expedition, there were 50 divers and 40 sib on board for a total of 90 crew members. It was the best crew I ever knew. I sailed with them for four years before withdrawing.*

PM: What were you doing before and after the pearling season?

A.S: *Oh, we would fish, work in housing, even transport water from Bassorah (Irak). We did everything that needed to be done. And one day, God sent us the oil which allowed us to rest. I got hired in the public service and since then we get by.*

PM: Did your income during the pearling season suffice for you and your family?

A.S: *Yes. I could earn up to 50 rupees*[6] *for a single expedition, but as a loan that was handed out by the captain. This would allow me to live for four months roughly and the rest of the time I would be at sea. Thankfully, my wife is good and not a big spender, like myself, keeping away from gambling and other foolish practices. God sent us many benefits and we were missing nothing.*

PM: You didn't need to do other jobs to supplement your income in order to raise your children, or to allow them to live comfortably?

A.S: *Not really, but I did work outside the pearling season as a mason and did little jobs to keep myself busy before receiving my first proposals for commercial expeditions. At this point my income and share rose to one and a half "Glata"*[7]*. Singing was a tiring job and the captains would fight between themselves trying to get the best singer by outbidding one another. You were chosen as a Nahham solely for your voice.*

PM: How did the sailors and the captain agree on a date to start the pearling expedition?

A.S: *Before the pearling trip, and when the weather became more suited to pearl diving, you could feel a real state of agitation in the population. Everybody would be excited and start to prepare themselves as they missed the sea. People would go down to the streets by the hundreds and start singing and celebrating the return of the season and the nearing of the pearling expeditions.*

PM: Do you remember one of the songs sung before the start of the season?

A.S: *There were a lot!*

PM: Do you remember one or two?

A.S: *It depends on the style you want. Midaf*[8]*? Khatfa*[9]*? Is there something you'd really like to hear?*

PM: I don't know, you tell me!

A.S: *They would usually perform some Fijiri*[10] *or Hassawi*[11] *during those occasions. They would also sing Haddadi to rest. In some pearling expeditions there were no resting periods so we wouldn't necessarily be able to perform that music. This is why they would be played and sung during celebration periods, like the ones preceding the start of the season, or during commercial trips.*

PM: When the day of the departure on the expeditions would come, how would this unfold?

A.S: *The parents and family would be on the pier and I would sing to them – and to my wife especially – a Nahma[12], stating "Farewell in peace, light of my eyes – Far from you, the lid of my eyes hasn't closed itself – You make me a promise that, when I would close my eyes, I would remain a corpse without soul. Take care of me, as I take care of you"[a] This is what we would sing when we would leave for the sea. It was a very sad melopee. We would put the boat on some wooden tree trunks and make it roll all the way to the water, where we would be towing it, allowing us to leave for months.*

PM: How was the "Chouna[13]" performed?

A.S: *We would sing a Nahma and ask for the Prophet to bless us.*

PM: How was the preparation of the trips organized? The food, diving instruments, and material needed on the ships?

A.S: *What do you want to know exactly? You are mixing up a lot of things. (laughs) For the food we would carry dates and rice in quantities according to the size of the boat. The fish we would cook and eat at sea after fishing them. The captain would attend to this and no one would come with his own food aboard the ship. He took care of the slightest detail aboard the ship and was concerned by all the aspects of life on the ships. From the usurious loans, to the "Khrab" (rigging), and all the little details on the boat. As soon as there was a sale of pearls happening, the captain would automatically take his share, which was equal to one fifth of the global revenue of the boat for every sale, once having deducted all the expenses necessary for the expedition. The remaining revenues would be distributed according to each individual's rank in the crew.*

PM: Were there specific songs performed during the hailing of the Khrab and anchor?

A.S: *Yes, we would play some Dawarris for that occasion, which is a genre with a really specific hand clapping rhythm.*

PM: How would you proceed once arriving on a pearl bed?

A.S: *While arriving there, and if there were a lot of oysters, we would sing a "Taksira[14]" and shout "Khalib" ("turn"). This would signal the start of the technique consisting of lifting one of the two anchors stabilizing the boat* *during the dives in order to allow the boat to rotate according to the currents, in a diameter of 10 to 20 meters, which would allow for multiple dives in an area with many oysters.*

PM: And if there were not many oysters on a pearl bed?

A.S: *We would just take the anchor up and continue searching for another pearl bed with more oysters.*

PM: And there would be no singing involved in this?

A.S: *No, of course all of this was done with songs and music.*

PM: Can I hear an extract of the songs when they were no pearls?

A.S: *What do you want me to tell you? Sorry, but it will be for another time, I have a meeting at the bank. (leaves abruptly and departs for the bank).*

image 6

image 7

[1] Honours to the sailor were made at sea directly here and in Safaniya, from the name of the region of the inner Gulf sea that gave his name to the largest off-shore oil field in the world today.

[2] Was a famous kuwaiti "Noukhaza" from the region of Fahaheel. He owned several pearling ships and was close to the circles of power and to the ruling family in Kuwait. He died in 1963.

[3] In 1917, one Indian Rupee was worth 0.314 USD. The salary mentioned at the time was between 2.5 and 3 USD.

[4] Grade above the Tabab (cabin boy).

[5] Divers assistants.

[6] Around 15USD in 1917.

[7] The name of the shares for the different crew members on pearling ships.

[8] Is a local deformation of the word "Mijdaf", meaning "an oar". It is the song chanted by the Nahham when the sailors are rowing and it is punctuated by group loud exhalations.

[9] Comes from the verb "Khatafa", meaning "remove". It is a very rhythmic chant of the Nahham punctuated by the Tabl drums and hand clapping while the sail is set.

[10] In Bahrain, "Fijiri" is a suite of chants regrouping Bahri followed by Adassani, followed by Haddadi, followed by Mkholfi and finally Hassawi.). In Kuwait however, those five genres exist under the denomination of "relaxing sailor songs" as "Fijiri" is used to describe another genre, unrelated to the five previously mentioned ones. In both countries, those songs have in common to be performed during resting periods of time and not while work is being performed on the boats.

[11] Is one of the five subgenres of the "Fijiri" suite of chants. The Hassawi is the ultimate chant in the order of passage of those songs.

[12] Similarly to the "song" for the "singer", the "nahma" exists in relationship to the "Nahham".

[13] Process of impermeabilization of the pearling boat.

[14] Song and technique performed when the pearling crews arrive on a richly furnished pearling bed.

[a]original version:
وادعتكم بالسلامة يا ضوى عيني
وخلافكم ما غمض جفني على عيني
واعدتني بالوعد لمن حفت عيني
ظليت يا سيدي جسم بليا روح
شد فرمن عقل وظل الجسم مطروح
كل العرب هودت وانا شقي الروح
يا نور عيني مثل ما راعيك راعيني

PAUL MATTAR
Is a Lebanese artist born in Heliopolis, Egypt in 1946. A contributor to the renewal of the artistic landscape in Lebanon since the 60s, he acted for television, theater or movies before becoming author and director. He directed a series of documentaries throughout the Arab world commissioned by UNICEF for educational purposes and also composed numerous famous songs in Arabic and French. During his travels, he conducted a thorough ethnomusicological study of the traditional songs and chants from the Gulf region, which he compiled into a book called "The Gulf of Chants" (خليج الأغاني), which was published by Dar Al Muthalath in Beirut in 1981. The collection of his recordings is archived at the Geneva Ethnography Museum. Today, he teaches at the Saint-Joseph University in Beirut and is also the director of the prestigious "Théâtre Monnot" and the founder of the "Maison des Arts et du Conte", which works to preserve oral transmission traditions.

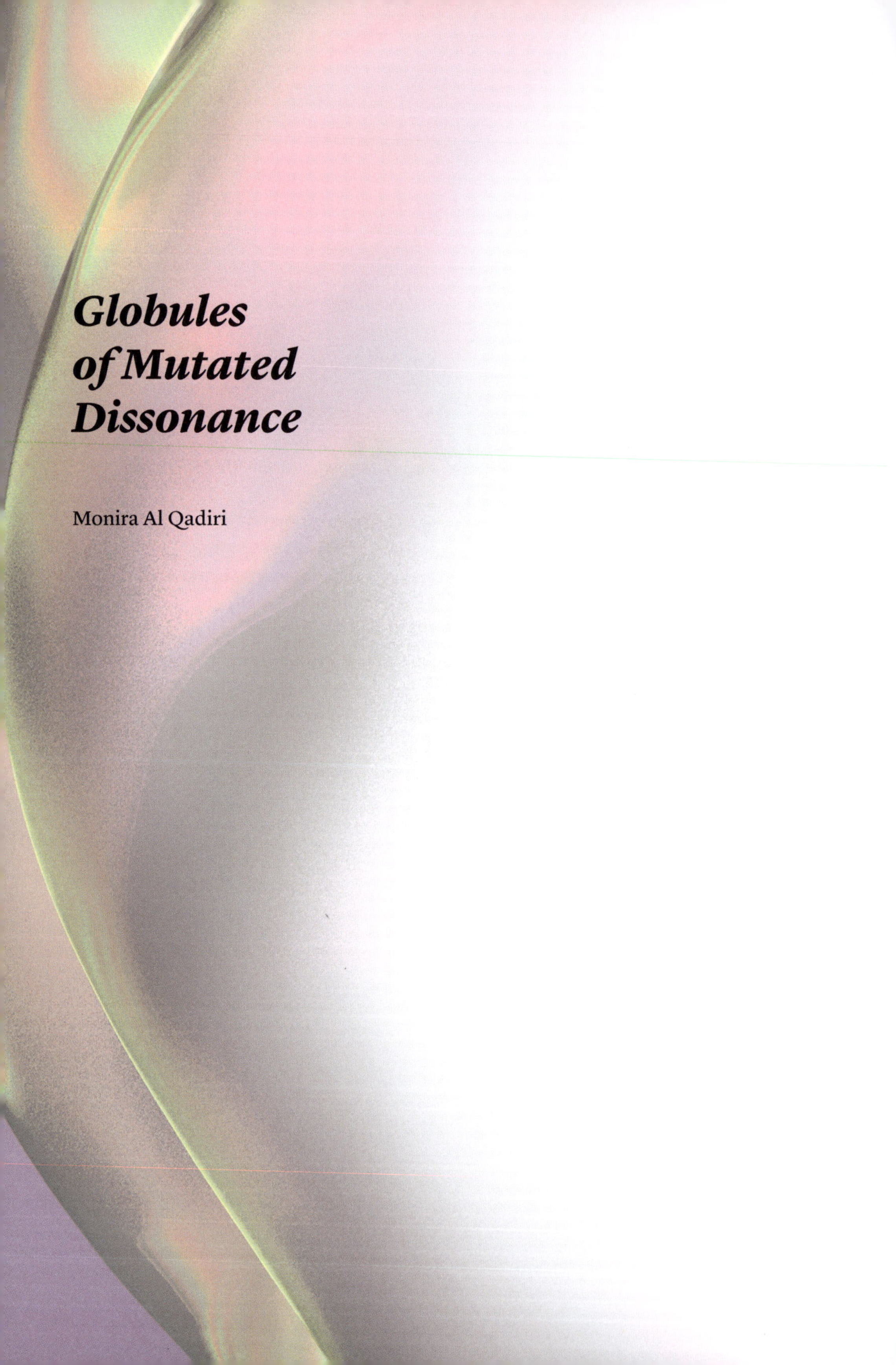

Globules of Mutated Dissonance

Monira Al Qadiri

image 8

"We were rowed ashore in the longboat with the traditional Kuwait style, the twenty stalwart men at the long oars dressed in their best robes, and all chanting lustily. They rowed very well and their chants were better than their songs. When they were not chanting they made a queer kind of low throaty growling sound like the distant rumbling of a squadron of bombing aeroplanes."

Supposedly, the 1940 book "Sons of Sindbad", by Australian explorer Alain Villiers, contains some passages about my grandfather, the resident singer on a Kuwaiti pearl diving boat he boarded from a port in Yemen, and his sea mates who provided the percussion and dancing accompaniments to his music.

"The musician was a large Arab with fierce eyes and a big black moustache, who played a guitar which looked as if it might have come from Europe. (I learned later that it had been bought in Basra, Irak.) He probably played very well, according to Arab ideas of music, but unfortunately those ideas were not mine, and he made matters worse by singing endlessly in an unnatural, rasping voice. Whatever it was he sang, it seemed excellent to his listeners, but I could have done without it. Ali whispered to me that he was a famous singer from Kuwait, but even this advertisement of his fame did not make his singing any more bearable. I hoped he was not part of the permanent equipment of the vessel. They said his name was Ismael. I was glad to see the sailors and a little man who looked like a cook come along with tiny drums, which were made from cylindrical pieces of Basra pottery, across one end of which had been stretched warmed kid's skin. There were about six of these drums and also some large tambourines. The sailors took turns at beating them, with their thumbs and forefingers, which they used with an excellent sense of rhythm. I liked the drums for they had a pleasing low note, and they helped to drown Ismael's music."

I had never met my grandfather, who passed away a few years before I was born. He was a harsh and difficult man according to what I've heard, and almost never sang a single phrase after returning home from sea, even though only my grandmother attested he had a beautiful voice that could be heard from miles away. To him, though, the singing was strictly labor music, to help the morale and psyche of his mates. His job for months on end, while riding the waves under the hot sun.

"It was heavy, brutal work. They stopped frequently to dance and sing, stamping the deck rhythmically with their great bare feet and clapping their tremendous hands so that the handclaps rang through the harbour, and the serang banged an indian drum. This dancing was good, far better than the formless shuffling of Sunday's performance, and it seemed to act as a tonic for them, reviving the sailors for their heavy tasks. They did nothing without a preliminary dance, and they kept up a melodic chanting all the time they worked."

I always fantasized about his life, but I found it mentally impossible to access, as a post-oil person myself, who has had their connections to the pearling past severed by the alien force that is petroleum. Did they really all risk their lives, day and night, for a glimpse of a tiny, shiny ornament? So that someday some faraway monarchs can sport them on their person, never knowing how people had literally lived and died for them to be extracted from the sea? Was it true that they were all slaves to one master – the Pearl[1]?

"After the feast we had coffee, then sleep; after the sleep, the midday prayer followed, and after that Ismael, our musician, would play on his damned guitar. Then all peace was ended. In six months I never came to like that music. So far as I could see, there was not a thing to like about it. One can be accustomed to Scots pipes and Siamese reeds, to Balinese and Javanese gongs. Even the Swahili, banning on their drums, produce some kind of rhythmic noise, and the Beduin's reeds were not wholly unpleasant. But Ismael and his guitar was and remained an affront to the ear of mortal man. Given the slightest encouragement, he also sang which was worse. His songs were interminable, plaintive, and most repellent, sung horribly in an unnatural and dreadfully unattractive voice. Yet everybody insisted that Ismael was a musician of note in Kuwait, and ranked among the supreme attractions of the vessel."

All of these stories feel like a form of fiction to me, despite having heard very animated familial recollections of his life for years. Perhaps I was so obsessed with him, now after having lived in Japan for so long, and found myself participating in the cult of ancestor worship so commonly seen in the east Asian cultural sphere. Who was this ancestor? Did he feel cynical, angry, vengeful towards the world that had forsaken him so, as many of the sea songs' lyrics described? Or was that only the plight of his pearl diver mates, while he only sat there singing and wailing on the sidelines as they jumped into the ocean time and time again, for he was the conductor of their work-life rhythm.

"They too shuffled barefoot over the carpet, ranging fore and aft, keeping time with the moustachioed ruffian's music. They walked backwards and forwards hand in hand along the carpet, while Ismael's black fingers tortured the strings and his cracked voice wailed. Each time they approached the musician they stopped a second or so before him, and cracked their fingers. Sometimes they agitated their bellies and whole bodies up to the shoulders, somewhat in the manner of a Moroccan dancing girl. It was a curious business.

Sometimes the singing sailors, unable to contain themselves at some particularly moving stanza from the moaning singer, would leap up and form in formation behind the two nakhodas, while they cracked their fingers and trembled violently."

Perhaps I am just interested in his machismo and his artistry, imagining that this past life inhabits my body still. But no matter how hard I try to envision it, there is this dissonance that overcomes my mental space very quickly and without mercy. The curse of the black pearl – oil – blinds me from my own historic imagination. I have become a mutant with no past. No history. No recollection. My body and mind are misshapen, distorted, never to be the same again.

"Ismael must have had something to put into those songs to hold his hearers, for the melody was always atrocious and the delivery was abominable.

It was, I suppose, inconsiderate of me to want him to stop when everybody else so enjoyed him. But he used to go on far into the night. Sometimes we had drums with the guitar, and this was better, for they helped drown the music. Often there was dancing, but it was always the same dull shuffling, agitating, finger cracking, hopping and jumping I had first seen in Ma'alla bay. We never had any dancing girls: they were kept ashore."

I own some pearls, and I touch and look at them often in order to try and find some invisible connection to him. Some are misshapen and deformed, undesirable by the market that only covets the perfectly round ones. Perhaps he encountered many of these along his travels in the sea. What if I carved these unwanted globules of nacreous lustre into the shape of oil drills? Maybe their distortions can merge with my own, to create a new mutated form, one that is closer to the fossilized version of my unnatural self.

The oil drills themselves have also been a subject of fascination of mine for some time, as they bore endlessly into the earth's crust covered in gold and diamonds, resembling octopuses and sea creatures and extraterrestrial beings. Because my personal narrative has been so shunned by the pearl, I found some solace in these machines, as they embody something more in line with my freak generation.

"Sometimes Ismael went off with the guitar to be a public nuisance somewhere, and on such occasions I was glad."

Maybe I can free myself from ancestral delusions by creating new delusions of my own, like the pearl-drill that is the only remnant of the past, as well as being an indicator of an oil-less future.

[1] In 1863 Muhammad Al-Thani, former ruler of Qatar told the british explorer and diplomat William Palgrave: "We are all from the highest to the lowest slaves of one master, the pearl."

MONIRA AL QADIRI
is a Kuwaiti visual artist born in Senegal and educated in Japan. In 2010, she received a Ph.D. in inter-media art from Tokyo University of the Arts, where her research was focused on the aesthetics of sadness in the Middle-East stemming from poetry, music, art and ritual practices. Her work explores gender identities, petro-cultures and their possible futures, as well as the legacies of corruption. She is currently based in Berlin.

The Pearling Industry on the Arab Coast of the Gulf

Dr Mark Hobbs

I first went to Qatar in 2011. It was August and the mercury was topping 40 degrees Celsius, the late-afternoon air stifling hot, impossible to breathe. It was also Ramadan, and the streets were empty, the city deserted. As we careered around roundabouts on the way to my hotel the taxi driver pointed out the sights along the Corniche: Souq Waqif, I. M. Pei's Museum of Islamic Art, the Amiri Diwan, the pyramid-like Sheraton Hotel, and ahead of us, the anarchic West Bay skyline, with its dozens of starchitect-designed skyscrapers, all vying to outshine each other.

Doha's West Bay skyline has become one of the Gulf region's iconic images—a symbol of Qatar's rapid acquisition of extraordinary levels of wealth, thanks to its huge reserves of natural gas. I was in Qatar for work: specifically two major museum projects, both of which were beneficiaries of the country's vast wealth, and both of which explored the role that first oil, and then natural gas, has played in the transformation of the tiny Gulf state. Both projects also explored Qatar's history before the discovery of oil in the 1930s, including the region's earlier dependence on the pearl fishing industry.

The story of Qatar's—and the wider Gulf's—reliance on their pearl fisheries is less well-known to outsiders, but is central to the cultural heritage of the relatively young nation states of Qatar, Bahrain, the United Arab Emirates, and Kuwait. References to pearls can be found all along the Arab coast of the Gulf: in prestigious real estate developments, along tourist trails and heritage sites, and in the ubiquitous pearl jewellery shops found in the open-air souqs and air-conditioned malls.

Throughout human history the pearl has been associated with wealth and beauty. With wealth comes aspirations of power, and with beauty comes notions of taste. Pliny the Elder described the ways in which the aristocracy of ancient Rome adorned themselves with pearls.[1] Sacred images of Saraswati, the Hindu goddess of knowledge, music, art, wisdom and learning, depict her holding a pearl necklace. Marco Polo described how, in the thirteenth century, the Mongol Emperor Kublai Khan bestowed gifts of pearls and other gems upon his loyal followers.[2]

The pearls discovered along the Arab coast of the Gulf were widely regarded as being the finest in the world. In his Historia Naturalis, Pliny wrote that the 'most perfect and exquisite' pearls came from Arabia.[3] Pearl fishing had been the predominant economic activity along the Arab coast of the Gulf for centuries, and its inhabitants and rulers were entirely dependent on them. In 1863, acknowledging his dependence on pearl fishing, the ruler of Qatar, Shaikh Muhammad bin Thani, told the English explorer William Palgrave that «We are all, from the highest to the lowest, slaves of one master, [the] Pearl.»[4] The Gulf's biggest pearl fishery was centred on Bahrain, with smaller fishing fleets operating out of the coastal towns of Kuwait, Doha, Dubai and Abu Dhabi.

A valuable source for understanding the economic importance of pearl fishing in the Gulf is the archives of the British East India Company and the British Government's India Office, held at the British Library in London. These records were created as a consequence of Britain assuming de facto control of the waters of the Gulf in the early nineteenth century, through a series of maritime treaties signed with the region's shaikhs.[5] In 1833 British officials estimated the export value of Gulf pearls at 300,000£ (approximately 36£million in present-day terms).[6] The beginning of the twentieth century saw a distinct upturn in the demand for pearls worldwide. A 1906 report estimated that the value of the Gulf pearl market—a market that accounted for half of all global pearl production—had risen to 1.4£million, roughly equivalent to 170£million today.[7] This upturn was brought about by growing global prosperity, particularly in Europe and North America, where a renewed interest in the 'Oriental' East was driving demand for the exotic goods that travelled along the Silk Road routes from the East.

Aside from the value of exports, the success of pearl fishing in the Gulf could be measured by the size of each port's fleets, and the numbers of men involved in fishing. In 1833 Lieutenant James Wellsted of the Royal Indian Marine estimated that there were 4,300 boats and 30,000 men employed in the Gulf's pearling industry.[8]

image 9

image 10

In 1930 Charles Belgrave, Britain's Advisor to the Government of Bahrain, estimated that there were 100,000 men employed in pearling in the Gulf.[9]

The Pearling Season

The main pearl diving season took place between May and October. Each day scores of pearling boats set out for the shallow banks off the coast. Each boat's crew consisted of a captain (nakhuda) and a team of divers and haulers. Wellsted witnessed pearling activity in the waters of the Gulf firsthand. He observed that:

«When a boat arrives at a spot considered from the nature of the bottom as likely to prove favourable, the boat is anchored, and the crew divide into two portions; one remains in the boat to receive the oysters, and haul up the divers, the others strip naked, and jump into the sea. A small basket, capable of holding from eight to ten oysters, is then handed to them, and suspended to their left arm; the nostrils are then closed with a piece of elastic horn, the diver places his foot on a stone attached to a cord, inhales a long breath, and upon rising his right arm as a singla, the rope is immediately let go, and he sinks to the bottom. After collecting as many as are within his reach, he jerks the line, and is drawn at once to the surface.»[10]

The pearling diving crews worked from morning to sunset. The pearl divers typically dived to a depth of fifteen to twenty metres, spending between one and two minutes underwater. Larger boats might spend several days on the pearl banks. When the boats returned to port in the evening, the pearl shells were opened under the watchful eyes of crew members. The nakhuda would then try to negotiate the best deal for himself and his crew with pearl traders.

Diving for pearls was a physically demanding task best suited to young men. It was also labour intensive and a seasonal trade, reliant on itinerant migrant labour. As a result, the pearling industry was to some degree dependent on an enduring slave trade in the Gulf that Britain, in spite of its hegemonic status in the region, showed little enthusiasm to entirely eradicate. Estimates of the numbers of slaves involved in the Gulf's pearling industry vary. In 1929 Britain's Senior Naval Officer in the Gulf estimated that a quarter of the Gulf's pearl divers (approximately 20,000 individuals) were forced workers.[11]

This figure of 20,000 does not, however, distinguish between those individuals who were slaves in the chattel sense, and those that were indentured labourers, of which there were many in the twilight years of the Gulf's pearling industry, when pearling profits collapsed. Distinguishing between one and the other was difficult, not least because their circumstances were more or less the same. These difficulties reflect the complexities of slavery in Arabia. It was very different in nature to the Atlantic slave trade, in which Europe's colonial powers, throughout the sixteenth to nineteenth centuries, transported hundreds of thousands of men, women and children from Africa to the Americas, primarily to work on sugar, cotton and tobacco plantations. The slave trade in Arabia existed for many centuries as part of a larger network of trade routes sometimes referred to as the Indian Ocean World. People were enslaved through war, conquest, colonisation, and in response to the demand for labour in industries such as pearling and date farming. In times of famine and natural disaster it was not uncommon for people on the Asian subcontinent to submit themselves or their dependents to slavery, because it offered better prospects for survival.[12] Slaves came from a variety of places. In the medieval period the expanding Ottoman Empire enslaved Europeans from the Balkans and Caucasus regions. East Africa was an enduring source of slaves, who were transported along maritime trading routes dictated by the monsoon seasons, as well as overland trade routes. Other slaves came from the Asian subcontinent and southeast Asia.

The best records we have of the lives of the Gulf's enslaved pearl divers in the early twentieth century are the manumission statements of hundreds of men that were recorded in the British Government's agencies in the region. Although the British Government had abolished the maritime slave trade, and took measures to suppress it wherever it appeared, it condoned the practice of slavery on the Arab coast of the Gulf. However, any slave citing reasons such ill-treatment by their owner could apply to the British Government for manumission. Manumitted slaves were issued certificates by the British Government.[13]

The manumission statements taken down by British Government officials in the Gulf in the early twentieth century suggest that many men seeking manumission were not slaves per se, but indentured labourers. For pearl divers to be indebted to their employers was common. The divers were offered credit by their nakhudas, to support their families while they were away during the pearling season, and to sustain themselves during the off season. This credit system meant that divers were perpetually indebted to their nakhudas, and were compelled to return to the pearling banks each year. And whenever the pearl industry's profits shrunk, diminishing returns meant that pearl divers—whether slaves or technically free—found their debts growing from one year to the next, no matter how hard they worked.

The decline of pearling

The plight of the Gulf's pearl divers was precarious: compelled to work in an industry ruinous to human health, with no guarantees of financial returns, and uncertainty over their most basic and inviolable right to freedom. The situation could only worsen as the 1920s and 1930s brought upheaval and rapid decline to the Gulf's pearl industry.

The value of pearls exports from the Gulf peaked in the years before the First World War. After the War exports rallied slightly before going into steep decline in the 1930s. By way of an illustration British officials estimated the pearl export market in Bahrain for 1926 to be in the region of 466,000 GBP (28 million in present-day terms). In 1935 this figure had shrunk to just 35,000 GBP (2,5 million in present-day terms), less than a tenth of its value a decade earlier.[14] A number of factors combined to decimate the Gulf's pearling industry. First, the First World War significantly reduced the global demand for luxury goods. The partial recovery in the early 1920s was swiftly wiped out by the worldwide economic depression that followed in the wake of the Wall Street Crash of 1929. In the meantime, refinements had been made to the production process of cultured pearls, pioneered by the Japanese entrepreneur Kokichi Mikimoto. These refinements meant that, from 1916 onwards, it was possible to mass produce pearls in offshore farms. By the late 1920s cultured pearls 'manufactured' in Japan and the South Seas, virtually indistinguishable from natural pearls and costing a third of the value, were widely available.

The decline of the pearling industry had a catastrophic effect on the inhabitants of the Gulf's Arab coast, who were almost entirely dependent on the pearl trade for their livelihoods. A British official noted in 1915 that were the pearl trade to stop, Bahrain would 'be reduced to about one-fifth of its present dimensions and the ports of Trucial Oman [Dubai and Abu Dhabi], which have no other resources, would practically cease to exist.'[15] 'The prosperity and almost the very existence of Bahrain' wrote Charles Belgrave in 1928, 'depends upon the pearl industry.'[16]

But good fortune lay around the corner. The 1930s brought momentous changes to the Gulf region, with the emergence of a new industry—oil—quickly taking over from pearling as the Gulf's main source of income. From the early 1930s onwards a series of oil concession agreements were signed between the region's Shaikhs and oil companies from Britain, Europe and the United States: Bahrain in 1930, Kuwait in 1932, Qatar in 1935, Abu Dhabi in 1939.

image 11

These concessions, and the first exports of oil, bought newfound wealth to the Gulf region. It also brought dramatic modernisation in its wake, with the arrival of a host of western innovations such as electricity, refrigeration, telecommunications, and the automobile.

Today's inhabitants of the Arab coast of the Gulf regard the 1930s as a heroic period in their history: a period of great hardship caused by the collapse of the pearling industry, of great sacrifices made by early pioneers who toiled in the desert under a hot sun in search of oil, and the drawing up of national boundaries and the foundation of modern nation states.

[1] Chicharro, Lucia Avial, 'Romans prized these jewels more than diamonds' National Geographic Magazine (2 April 2019).

[2] Marco Polo, Travels in the Land of Kublai Khan (London, 2005), 54.

[3] Kunz, George Frederick, and Charles Hugh Stevenson, The Book of the Pearl: The History, Art, Science and Industry of the Queen of Jems, (New York, 1908), 85.

[4] Hopper, Matthew S., Slaves of One Master: Globalisation and Slavery in Arabia in the Age of Empire (New Haven, 2015), 82.

[5] Many records from the East India Company and India Office archive that relate to the Gulf have been digitised and published online since 2013 on the Qatar Digital Library (https://qdl.qa/), a partnership project between the British Library and Qatar Foundation. References to East India Company and India Office materials in this article cite the original held at the British Library. Digital copies of all materials citied can be found on https://qdl.qa/.

[6] This and subsequent present-day figures based on calculations made using the CPI Inflation Calculator (www.officialdata.org)

[7] 'Gazetteer of the Persian Gulf. Vol I. Historical. Part II. J G Lorimer. 1915', British Library, India Office Records and Private Papers, IOR/L/PS/20/C91/2, 2000; Hopper, Slaves of One Master, 100.

[8] Wellsted, J. R., Travels in Arabia, Vol.1, (London, 1838), 264-5.

[9] 'File 8/3 Pearling industry', British Library: India Office Records and Private Papers, IOR/R/15/2/122, f.49r.

[10] Wellsted, J. R. Travels to the city of the caliphs, along the shores of the Persian gulf and the Mediterranean Vol.1 (n.p., 1840), 121-2.

[11] Hopper, Slaves of One Master, 86.

[12] Engerman, Stanley L., Slavery, Emancipation, and Freedom: Comparative Perspectives (Baton Rouge, 2007), 24.

[13] Hobbs, M, 'Manumission Statements: Insights into the Lives of the Gulf's enslaved Population', Qatar Digital Library (2019).

[14] 'File 10/4 I Trade Reports', British Library: India Office Records and Private Papers, IOR/R/15/2/1344, f.208r; 'File 10/4 II Trade Reports', British Library: India Office Records and Private Papers, IOR/R/15/2/1345, f.155r.

[15] 'Gazetteer of the Persian Gulf. Vol I. Historical. Part II. J G Lorimer. 1915', British Library, India Office Records and Private Papers, IOR/L/PS/20/C91/2, 2220.

[16] 'File 10/4 I Trade Reports', British Library: India Office Records and Private Papers, IOR/R/15/2/1344, f.229r.

MARK HOBBS

Mark Hobbs is a London-based writer and historian, with over ten years' experience working in the cultural heritage sector. He has worked for heritage consultancy Barker Langham, and a number of prestigious institutions including the Royal Academy of Music, the British Library, and the Royal Horticultural Society. At Barker Langham, he worked as a curatorial consultant for the Bin Jelmood Museum in Qatar, which seeks to raise awareness of the important social, cultural and economic contributions that formerly enslaved peoples have made to the history of human civilisation. Mark's writing has been published in the journal Urban History, the Public Domain Review, and the Paris Review.

image 12

Trading Chants & Pearls: Visiting Talal Mattar

image 13

image 14

OLIVIER DUPORT/FLEE: Can you introduce yourself?

TALAL MATTAR:
I am Talal Mattar from the Mattar family, who has been in this business for over 200 years. My family used to be pearl merchants - we call it "Tawash" in Arabic. We used to work only in loose pearls and necklaces. In 2004 we started in jewelry and now we do both: wholesale and jewelry.

OD: Your family has been trading pearls forever?

TM: *I do have letters that date back to then, even from Paris, from the Hotel Bohy Lafayette, addressed to my great-grandfather in 1884.*

OD: Did they trade with people from all over the world?

TM: *Most of the people interested in pearls used to come to Bahrain, which was one of the strongholds for it. They didn't travel before, as people would directly come to them.*

OD: Any pearl divers in your family?

TM: *No no, only merchants.*

OD: How would you describe your relationship to pearl diving music?

TM: *As we are pearl merchants, it is all connected. Pearl diving music can be divided into two parts: the music played on board, and the music played on land during the off season in the Dars. We were born with music being played daily from my grandfather's time. We are attached to this music as it is our heritage, our culture here in Bahrain. It's nothing imported, it is our family and nation's culture. I do not only have a close relationship to pearl diving music but also to its musicians here in the region. This link dates back to my grandfather - we all had great connections to them.*

OD: How did you learn the music?

TM: *We grew up learning percussion. My father and grandfather all knew it and it was passed down between generations. Even my sons are very fast at learning it, it is easy as they are used to this kind of music. We feel it, for us it's easier to play this music than any other in the world.*

OD: You mentioned a common heritage linked to this music.

TM: *Of course, especially in the old times as there was no other entertainment, no restaurants, no lounges. Before there was only one place open at night: The Dar. This was the only entertainment at the time.*

OD: Why do you play this music?

TM: *Because we like it! Nowadays it is very rare to see people who play it well, actually. The other reason is that we have to keep rehearsing to get a proper result, as it is joint work. Indeed, the whole group needs to sing at the same level, to stop at the same time, to play at the same tempo. Furthermore, we don't read and write music, so a proper result can only be achieved by jamming and rehearsing. Otherwise it will be lost. We play everywhere although it's usually in the Dars. As soon as we are more than 15, we immediately play Fijiri. We also play other stuff, but it usually always starts with this and everybody needs to know how to play it.*

OD: How regularly do you play?

TM: *Before Corona (Covid-19), it was at least once a week. Now it depends on the regulations.*

OD: What's the minimum number of persons required to play?

TM: *At least 10 to 15. However, the more people, the more powerful the music. It is like football, if you have 11 players, it's better than having only five or six on the field (laughs). You cannot play if your team isn't complete.*

OD: What captivates you the most about pearl diving music?

TM: *I don't know, because it is something we feel and because we witnessed this music being played as kids, unlike the younger generations. In school they brought us every Wednesday to the same Dar to listen to this music. This created a specific connection for us. Young people needed to learn from scratch but luckily, some got really good at it and now our group has expanded to 25 really good players.*

OD: You work with pearl divers, who bring you pearls. Do some still work the traditional way?

TM: *Nobody does - and why would they? You have equipment that makes your life easier, why would you make it tough again on purpose? There are now more than 2000 divers in Bahrain and you don't even need any equipment when you go in shallow waters. In deep waters, they simply use scuba diving equipment because the water gets too cold as you go deep.*

OD: What do you think the future holds for pearl diving and for its music in general?

TM: *I think a boom is coming, as the competition today is getting scarce compared to a couple of years back. Diamonds are losing their value nowadays because of artificial ones and because of CVDs*[1] *, so I think that the future will be bright for natural pearls. 100 years ago, the invention of cultured pearls had a devastating impact on the pearl market. Now artificial diamonds are affecting the diamond industry the same way. Regarding the music, I see a young generation that has interested itself a lot in this tradition and I am very optimistic for what the future holds, especially as now we have some educated musicians among ourselves who can read and write music. This will help us in the future to pass this music on and to facilitate its teaching.*

OD: You are trying to put together an archive of this music. Could you tell us more about it?

TM: *We don't read music so it is interesting to record it. In order to do that though, you also have to be lucky as sometimes 20 people are playing without following notes and you cannot control them all. Sometimes some will be very happy and will play a bit louder, some others will cough at times or play at higher pitches, the singer could be in a bad mood... There's a lot of different elements to take into consideration when you are recording and this is why we always capture on tape what we play. I have more than 500 recordings of this music I've made and out of them, only five or six are truly successful. The rest there is always something wrong with them.*

OD: What is the process of buying pearls from a diver?

TM: *First of all, when a diver comes to me, I have to buy whatever he has. I cannot cherry pick. If I take only the big and best ones, what is he going to do with the others? The vast majority of pearls they get are seed pearls*[2]*, which* *means they have no value. You have to evaluate the whole lot. Of course, the main factor that will increase its price is the presence or not of bigger pearls. You might buy five or six grams of pearls for a single one. It's the first thing you look for. As we say here: everybody looks for his own profit, and that's especially true when it comes to pearls - because if you don't buy when the pearls are being presented to you, you don't know when you'll get another opportunity to do so. It is the randomness of nature that dictates in contrast to diamonds. Whatever comes from the sea, you have to work with it.*

OD: Are there no pricing methods or references for those exchanges?

TM: *No, but there are five major factors to pay attention to when it comes to pearls: size, weight, shape, colour and luster. There is also a psychological part of course. I prefer creamy pearls, but other people might have other tastes, and this is why it is impossible to have standards as there are no two pearls alike in the world, even if they came from the same oyster.*

OD: Were there ever any pearls you wanted to keep for yourself?

TM: *I always kept some for myself. I regularly see pearls that I feel I have never seen in my life, even small ones. Sometimes it's a unique shape or colour, and if you sell them you will not be happy of the value you will be getting for them, so it's better to keep them for yourself (laughs).*

OD: Coming back to cultured pearls, what do you think of them?

TM: *I don't see cultured pearls as pearls. If you can drive a Rolls Royce, would you drive a Ford? You wouldn't even look at it. Cultured pearls don't impress me at all and even during conventions or (gem) shows. They don't. I have the valuable thing, why should I bother with this man-made thing? Before, cultured pearls used to be our competitors but currently because of China, Vietnam, the Philippines and the mass-cultivation they do, the cultured pearl value has dropped to near zero. The cultured pearls that Mikimoto invented used to go for 200 dollars, now they go for two dollars*[2]*. It doesn't compete against natural pearls anymore.*

OD: How did you cope when cultured pearls arrived on the market?

TM: *My grandfathers loved pearls, and together with lots of other merchants they led a common case against Mikimoto in court in New York. The court ruled in favor of Mikimoto, but despite that, pearl diving in Bahrain continued until the late 50s, even if cultured pearls arrived on the market as*

image 15

early as 1916. People simply didn't pay attention to them. The main impact on the industry came from the oil discovery. Most divers were used to working for four months straight on the pearling boats and with oil, they could afford to work during the day and to come back home to their families in the evenings. At this point, nobody would dive for pearls anymore - except for some people doing it as a hobby up until the 90s/early 00's. But recently, the fleet of divers - men and women - expanded and reached the number of 2000, which is significant!

OD: Do you think the fact that Bahrain has always remained loyal to natural pearls gives you an advantage today?

TM: *Of course. You know, there is a law here in Bahrain that forbids anyone from dealing cultured pearls on national territory. You can be jailed for more than 10 years if they catch you with large amounts of it. This helps a lot, and we are the only country in the world with such a legal framework. If you import pearls, they have to get tested and certified before actually entering the country. If they turn out to be cultured ones, they get rejected from Bahrain.*

OD: How do you actually assess natural pearls from cultured ones?

TM: *80% of the pearls we see don't need testing. When it comes to a finished product, though, like a necklace for example, you need to authenticate the pearls for the sake of both the consumer and yourself as a seller, to be on the safe side - by receiving a document stating that the pearls are natural ones. This guarantees that in the future, the client doesn't come back to you with claims about the nature of the pearls. For the other remaining 20% of pearls, you need high-end machinery to tell them apart.*

OD: Do you wear pearls yourself?

TM: *No, I don't wear anything - no watch, no rings, nothing. I'm very free (laughs).*

OD: You mentioned you were teaching this music to your kids. How do you make sure that this legacy is being transmitted from one generation to the other?

TM: *For our kids' generation, it is harder to learn this than it was for ours, because they have distractions today we didn't have in the past. You have to convince the newer generations another way. Teaching them to play the drums first in order for them to then discover the world and business of pearling is a good way to do it. You cannot force the kids to do it - it has to come from them.*

image 16

image 17

image 18

[1] CVD Stands for chemical vapor deposition, a production process for synthetic diamonds (also referred to as laboratory-grown diamond) which are made of the same material as natural diamonds: pure carbon, crystallized in an isotropic 3D form.

[2] Seed pearls are pearls which are smaller than 2mm in radius.

[3] Before mass-production started in China, Vietnam and in the Philippines, the retail value of the common 7mm necklace was not less than $200, which is now sold in China for $2.

TALAL EBRAHIM MATTAR

Belonging to the sixth-generation pearl merchant from one of the major Bahraini families active in the sector, Talal Mattar expanded the family venture by founding Mattar Jewelers in Manama, two years after joining his father business (2002). An important promoter of the national pearling heritage and legacy, he is also a percussion expert, whose love for music and domestic rhythms equal his shared passion towards pearls. He currently dedicates his free time and energy towards the development of a musical archive focusing on the chants and rhythms of Bahrain.

The Pearl of Great Value

Charles M. Stang

What is it about the pearl that captures the human imagination? Is it that a perfect sphere emerges from the ragged and misshapen shell of a mollusk? That a thing of such beauty comes from what seems like formless filth? Or that its beauty owes to the introduction of an impurity, a bit of sand over which an oyster coasts a milky white surface? Our eyes are drawn to that surface, somehow both luminous and opaque, shining with light and yet obscure to our vision. Part sand and part sea, simultaneously earth and water; an accident of nature, but an accident that seems to perfect nature; a contradiction, a paradox, a mystery.

People have been diving for pearls since the Neolithic period[1]. The Arabian Gulf and the South Indian coast were the preeminent diving sites of the Old World until the sixteenth century, when New World pearls flooded the global market. With the invention of cultured pearls in Japan in the late nineteenth century, the traditional practice of pearl diving fell into obsolescence.

Pearl diving is difficult and dangerous work, and in antiquity often fell to indentured or enslaved men. Sadly, their voices are lost to posterity and with them the music they played and the songs they sang[2]. In the ancient world, we know of the pearls, and sometimes their divers, from people far removed from the hard work of harvesting them: first, from the records of the nobles and royals who adorned themselves with them; and secondly, from ancient Christian writers for whom the pearl and its diver became important metaphors for theology and spirituality[3].

In the ancient world, no one valued pearls more than the Persians: it was a favorite commodity among their kings, across dynasties, including the Achaemenid (550-330 BCE), Parthian (247 BCE-224 CE), and Sasanian (224-642 CE) eras[3]. Just before the Sasanian King Peroz (r. 459-484 CE) died in battle against the Hephthalite Huns, he is said to have cast away his famous, huge pearl-earring so that none of the Huns might claim it as bounty. The Romans, having learned of his defeat, offered the Huns great sums for the earring: some say the Huns never found it; others that they did but sold it to Peroz's son instead. The Romans were eager to recover the earring because already by the fourth century CE the pearl was synonymous with the proverbial wealth of the Persian king. It would have been a prize for a Roman emperor to flaunt this symbol of Persian power. The Persian king not only wore pearls himself, but assigned pearled jewelry and belts to noblemen and women in his court as a sign of favor, prestige, and their loyalty to his crown.

The Persian fashion spilled over to their neighbors, so that not only Romans, but also Arabs, Armenians, and Sogdians[4] (among others), were soon swept up in the fad, and its associations with legendary wealth and power. The international pearl trade, which was well underway by the first century BCE, was promoted and increasingly controlled by the Sasanians between the third and seventh centuries CE. One Sasanian king, Ardashîr (r. 224-240), is credited with founding a number of cities on the Persian Gulf to promote maritime trade, especially in pearls. During these same centuries, the Gulf became home to a number of Christian communities, for whom pearls and pearl diving came to have special significance.

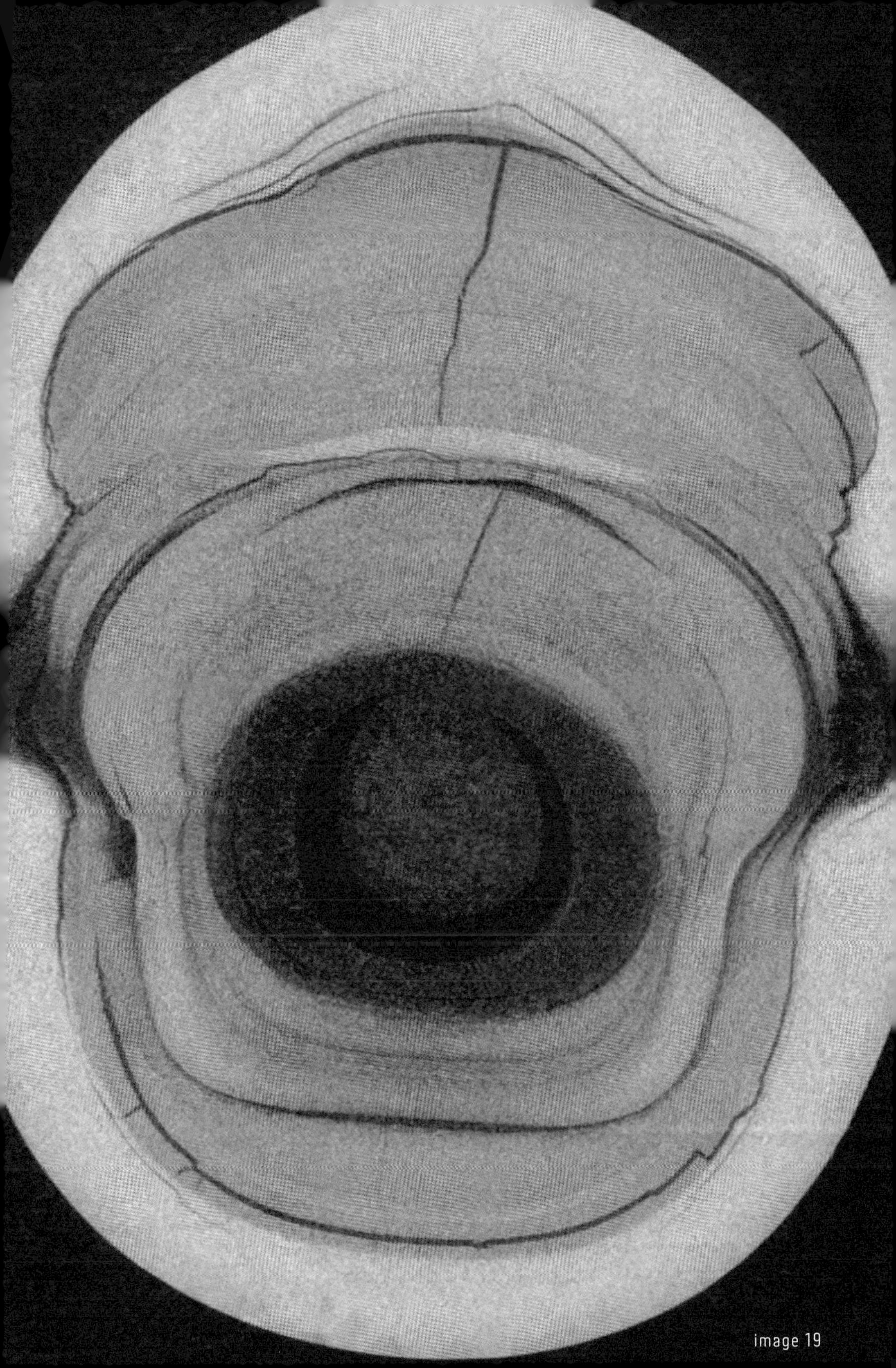

image 19

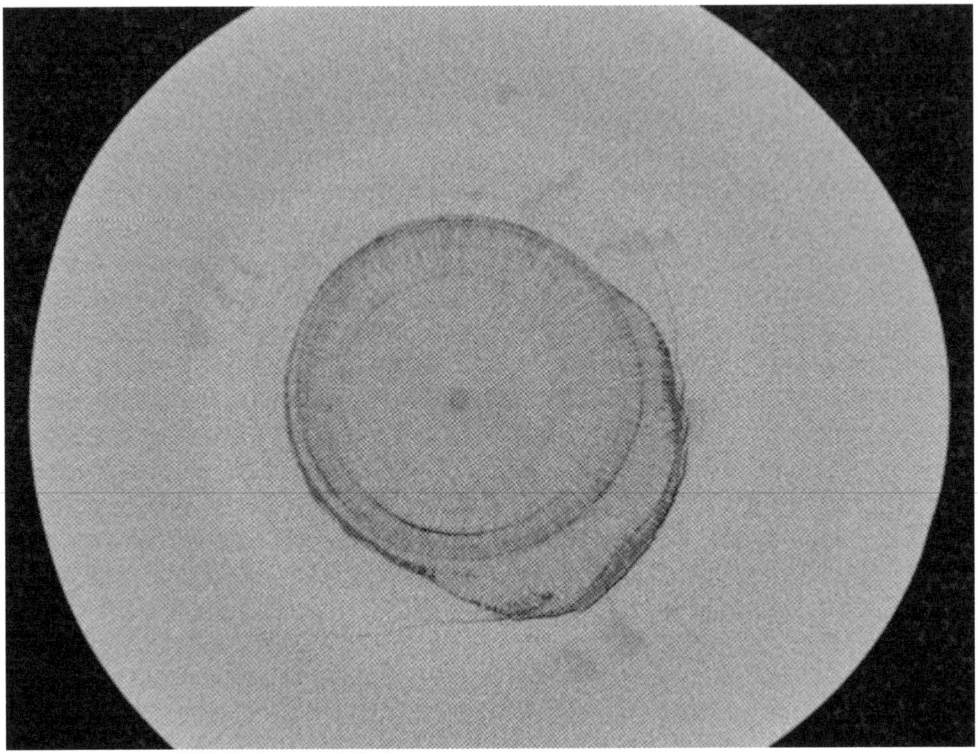

image 20

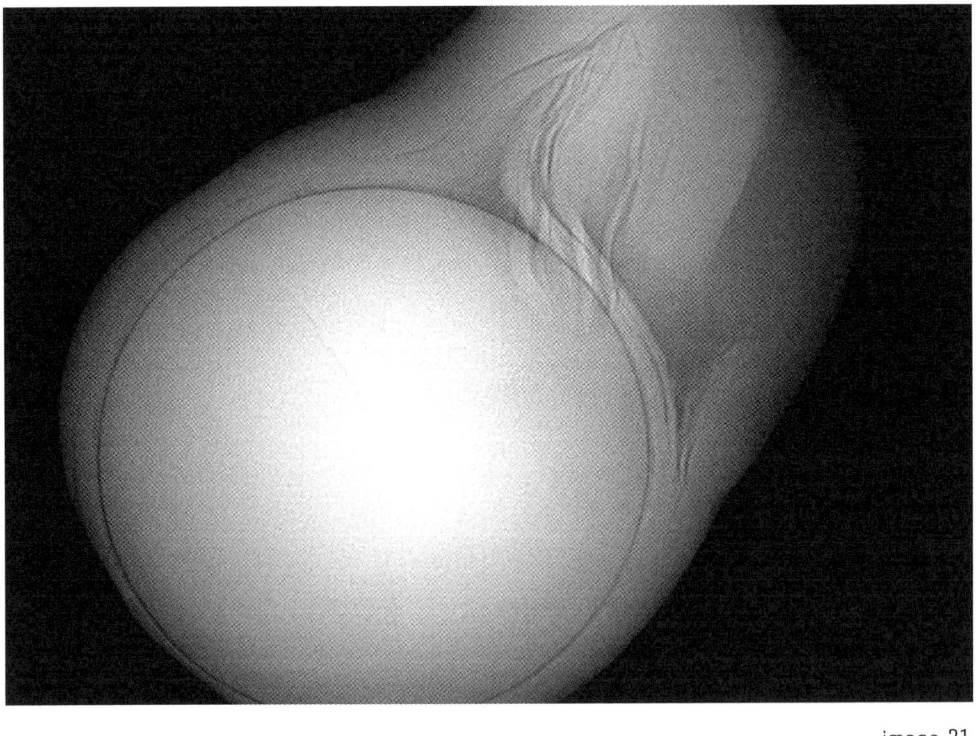

image 21

In the Gospel of Matthew, Jesus offers one of many parables about the kingdom of heaven: "the kingdom of heaven is like a merchant in search of fine pearls, who, on finding one pearl of great value, went and sold all that he had and bought it" [6]. As with most of Jesus's parables, the meaning is not immediately clear. The question most readers wrestle with is this: what is this one pearl of great value? Whatever it is, the demand is clear: to enter the kingdom of heaven one must be like a merchant who sells all that he has so as to have that one pearl.

When Christians reached the Gulf in the fourth century, their musings on the mysteries of the pearl encountered the hard reality of those who dove for pearls, and those who traded in them. Jesus's parable came alive in new ways as these Christians interpreted the pearl divers in light of their own religious tradition, and in turn reinterpreted their own religious tradition in light of the same.

We have evidence of Christians in the Gulf as early as the fourth century, and as late as the ninth century. The Christians who emigrated to the Gulf were not Greek-speaking Christians from the West, but rather Syriac-speaking Christians from Syria, Mesopotamia, and Persia [7]. Tradition has it that monasticism came to the Gulf from Egypt. The man who said to have brought it eastward from Egypt is named Mar Awgen (d. 363). The story goes that he was a Christian pearl diver in the fourth century, living on an island in the Suez, diving for pearls and distributing the proceeds of his labor to the poor. He then traveled to the western deserts of Egypt, where he met one of the famous founders of Egyptian monasticism, a monk named Pachomius (c. 292-348). Pachomius commissioned him to take seventy of his own monks and to establish a community in northern Mesopotamia. Whether this traditional story is accurate or not, we know that monasteries of the sort Mar Awgen established proliferated throughout Mesopotamia, and down the Tigris and Euphrates, all the way to the Gulf, where they came to line the eastern shore. From the very beginning, then, the history of monasticism in the Gulf is connected to pearl diving. That connection will only grow stronger as the Christians of the Gulf become more familiar with the trade, and some writers turn to pearl diving as a metaphor for their own mystical efforts.

One of the distinctive features of the Syriac Christianity is its tradition of theology expressed in poetry. The most celebrated poet-theologian is Ephrem the Syrian (c. 306-373), who wrote a series of five hymns on the symbol of the pearl at the same time as Mar Agwin, the former pearl diver, was allegedly bringing monasticism to the East [8]. Ephrem says that while precious stones were sufficient to represent the angels, only the pearl is a worthy symbol of Christ himself. The piercing of a pearl with an awl so as to string it on a necklace, becomes for him a symbol of the crucifixion. Although he never witnessed pearl divers at work, he imagines himself as a diver. At one point, he holds a pearl in front of himself and asks after its mysteries. It speaks to him, and says that just as the divers who retrieved her, a daughter of the sea, were astonished at the inexhaustible depths of that sea, so Christians should not presume to know the nature of God, whose depths are beyond any and all understanding. In this case, the pearl becomes a witness to God's unknowable essence and inexhaustible depths.

Syriac Christianity was also renowned for its rich mystical tradition. These mystics came to understand themselves as pearl-divers and pearl-merchants, appropriating this ancient trade as a powerful metaphor for their search, in this world, for purity, illumination, and union with God. The so-called "golden age" of Syriac Christian mysticism spanned the sixth through the ninth centuries[9]. That golden age peaked in the seventh century, and at its summit stands Isaac of Nineveh. Isaac was neither born nor raised in Nineveh, but rather in Beth Qatraye (modern day Qatar). Christianity has a longstanding practice of naming bishops after their episcopal sees; in this case, Isaac was ordained the bishop of Nineveh (modern day Mosul) in the year 676 – hence he is called Isaac of Nineveh. He had been a monk and a teacher in Beth Qatraye for many years, but he did not take the role well. After only five months, he abdicated his episcopacy, and retired to the mountains of Khuzistan on the northern shore of the Gulf, where he led a solitary life.

We know very little about Isaac's life. But we do know that he was born and raised on the Gulf, within sight of the sea. As one scholar has remarked, Isaac's writings are full of references to the sea: "he speaks of ships, of captains and sailors, of sea storms and winds, of divers and oysters plumbed from the depths of the sea"[10]. Isaac was a child of the seashore, and the pearl diving trade presented itself as a poignant metaphor for the monastic pursuit of holiness. He wrote, "If in each oyster a diver was to find a pearl, then every man would quickly become rich. And if the diver immediately got the pearl and the waves did not beat him and the sharks did not encounter him, he would not have to hold his breath to the extent he suffocated, and he would not be deprived of fresh air which is available to all and he would not go down to the sea bottom – then more often than lightning strikes, pearls would appear in abundance"[11]. But, of course, a diver does not find a pearl in every oyster. He must search and scour for a single pearl among many oysters. He must set himself apart from his fellows and suffer as he trains his breath and his body. The pearl diver thus becomes a symbol for the monk and the mystic, and the sea with its dangers becomes a symbol for the world and its attachments that would thwart his pursuit. In other words, Isaac saw the pearl diver's struggles, and saw them as equivalent to his own struggles to achieve purity, illumination, and union.

On another occasion, Isaac makes the analogy between the diver and the monk even more explicit, "The diver plunges naked into the sea to find a pearl; and the wise monk will go naked through the desert places to find the Pearl, Jesus Christ himself"[12].

In a variation on this same saying, Isaac says that "a swimmer dives naked into the sea until he finds a pearl, and a wise monk, stripped of everything, journeys through life until he finds in himself the Pearl, Jesus Christ". The pearl is still identified with Jesus Christ[13]. But here the desert has been replaced by the monk himself, or perhaps even better, the monk himself has been revealed as the true desert, the true desolate place, he in whose desolation a pearl lies somewhere hidden. The mystery of the Incarnate Christ is to be found not out in some exotic or forsaken place, but within. Isaac suggests that mystical union is found by turning inward, and finding that Christ already lives within, waiting to be found, as a pearl waits to be found by a diver.

Isaac is not alone: other mystics of his era speak of pearl diving as a metaphor for the mystical life. John the Venerable, in the eighth century, writes, "these precious pearls are gathered and stored among the treasures of his mind by the merchant who is occupied with prayer, the strenuous diver captivated with desire for the sea that washes him"[14]. His contemporary, Joseph the Visionary, spoke of the efforts of the solitary monk as "the labour of the merchant up to the time when the pearl of great price falls into his hands."[15] While Isaac was drawn to the pearl divers, these two authors, perhaps in keeping with Jesus's parable, have turned to the pearl merchant of the Gulf to help understand their practice and piety, their monasticism and their mysticism.

I have presented two sets of eyes with which to contemplate "the pearl of great value" and its many meanings in antiquity. In the eyes of the royal Persians, for whom pearls are symbols of imperial power, wealth, and influence, the divers themselves disappear as kings and nobles trade in their precious haul. In the eyes of ancient Christians, for whom pearls are symbols of the mysteries of the faith, preeminently the mystery of the Incarnation, the pearl divers reappear, but understood now as types for the monk and the mystic. In neither case, sadly, do we better understand who these divers were, and how they understood their difficult trade and its treasure. For that task, we must turn from antiquity to modernity, and listen not only to the words preserved by literate elites, but to the lyrics and rhythms of the divers' own songs.

In conclusion, I wish to raise the question of the place of these ancient Christians in the history of the Gulf (or Beth Qatraye, as they call it), including its distinct tradition of pearl diving. For decades, archaeologists have been doing important work bringing the material remains of these communities to light. Historians have been collecting evidence, documentary attestations of these Gulf Christians—putting flesh to bones, so to speak. In addition, textual scholars have been collecting, editing, and translating the Beth Qatraye canon of monastic and mystical literature[16]. Their research makes this story better available to a wider audience, including the citizens and residents of the contemporary Gulf.

Why might that be important? First and foremost, because this history should be embraced as a part of the Gulf's own heritage, as a testimony to its own religiously pluralistic past, and a resource for thinking about pluralism in the present, and the future. The Gulf has at times been home to all three of the Abrahamic faiths. Of those three faiths, the Christian history of the Gulf boasts one of the greatest monastic and mystical theologians of the first millennium, Isaac of Nineveh. What would it mean for the Gulf to claim Isaac and this broader heritage as its own? What would it mean for the Gulf to claim this entire Christian canon, and the communities that produced it, as its own? Just as the Greeks, who are now Christians, claim Homer and Plato as part

image 22

of their heritage; and just as the Egyptians, who are now Muslims, claim the Pharaohs and their civilization as part of their heritage; why should the Gulf not claim Isaac and his Christian tradition as part of its own heritage? To claim this history would be to see the monks and mystics of the Gulf as part of a broader history of diversity and pluralism in the region, not surprising in fact, given that the Gulf is, among other things, a series of ports, where not only goods but ideas were traded, and thus where not only monks but merchants were missionaries.

Finally, if we were to situate this Christian mystical tradition squarely in the Gulf, what would we see or understand about it that we have failed to see or understand? In the case of Isaac, recognizing him as a son of the Gulf encourages us to read his mystical theology through the figure of the pearl diver. But what if we read Isaac and the other Christian writers from the Gulf with an eye to the wider landscape they were raised in – looking out for language of winds and seas, oases and deserts, ports and trade? In other words, have western readers of Isaac missed crucial aspects of his writings because we have lifted him out from his cultural context? What would it mean to see Isaac, and the Syriac mystical tradition of which he is the most famous representative, through the unique eyes of the Gulf experience? What would it mean to see him through the eyes of its pearls?

image 23

[1] R.A. Carter, "Sea of Pearls: Seven Thousand Years of the Industry that Shaped the Gulf" (London, 2012). See also R.A. Donkin, "Beyond Price: Pearls and Pearl-Fishing, Origins to the Age of Discoveries" (Philadelphia, 1998).

[2] For a memoir of a modern pearl diver, see S.M. Al-Shamlan, "Pearling in the Arabian Gulf: A Kuwaiti Memoir", trans. P. Clark (London, 2020).

[3] See Brian Colless, "The Wisdom of the Pearlers: An Anthology of Syriac Christian Mysticism" (Kalamazoo, MI, 2008).

[4] See Joel Walker, "Luminous Markers: Pearls and Royal Authority in Late Antique Iran and Eurasia," in Nicola Di Cosma and Michael Mass (eds), "Eurasian Empires in Late Antiquity: Rome, China, Iran, and the Steppe" (Cambridge, 2018) 253-267. The Achaemenid the first Persian empire, whose territory at its height stretched from Eastern Europe to the Indus Valley. The Parthian Empire controlled a smaller territory than did the Achaemenids, whose heirs they claimed to be. The Sasanian Empire, sometimes called the Neo-Persian Empire, endured the longest of the three, and was the last before the arrival of Islam in the mid-seventh century.

[5] Sogdia was an ancient Iranian civilization situated in Central Asia. Sogdians were well known as merchants, transporting goods between Persia in the West and China in the East.

[6] (13:45-46)

[7] Syriac is a dialect of Aramaic that emerged in the first centuries CE, perhaps in Edessa, and became a major literary and liturgical language for Christians throughout the Middle East between the 4th and 8th centuries. In late antiquity, Syriac-speaking Christian communities were established as far west as Asia Minor and as far east as China.

[8] The five hymns "On the Pearl" are Hymns 81-85 of "The Hymns on Faith". See Jeffrey Wickes' translation (Washington, DC: The Catholic University of America, 2015), pp. 377-392.

[9] For an anthology of the spiritual tradition that led up to this "golden age," see Sebastian Brock, "The Syriac Fathers on Prayer and the Spiritual Life" (Kalamazoo, MI: Cistercian Publications, 1987).

[10] Metropolitan Hilarion (Alfeyev) of Volokolamsk, "In Search of a Spiritual Pearl: St Isaac the Syrian and His Works," in "St Isaac the Syrian and His Spiritual Legacy: Proceedings from the International Patristics Conference, Moscow", 2013 (Yonkers, NY, St Vladimir's Seminary Press, 2015), 13.

[11] Part II, Hom. 34:4; quoted in ibid.

[12] Quoted in Colless, "The Wisdom of the Pearlers", 1.

[13] Homily 48 from "The Ascetical Homilies of Saint Isaac the Syrian", translated by the Holy Transfiguration Monastery (Boston: The Holy Transfiguration Monastery, 1984).

[14] Quoted in Colless, "The Wisdom of the Pearlers", 1.

[15] Ibid.

[16] See Mario Kozah, Abdulrahim Abu-Husayn, Saif Shaheen Al-Murikhi, Haya Al Thani (eds), "An Anthology of Syriac Writers from Qatar in the Seventh Century" (Piscataway, NJ : Gorgias Press, 2015); and their accompanying collection of studies, "The Syriac Writers of Qatar in the Seventh Century" (Piscataway, NJ : Gorgias Press, 2014).

CHARLES STANG

Professor of Early Christian Thought and Director of the Center for the Study of World Religions at Harvard Divinity School, Charles Stang's research and teaching focus on the history of Christianity in the context of the ancient Mediterranean world, especially Eastern varieties of Christianity. More specifically, his research addresses: the development of asceticism, monasticism, and mysticism in Christianity; ancient philosophy, especially Neoplatonism; the Syriac Christian tradition, especially the spread of the East Syrian tradition along the Silk Road; other philosophical and religious movements of the ancient Mediterranean, including Gnosticism, Hermeticism, and Manichaeism; and modern continental philosophy and theology, especially as they intersect with the study of religion. His most recent book is Our Divine Double (Harvard University Press, 2016).

image 24

Leaking Pearls

Talin Hazbar

Looking at the systems and the invisible borders within a fluid space, how do we create a system and how do we define it? What does it mean to be a host, and what does it mean to be a guest? What is the transitional state in which one becomes the other? What is our relationship to a space which is always in constant flux? How can we navigate through it? How much can we anchor and depend on the unseen and untouched grounds?

The marine ecosystems served important roles in the social, financial and cultural development of the Gulf communities. Fishing and pearl diving were the source of livelihood to many. Pearls and the dependence on pearl diving in the Arabian Gulf reshaped and transformed the region before the oil boom. The stories, the struggle, the pride, the economy and the growth of the region is strongly connected to the sea as a whole and oyster-beds in particular.

An oyster bed is determined by the geological structure of the seabed, the temperature and the depth of the water. Within the indefinite and the extended seabed, oyster beds were identified and recorded in terms of the quality of their pearls, the density of their oysters, and the high ratio of pearl discoveries made during the pearl collecting season within a particular location.

The parallel between an oyster bed and the diving industry lies in a focal point being community and nurturing environment. Oysters and the growth of pearls depend on the marine ecosystem's health. Fishermen and divers depended on strong connections within the crew. In both cases, the wait and the fact of trusting the unknown were always present.

Leaking Pearls is a work that looks at the tight knit of an organic system. The work recreates an oyster bed, formed to stimulate a sea bed, through spheric units woven together into a malleable fluid structure. The structure explores how ephemeral and amorphous objects would shape and react to various stimuli, internal and external while submerged in sea water. The sea and the ecosystem will transform the submerged structure as a whole and the unit in particular. The malleable structure is expected to be influx as it settles within its new environment and eventually remap where it falls on the seabed. It will in return live to create a taxonomy of the current marine life.

The structure of the piece provides a space to contemplate on the multilayered relationships of oysters, pearls and the pearl diving practice. It meditates on the cycle of host, guest, and the organic growth and transformation of the relationships within a cycle, looking at the complexities and the ecological implications formed by a system.

The unseen seabeds, despite being in constant flux and change, were also in a state of stillness allowing growth. It's a fluid infrastructure, which keeps on producing and systematically responding to the tests of time. The aim is to study the fragility of the micro scale unit, and the surface's overall adaptive mechanism through time. From a woven light and adaptive structure to heavy, stiff and structured surface. Understanding time, through its weight and materials, understanding value through its surface transformation and points of rigidity. The piece aims to reimagine the earlier seabed locations, how they were defined and how they have evolved.

As such it raises questions on the invisible borders within a fluid space, the value of these sites in the open sea, and our regulated system to find means of life. The process of this project and the uncertainty also raise questions that may or may not be answered; What is an ideal state versus an idealized state? How do we exist within the systems we create and how do our systems coexist within ones larger than us?

This structure will be submerged in the sea waters, and will remain an underwater guest and then a host, eventually, until a date for a physical exhibition is set.

TALIN HAZBAR

Landscapes and natural formations influenced Talin Hazbar's understanding of matter as volatile and mobile, continuously moving and adapting. Exploring and understanding the surrounding landscape, its intricate materials and the relations between the two has been at the core of Hazbar's practice. Her interest in nature and the ephemeral structures stems from nature's ability to operate and behave both at a microscopic and a grand level simultaneously. Her practice framework is focused on redefining the idea of molds and systems, and exploring the space between material contingency and malleable molds, to achieve articulated, coherent and responsive structures. Hazbar's work and processes aim to showcase the overlapping boundaries in nature, history, ecology and the formation of society.

image 25

Cultivating Pearls in the Gulf: Interview with Abdulla Al Suwaidi

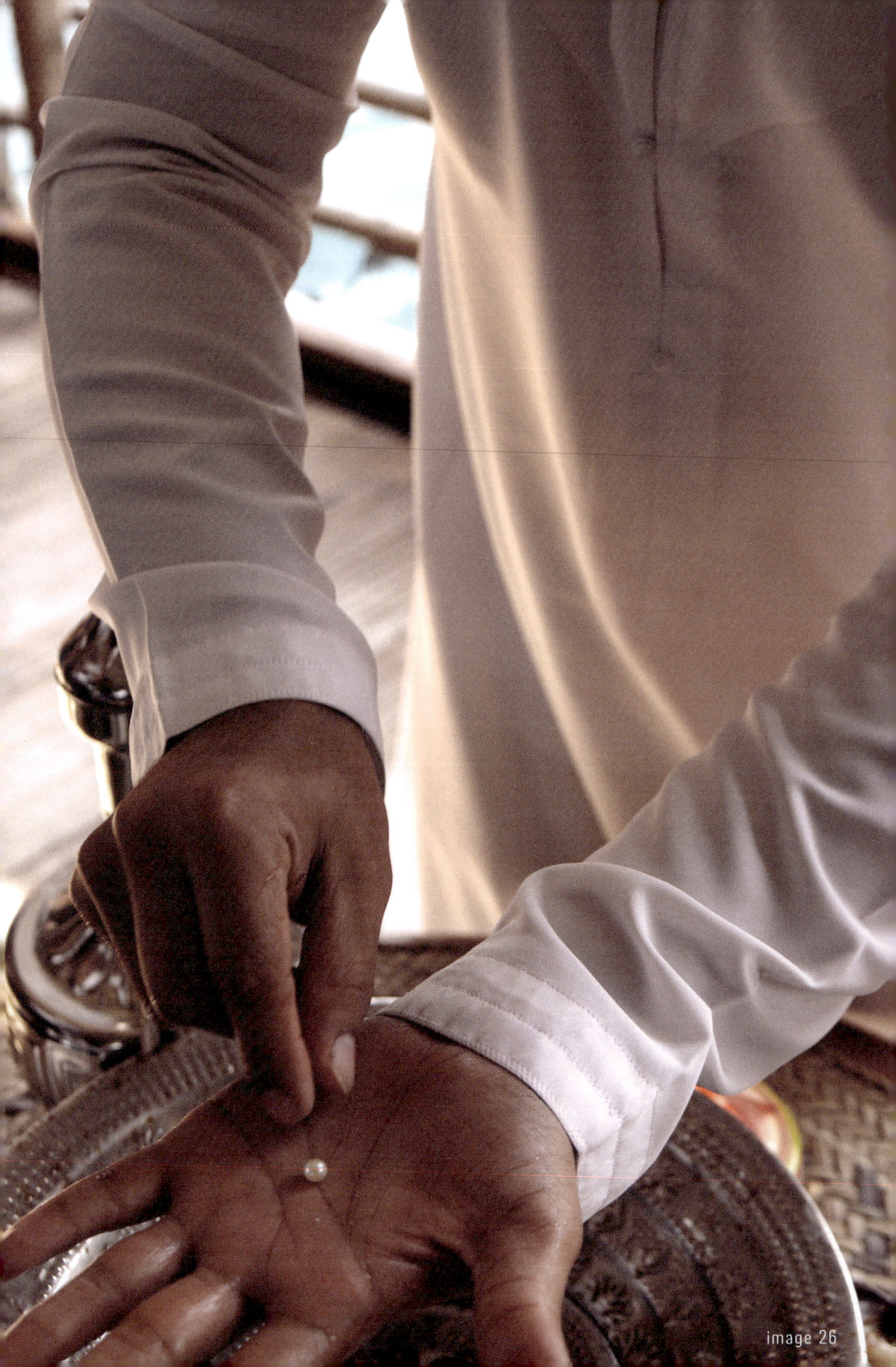

image 26

OLIVIER DUPORT/FLEE: Can you introduce yourself?

ABDALLAH SUWAIDI:
I am a pearl diver, passionate and connected to the past and with the great legacy of pearl diving. I see myself belonging to the old times, not the new ones. I don't wear a watch, I don't go with the brands. I am what my grandfather was: a pearl diver. When I see the way we live our lives today, it is completely different to the old life. And that old life is my passion.

OD: You started the project of a pearl farm here in Ras al Khaimah which is the only one of its kind in the whole Gulf. Could you tell us more about it?

AS: *I've dived for pearls for the last twenty-five years. I did a lot of thinking and had a lot of ideas to attract people to see the importance of our history. Rarity and scarcity of the natural pearl have forced me to consider using technology and research to maintain the legacy of our ancestors. People are now driven by the defense of the environment and are worried about preserving it. This is a modern component that can help preserve the legacy of pearl diving.*

I've been doing this because my generation is the last one to have witnessed and seen people diving for pearls at the end of the 1940s. My child and his generation haven't seen my grandfather diving, as I did in the early 1970s. We are a generation stuck between the collapse of the pearling legacy and its potential resurrection. That is, only if we do something to transmit it to the next generations. This is why I find myself responsible to do so and why I started the farm.

OD: It's a huge responsibility to be handing over this heritage to the next generation. Do others in the Gulf share this belief in the importance of passing it on?

AS: *For me, pearl diving in the Gulf is like an intangible magic. No matter the generation, they will be connected to pearl diving. Young or elderly, if you ask anybody here in the Gulf what they are in terms of identity they will answer you: pearls. But if you ask them how this happened, they might not be able to answer, yet they will have kept carrying on this magical legacy. Why? Because somehow it's passed on from generation to generation as every family counted, whether a diver, a hauler, a sailor or a singer or a cook or a captain, navigator or pearl trader. This has shaped life in the Gulf socially, economically and even politically.*

Going back in history, you'll see that the Greek, Roman, Persian, Arab travellers like Ibn Battûta, Al-Mas'ûdî, Al Idrissi, all passed through and spoke about this area, followed by the Portuguese, Dutch, Italian, French, British. The whole world had understood the beauty of the elegant pearls which had brought them all the way to the Gulf. We were globalized even before what people refer to as globalization. We are connected with the world, and that is due to the magic of the pearl. If you ask many people in the Gulf if they have seen pearls, many will answer positively, but the truth is that they don't know the true Arabian pearls. Pearling has come this far after thousands of years and now risks getting cut off from new generations. I realized that pearls could come to an end and could be forgotten along with their songs, poems and stories. I could be the person to give the kiss of life to pearls and to revive the legacy.

OD: Do you think it is working? Are the younger generations receiving this message and are you connected with other people working to achieve the same goal?

AS: *My simple answer is that, in the English ports back in 1906*[1]*, 74,000 men went to pearl diving season in the whole Gulf, starting from my lovely pearling village Al Rams*[2]*, all the way to Kuwait. Today, in the UAE (United Arab Emirates), there are probably maximum two or three pearl divers left. There used to be more, but they are dying and I am probably the youngest at the age of 47. This is my biggest challenge, how to pass it on to the next generation. The farm shows the legacy and the story of pearl divers in order to attract people and to share this knowledge. Pearls are one of the strong gems that can unify us.*

OD: What do you perceive as the biggest challenge in passing this legacy on to younger generations?

AS: *Modernity and traditions probably did conflict in the past. Today they are complementing each other. We can not live without modernity nor without the great tradition we have. Maintaining and preserving it requires a complex environmental equation. Producing a pearl naturally or by cultivating and seeding the oysters is a positive environmental signal. Failing to do that means that the ecosystem is not clean, explaining why oysters can not survive in it. To me, the biggest challenge in the future is how we maintain and take care of the environment. Less trash in the sea, no chemical waste, limiting the factors that cause pollution – like big ships that travel in the Gulf and dump their waste there – are all ideas to protect the sea from suffering that will definitely*

image 27

affect us all one day. Preserving and moving forward is what I've done at a small scale, and I hope that it will inspire others to do the same or even better. Julphar[3] *was one of the pearl trading hubs in the world. I've tried to preserve it and to present it to the world. Let's see how Abu Dhabi and Dubai manage bringing this beautiful legacy forward. I believe one day they will celebrate this unique culture.*

OD: Cultured pearls have been considered a major issue in the Gulf as their invention affected the market tremendously. Was your initiative at the pearl farm met with resistance or criticism?

AS: *Absolutely, I had a lot of challenges explaining my work to people. I had some media attacks, but these attacks were never supported with claims as I am bringing an argument forward and know why I am doing what I am doing. I ask them: If you celebrate the natural pearl and want to maintain it, what do you want to do about it and how are you going to move forward with it? I get no answer and nobody wants to do anything.*

There are people who have manipulated the names and definitions of pearl culture to link it to the artificial pearl which is completely false. Natural pearls that divers get from the bottom of the sea have a likelihood of 1% to be founds in oysters. So only one of a hundred oysters will bring a pearl. You'll be killing 100 oysters just to end up with one pearl and this is what has been happening in the past. They harvested the seas as one harvests the land and now from 74,000 divers in the Gulf, only a few remain active. The second type of pearls are cultured pearls invented by the Japanese pearl farmer Mikimoto in 1955, who attempted to seed a foreign body inside the oyster and with that, pearls were harvested with human intervention. Today 95% of the pearls sold around the world are cultured. Who can afford natural pearls today? No one. One gram is sold for a minimum of 2,000USD and goes up to 4,000USD depending on the type, size, luster and shape of the pearl. Finally, there are artificial pearls, made out of glass or a chemical component, that look like a pearl without being one. Artificial pearls are not cultured pearls, but the use of this concept created confusion that drove the natural pearl prices up while degrading the cultured pearls to the level of the artificial pearls. I know this strategy and this is nothing new. This has been the case since cultured pearls were invented.

The solution is to present both natural and cultured Arabic pearls that are affordable for the public. This is my biggest challenge in order to make this legacy sustainable. In order to do that, you need to focus on all people, not just on the rich and celebrities. I want to prove that our beautiful Gulf is still producing the best pearls. I provide an alternative. A cultured pearl from the same oyster that genetically belonged to the natural pearl. To do that, we breed it in the same area and environment in which natural pearls grow. This is the way to combine modernity and tradition and the way to make it a sustainable project.

OD: Have you been able to convince your critics of this solution?

AS: *The conversation will never stop and I don't have the time for it. I am 47 years old and I'd rather concentrate on growing what I'm doing.*

OD: Why do you think there is a lack of institutional support for your initiative in comparison to other important traditions in the region, such as falconry or camel racing?

image 28

image 29

AS: *Priorities. Pearling isn't one. Falcons have a lot of fans and their number is growing constantly. Pearl diving is not a priority and this chapter has been considered closed. I don't accept that, and I intend to prove it by starting my next project which will be a pearl diving academy, where people will learn how to dive the traditional way (with no assistance) and the modern one (with scuba diving gear). This is currently what I am doing most of my days and I know that one day pearl diving will become a priority again.*

OD: You mentioned commercial sustainability, but what about the ecological one? Are you still investing in research on development related to that?

AS: *I started working on pearl diving in 2003. The first seeding*[4] *was in 2005 and our first pearl was found three months after that. To me, and to foreign observers, it was nothing short of a miracle. We couldn't believe it. We tried again and again, and the first pearl coating started from the first month on! So from 2005 to 2018, it was only testing, testing, testing. A very long journey of collecting information for myself to satisfy my need of knowledge.*

You see, my project implies a deep understanding of the surrounding environment. Temperature, oxygen and salinity of water are crucial factors. Stopping Research and Development would kill the project. It is too important. One day, I would like to open my research laboratory to share this research with marine biologists and gemologists from all over the world to experiment and conduct research with me. I am sure they would be very much surprised by what they see. We cannot do anything with the actual environmental challenges as they are global, but we can think about simple ideas based on natural resources to overcome natural disasters.

OD: How do you plan on transmitting the music of pearl divers as part of the larger heritage of pearl diving in your projects?

AS: *I haven't been thinking about it before meeting you today. We are not perfect and there always is something missing. With knowledge sharing we can bridge this gap. Music turns out to be very important as it brings motivation on the boat while being alone in the middle of the sea. The connection to the families and the coping with the fear and uncertainty of such a voyage, the wish to find the pearl that will provide for the whole season, or long days waiting for wind to blow their sails – there was a lot at stake in this music. The lyrics of the compositions based on Arabic poetry are extremely important. It is an inspiration to explore the inner emotions of the divers and the whole crew and to capture these beautiful gems that are pearls in order to sustain themselves in a time when there were no other resources available. All poetry and stories revolved logically around this quest of the precious pearl hiding somewhere in the neighbouring sea.*

OD: Do you think you'll ever stop diving?

AS: *Only death will stop me diving. This is why I wish to die at an age where I won't depend on others. I believe it will be at the age of 86 and hope Allah will bless me with that. Diving is good for health and allows you to disconnect with the world. You create your own world in the depths without the noisy, crowdy disturbances of the modern world. During the lockdown I couldn't take the idea of staying on land. The farm was closed from receiving visitors but work didn't stop. We continued diving, taking care of the oysters, cleaning them and the nets, and knew that we would be harvesting the pearls when coronavirus is up.*

OD: Do you see this underwater world as a refuge?

AS: *Not only. The pressure we get in our lives disappears with the pressure you experience while going down to the bottom of the sea. All your tension is released and the moment you land on the bottom is the restart – the reset to your manufacturer setting – and you come back up every time a different person. That's why you want to do it over and over, whether you are a traditional diver or a scuba diver. Going down is a great relief. If you take a bottle with you it will release all tension before filling up again. The same thing happens with humans, but you get rid of all negativity during the process. The energy is completely different at the bottom of the sea than the one from the land. You need to watch out.*

OD: You have never had an accident diving?

AS: *Never. I was scared lots of times but never hurt myself. My hearing is still very good, although my vision decreased because I used to dive without goggles. Today I just do it to maintain myself, so I only dive from time to time for about fifteen minutes and about 10 meters deep. My grandfather did it for days because they needed it to survive. Many people think that holding your breath under water is the same as holding your breath on the land. It is not. Once in the depths, you have more air to breathe.*

OD: Do you think your children will be able to take this legacy over?

AS: *I wasn't forced to follow the footsteps of my grandfather. I searched and still search for it myself. My children will see what I've done and similarly they will have the choice to continue my work or to engage in another path. If they don't, someone else will, I have no fear about this; things will move forward. How did we maintain thousands of years of writing and pearls in the Gulf throughout history? There is a reason for this.*

[1] When most of the Gulf countries were under British dominion.

[2] Little seaside village next to Ras Al Khaimah in the north of the UAE.

[3] Former name of Ras Al Khaimah which also literally means "pearl" in Arabic.

[4] Process for the cultivation of oysters.

ABDULLA AL SUWAIDI

Is the grand-son of Mohammed Bin Abdulla Al-Suwaidi, famous pearl diver of the golden "Julphar" dynasty in Ras Al Khaimah and one the few remaining pearl divers in the UAE as well as the founder of "Suwaidi Pearls", the only cultured pearl farm in the whole Gulf region. After receiving his degree in Political Science from the American University in Washington, he joined the diplomatic service for which he served in Japan and Australia before returning to the UAE. There he spearheaded several projects for the account of the Ministry of Social Affairs before starting the pearl farm and trading company in Ras Al Khaimah in 2005. At the head of the unique farm of that kind in the region, he is constantly pushing for new initiatives centered around the preservation of local heritage while applying technology and conducting research when possible.

A Diver's Way: "Major Ali"

OLIVIER DUPORT/FLEE: Could you introduce yourself?

MAJOR ALI:
My name is Major Ali and I am the president of the Emirates Marine Environmental Group (EMEG). I started to deal with the environment and traditions a long time ago. In 1971, I started diving because of the many stories from my grandfather and father, and wanted to know what was down there. I wanted to see the pearls. When I started to dive, I opened thousands of shells without finding anything! My grandfather told me: "When you work with the sea, you have to be patient".

Soon after, I found the first pearls of my life, beautiful ones and that is how my pearl diving journey started. I call it "Al Wasl", which is the name of old Dubai today. I would take my friends and we would go to neighbouring islands by boat, around fifteen hours away, and there, we started to dive for pearls.

OD: How old were you when you dived for the first time?

MA: *I was 18 when I started.*

OD: Did pearl diving motivate you to become the head of the EMEG and protect the environment?

MA: *Well, you know Mr. Cousteau*[1] *was our Godfather. I went in '88 to Egypt and met him in Sharm el Sheikh. He inspired me to take care of the environment, and, returning from that trip, I started the Emirates Diving Association. After the Gulf war in 1995, I started EMEG. During the war, I was in the navy it was really dirty. After that, I started to take care of the environment and of pearl diving traditions around the whole UAE.*

OD: You are one of the last remaining divers. How do you consider the evolution of the last fifty years on that level?

MA: *Fifty years ago, pearl diving stopped, because oil, and the money linked to it, arrived. You know, diving is difficult... Since that time, I have been thinking about the future. Oil won't always be sustainable and its price fluctuates. One day it will be finished, and this is why I plan to teach the children. When it does, we can still dive for pearls and this is why I want to create a new generation of pearl divers.*

image 30

OD: How do you transmit this tradition? You told me you have children with you on the boat sometimes. Do you teach them?

MA: *In summer there is no school and we have kids coming here. The first was actually my son, who would bring his friends. But, before pearl diving, you have to learn how to swim properly and to be in good physical condition. Also, there is no telephone allowed for the kids, and we also forbid other bad things like fast food, Pepsi... When they come here, they are unhappy during the first three days because all of this isn't allowed and you change their lives. Step by step, after a week or so, they begin to like it and sleep over on the boat. They wash their faces in the sea, they eat dates, fish and rice, that is all. After 20 days, they don't want to leave anymore. I think this is because of the roots they have from their grandparents. It is amazing when you see their skills growing better and better as we teach them how to sing. They always sing to make the job easier, just like in the past. This is nice, I hope it will continue in the future. I have 2,000 kids doing that yearly, and young local ladies are also welcome of course.*

OD: Music is a central element to pearl diving, I was wondering if you sing?

MA: *Sure, when we start the pearling trip, we say "God, make it easier for us". For each thing we do on the boat we have another song. Many nice songs give courage and motivation to the crew to work, especially when you carry the anchor, which is very heavy.*

OD: There is a lot of poetry associated with pearl divers' music. What does the pearl mean to you?

MA: *Pearl, we think - and the Indians too -, helps the blood circulation. In Bombay, they would wear a lot of pearls to improve their blood circulation. It is the best thing you can wear, especially for ladies. You don't need gold or diamonds, you pick a pearl and wear it like it is. This is the great thing about pearls, they have a long life and keep their value forever.*

OD: Do you still dive the traditional way? Isn't it dangerous?

MA: *You go fast and this is when, sometimes, you get attacked by sharks. They usually only attack if you carry food or fish and there have been only a few attacks reported on divers in the past. They are a part of the sea and, as a pearl diver, you have to live with them. The sea belongs to another species. When we enter, we must behave, like when we go to someone's house. I myself, have a big diving history with around 10,000 dives under the belt (laugh).*

OD: You use a nose clip, a basket for oysters....

MA: *(interrupts) Also the weights*[2] *...*

OD: You go down quickly – how deep do you go?

MA: *My grandfather did 40 meters. Me, I do 10, maximum 15 meters, not more because these are the best places to find oysters. Some are full of them, where you can fill a basket in two minutes. Sometimes, you find some here and there and you might take three minutes or four minutes until you fill your basket.*

OD: That must be exhausting. How many dives do you do in one day?

MA: *In the past, they would do up to 200 dives in one day. For us, it is different, we do it more for fun, so maybe 10-15, maximum, a day.*

OD: Do you have a diving crew?

MA: *I do it with my team of about 10 people, because they are trained in pearl diving. We need the group, as one part of the group is diving, and the other assisting. Each diver has a helper, that is to also control the steering and support the captain. Pearl diving is a team's work which never bores you. Sometimes we dive for up to two months and nobody wants to go home.*

OD: What do you think of cultured pearls?

MA: *I don't like this at all because it destroys our culture. When artificial pearls arrived on the market, pearling collapsed. We would have suffered if oil hadn't arrived soon after. We would be dying. I am focusing on natural pearls, raising awareness about them. Cultured pearls are cheap and not good. If you take them between your teeth, they break! I like natural pearls and I want to get more of that kind. I conducted research to grow more natural oysters and hope to see more of that kind in the future.*

OD: Yet, natural pearl diving is taking a toll on oyster beds with only a 1% ratio of pearl per oyster. How do you ensure that this tradition remains sustainable, ecologically speaking?

MA: *Now with x-ray scanners you can tell if an oyster holds a pearl before opening it. You can replicate this process to thousands of oysters without damaging the oyster beds more than required. Otherwise, we would end up with an overfishing problem like in the past... It's sustainable thinking.*

image 31

OD: Do you think that cultured pearls affect the perception of natural pearls as well?

MA: *Yes, but eventually, people will realize the difference between both. Now people are coming back to natural pearls.*

OD: You mentioned you served in the war. Did that inspire you to be more active in the sustainable side of life?

MA: *Yes, especially during the Gulf war, because during this conflict, lots of oil got dispersed everywhere in the surrounding nature. It was terrible to watch, animals were dying. This is why I started the environment society. Our first focus was to make the sea clean and educate people, so they don't throw garbage in the sea. We started taking care of the marine ecosystem and we managed to change a lot of things. Before, some people thought of the sea as a trashcan and would throw away lots of rubbish in it. Now, it is forbidden and mentalities are changing. Today we teach the importance of taking care of turtles, sharks and dolphins. As an example, before, in Dubai, there weren't any turtles, now we have 52 that were born on this beach because I care about them. With our educational programs for the kids, they come, see the eggs and when the turtles are out, they release them to the wild. What is happening is amazing! I dedicated my life to the environment and to the teaching of our traditions. I am 63 now, and I am still diving, filming, helping because I don't smoke or drink and eat natural things (laugh).*

OD: The pearling culture is indubitably one from the Gulf. What is your relationship to divers from other countries?

MA: *We have a good relationship, especially with Bahrain. They have fresh water under the sea beds and this is why oysters grow better there, because salinity is down, and more plankton grows to feed them. We used to go to Bahrain and Kuwait to dive with them and they are coming to us. It is an open sea!*

OD: What about the current tensions in the Gulf with Qatar[3]: Is it affecting your work or is the sea something apart?

MA: *It is affecting our work for sure, but I think next week they are signing an agreement[4] and we will be done with this problem. The Gulf is one, and it connects all to each other, even with Iran.*

OD: Talking about Iran, are most of the sea beds on the Arabian side of the Gulf or you can also find some on the northern part?

MA: *You can find some on the other side, because they have some islands. The Gulf's waters are shallow but there it is deep, which is a problem for the growth of oysters. But, on some of the islands like Kish, Abu Mussa, Thumb, they are oysters and very good pearls. The Gulf on this side is a bit different.*

OD: Do you plan to ever stop diving?

MA: *Never! The sea is my life. If I don't go to the sea, I die, like a fish (laugh). When I was young, they would call me the English boy, because I would go to the beach everyday, and my hair would become lighter!*

OD: What do you think the future holds for pearl diving in the Gulf?

MA: *I see a bright future ahead. It is coming back. In Bahrain, they have 1,000 boats[5] doing pearl diving and last month they launched big ones. It's an important fleet and they are getting good money out of it. It is natural and they sell it to the market which, in return, is growing. This is what I want to do in the UAE so that we don't have to only rely on oil, but also have something else to increase the revenue of our country.*

OD: Have you noticed the impact of climate change on pearling beds and pearls? With warmer waters, you get more algae, which could potentially affect oysters...

MA: *Well, I have done research for three years in Abu Dhabi, near the Islands, asking the old people how they would find pearls. They would find pearls everywhere before – big pearls. Now all are small, and the oysters too, because of algae and a higher salinity. Salinity makes less plankton and the oyster can't eat enough. We will hopefully do something to help them.*

OD: With the help of technology and science?

MA: *My dream would be to do a research trip. You know who taught me all of this? Cousteau. Back in Egypt, he gave me his book and I stayed with him for about 15 days. He taught me everything. Before dying, he told me "You need to do research to study this (the environment in the Gulf)" and I would like to do a comprehensive study around the Gulf. Hopefully this is going to happen...*

[1] Jacques-Yves Cousteau, was a French naval officer, explorer, conservationist, filmmaker, innovator, scientist, photographer, author and researcher who studied the sea and all forms of life in water.

[2] Traditionally, a belt of weights was attached to the divers waist to allow them to sink faster and with less effort.

[3] The Qatar diplomatic crisis was a diplomatic incident that began on 5 June 2017 when Saudi Arabia, the United Arab Emirates, Bahrain and Egypt severed diplomatic relations with Qatar and banned Qatar-registered planes and ships from utilising their airspace and sea routes, along with Saudi Arabia blocking Qatar's only land crossing.

[4] Following the joint mediation of Kuwait and the USA, a deal was brokered on the 4th of January 2021 resolving the crisis with Saudi Arabia ending its blockade.

[5] Note from the editor : figures couldn't be verified.

ALI SAQAR AL SUWEIDI (MAJOR ALI)

A retired major from the UAE navy who served during the Kuwait war, Major Ali was a sailor from the age of five. Today, he is the president of the Emirates Marine Environmental Group (EMEG) and one of the few pearl divers active in the country. Born in 1957 in Dubai, he has dived for pearls for as long as he can recall and has now dedicated his life passing this tradition on to younger generations. A true environmental activist with Jacques Cousteau as reference, he created the Jebel Ali Wildlife Sanctuary south of Dubai back in 2018, where he welcomes children and scholars every summer to teach them about pearl diving and its related traditions.

image 32

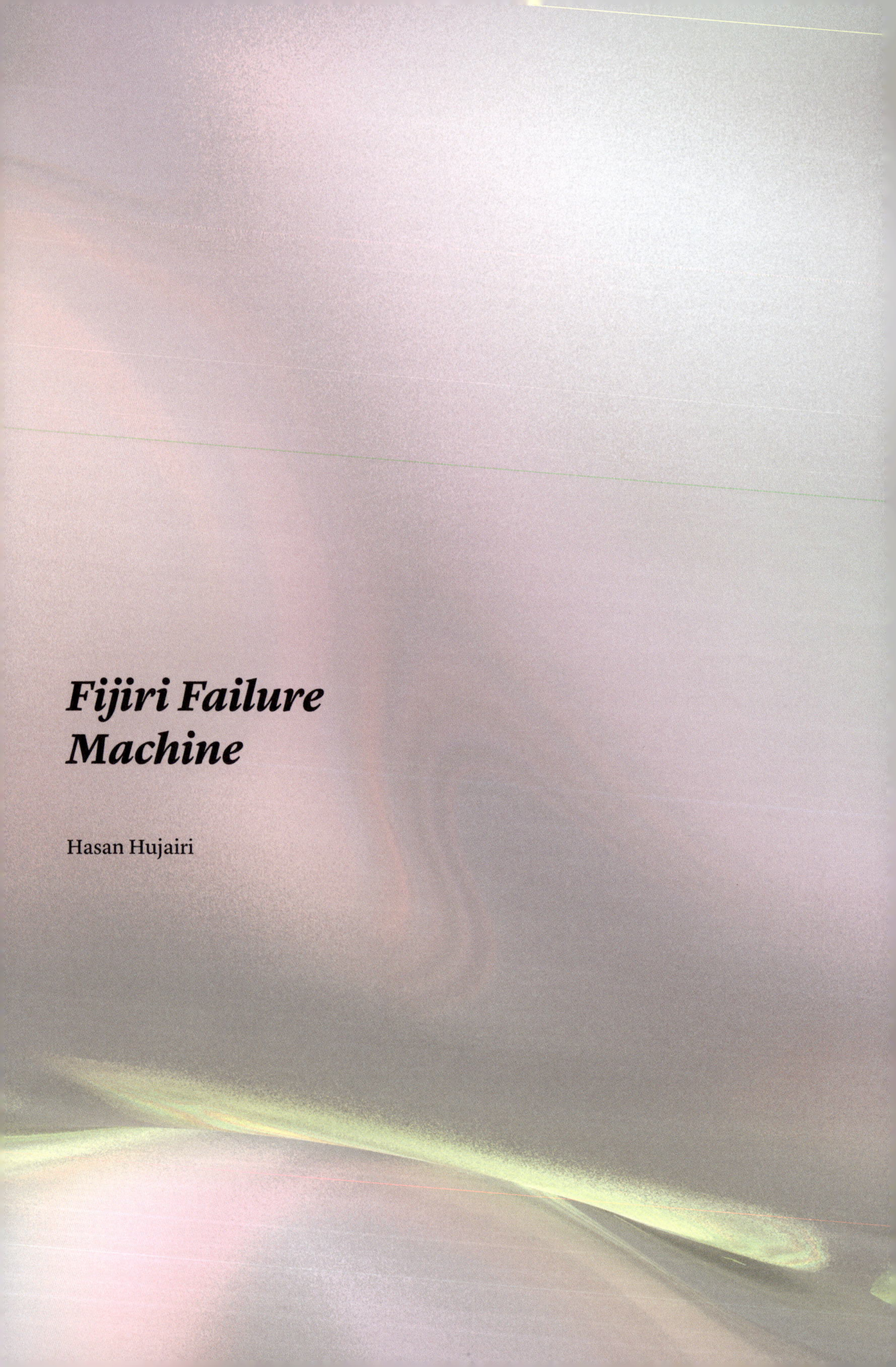

Fijiri Failure Machine

Hasan Hujairi

Over the past ten years, several of the projects I have been involved in concerned pearling culture to varying degrees. Some of those projects were initiated by visiting artists to Bahrain, some by cultural institutions, and others by myself for my own practices in music and art. The first of those projects took place back in 2011, when a well-known artist from the MENA region visited Bahrain to adapt an existing historic text into the format of Fijiri (which is perhaps problematically described as pearl diving music). That experience strongly influenced my views on the potential of this unique form of music for creative adaptation. That experience, however, also showed me how exploitative making use of such a culture could be. I felt so conscientious about exploitation to the point that I deeply resented my own role in enabling the visiting artist in that project. I also felt like I could no longer engage with those particular musicians again because of how ashamed I had felt after seeing how the visiting artist had used them. It was only ten years later that I was able to reengage with those same musicians when another foreign artist came to Bahrain to research the possibility of working with them.

In my own explorations of Fijiri and the history of pearling in Bahrain, my personal art and music projects tackled matters from a different angle. Although Fijiri seems to be celebrated - at least according to the officially-peddled narrative - as the national music of Bahrain, it has always left me with a mixed set of impressions orbiting around one notion: alienation. It took me years to come to terms with this alienation I perceived, and that it was not particularly my own misgivings that led me to see things in such a way.

Alienation is one of the strongest sentiments I have around Fijiri and its association with pearling. Although I had been studying this music for over a decade, and despite everything, I always found that I could never fully grasp its intricacies due to its extramusical elements connected to mannerisms, language, culture and dance that are beyond my reach. I think that this is because I had never physically engaged with the music. I now realize that it requires a corporeal knowledge that comes through engagement. My sense of alienation also comes from not being from a family that practices Fijiri, and much of what I have noticed is that - at least in the

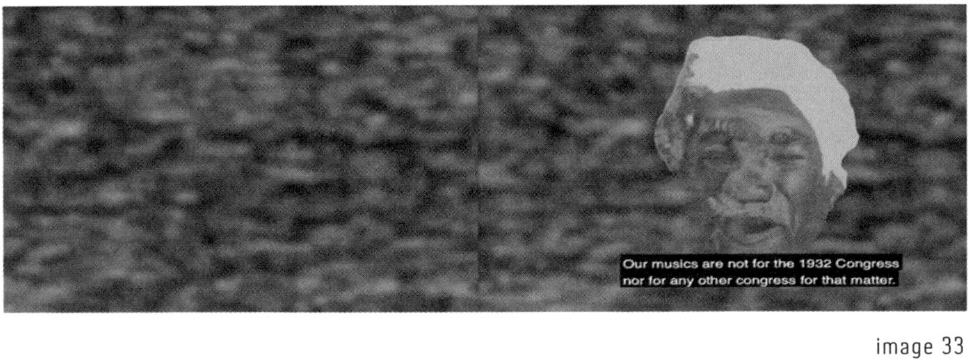

image 33

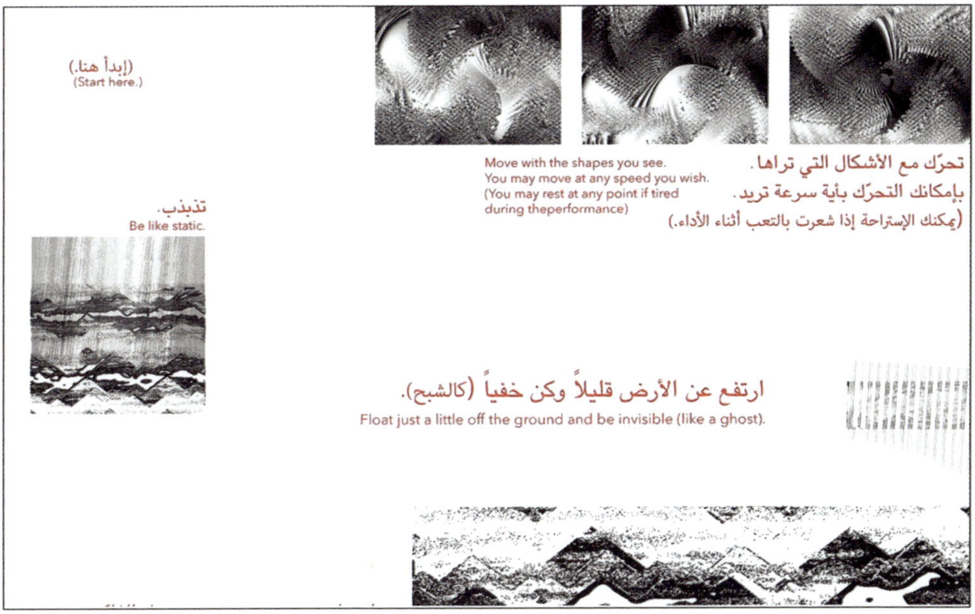

image 34

case of Bahrain - it is often a matter of oral tradition passed within male members of certain families. The largest source of alienation, however, stems from a sense of a collective-sorrow and collective shame coming from the knowledge that the entire pearling industry and its associated cultures were built on exploitation and slavery, and yet they are publicly celebrated without acknowledgment of its darker histories. All these conflicts are, to me, essential and as of yet generally remain unaddressed.

For the reasons mentioned above, in developing a new work around the notion of Fijiri and pearl diving cultures, I find that what is most urgent is a need for a mental framework that serves as a work in itself. Although this may seem as an unfair generalization, I find that there are a few approaches taken by artists in their referencing of this culture. Some artists decontextualize aspects of the music to create an entertaining spectacle, others acknowledge the history yet choose a form of creative misunderstanding in order to mix and match new images over archival audio (or vice versa), others use it in form in fusion-encounter based projects, and there are also others who approach it from an anthropological show-and-tell. Despite my critiques of the different approaches, existing works still stand and have their merits. I myself have not come up with an alternative approach in my own works that I find to be a major departure, but in a sense, that search for my alternative approach is my concern and the concern of this project.

The work I am proposing as part of the larger project is one centered around dissecting the idea of failure. The failures I am particularly interested in are those of my own doing: through my own alienation from this tradition (despite my attempts over a decade to break into it), through my inability to corporeally engage with it, and through the conditions that exacerbate my sense of failure towards this tradition.

In order to do this, I developed a software patch using Max/MSP that behaves as its own speculative 'failure machine'. The premise behind this failure machine involves digging into the very physical nature of the sounds of Fijiri, looking for the essence of my source of failure. By this, I look at the rhythmic prosody in the language used, the ghost-spaces in between the rhythms, and any tacit nuances that may be found in the data used to train the software. The result, I speculate, would lead to a catastrophic exaggeration of my past failures, translated into sonic pulses that never were in Fijiri music to begin with. The result would be an infinite, generative error-informed sound work that is perhaps a negative imprint or an unheard, ethereal space within the Fijiri tradition. At the time of developing the proposal for this project, I have been looking at the sonic DNA of archival and field recordings. I am now also considering developing this into a machine that is also aware of what is being said and how that would be misinterpreted by the Fijiri Failure Machine.

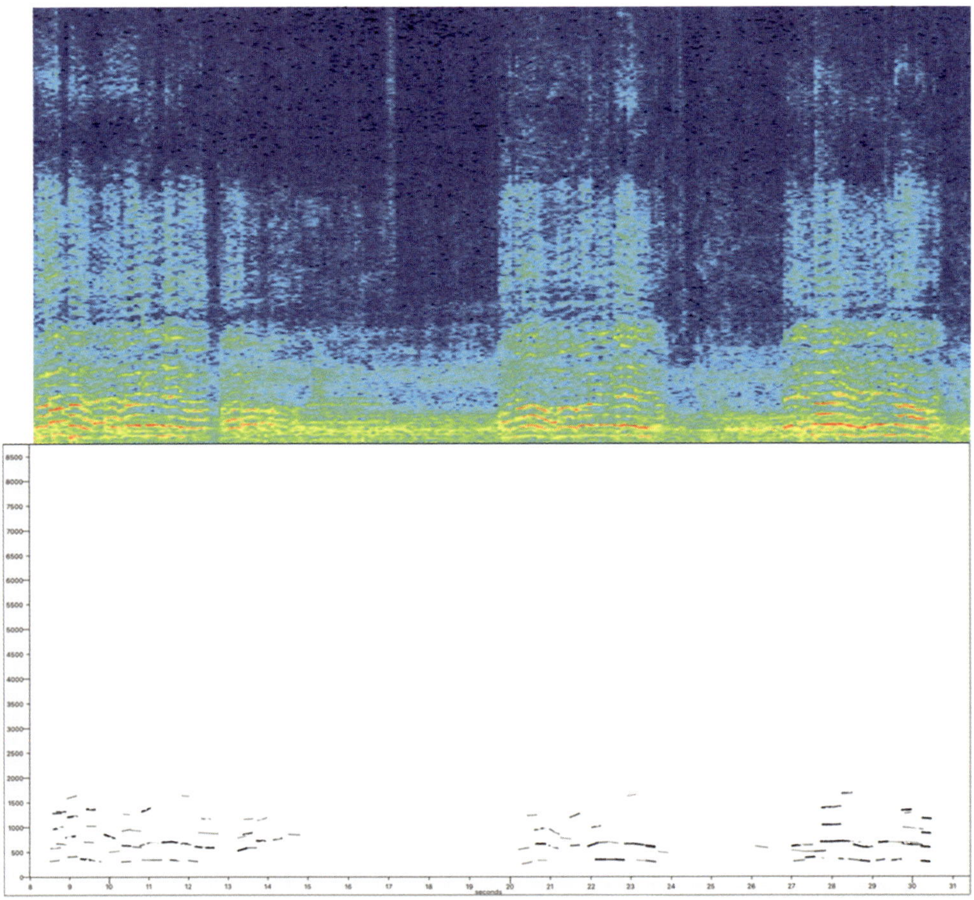

image 35

Ultimately, the Fijiri Failure Machine is a conversation that I need to have with myself. It is a work that converses with my practice thus far, and it potentially could be the start of a new direction in where I would like to take my work. It is my hope that the historiographic nuances of Fijiri and pearling culture would not serve as an endpoint in this work, but rather a foundation that would allow new explorations and speculations, with this work being one such example. Sonically, I would like to see how this 'failed Fijiri' would sound, whether it would take on a new meaning once it is divorced of its context and nuances, or whether even in failure the resultant franksenstein's monster-Fijiri would still have something meaningful to offer. For now, all I can do is look into the prejudices of the Fijiri Failure Machine and imagine what the results would be.

HASAN HUJAIRI
(b. 1982) is a Bahraini artist, composer, and writer. His work often explores the notion of the outsider, confronting (historiographic) superstructures, and the nature of constructing narratives within time. He holds a DMA (Doctor of Musical Arts) in music composition from Seoul National University (Seoul, South Korea), where he researched reorienting the narrative associated with the maverick composer tradition to be more inclusive of composers working outside the Western classical music tradition. He also holds a Masters of Economics from Hitotsubashi University (Tokyo, Japan) in economic history and regional economics, and wrote his thesis on the significance of conceiving the Gulf region in both its littorals within a Braudelian historiographic framework.

image 36

Preserving A Legacy: A conversation with Noura Al Sayeh

OLIVIER DUPORT/FLEE: Could you briefly describe what the Pearling Path is?

NOURA AL SAYEH:
The Pearling Path is a world heritage site. The idea behind it began in 2009, launched at the initiative of Sheikha Mai bint Mohammed Al Khalifa, who wanted to register the city of Muharraq[1] onto the world heritage list, as it is one of the best-preserved Islamic cities on the Arabian side of the Persian Gulf. The outstanding universal value of Muharraq[1], its pearling heritage and the idea to inscribe a superimposed path on the historic urban structure of Muharraq - a path that narrates the history and legacy of pearling in the city - was born. It connects seventeen properties within the historic city of Muharraq, starting from Bu Maher fort on the historic coastline, from which the Dhow boats and pearling fleets would depart, and leading to a row of more modest sites that may not necessarily be the most extraordinary in the city of Muharraq, but are important to its historical pearling narrative. From the houses of pearl divers to those of the captains, the merchants, to their Majlis[2], etc... It is through these different houses that the entire story of pearling in Muharraq is told. What is really interesting about this project is that it is a superimposition of narratives onto a built fabric.

OD: What is your link to the project?

NS: *I'm an architect myself, and started directing the project in late 2015. I have quite a loose role, in the sense that - thankfully - a lot of it is self-initiated. When I took over, it was an interesting time as the funding for the project had just been unlocked and it was possible to turn the management plan into a reality. As an architect, it was interesting as the project changed a lot, and in long-term urban rehabilitation projects, this is one of the main things one needs to keep in mind, as they take a lot of time to be implemented. It is a vital necessity to constantly reevaluate and reassess the situation, and check whether the initial plan is still valid or needs to be remodeled with regards to a changing city.*

OD: Was there a turning point in the project? You've been there almost six years, after all...

NS: *Already six years? (laughs). Years tend to go by rapidly... I think one of the most important aspects of the project is the interaction with the community, which I find essential. Whether you like it or not, these kinds of projects are made for the community... They are an essential player. One of the very important*

image 37

components of the project was to introduce specific urban regulations that would take into consideration the historic nature and fabric of the city, which did not exist before. It was very tedious work conducted by my colleague Ghassan Chemali, which, as with many parts of the world, came with a lot of frustrations for the local residents - with no compensation system for the eventual loss of value that would happen during this phase. In the long run, we are quite confident that the value will increase because of the specificity and the quality of life that the project encourages. But that period was a difficult one especially, because at the time when none of the construction work had started yet, people began to anticipate a lot but did not see so much moving on the ground, while the regulations came with immediate effect, making them feel like they were losing out on the whole thing.

We immediately started to communicate, although it's a difficult project for that to be done. It does not have a strong image, in this part of the world especially - where you can see really big real estate projects with lots of money and easy images to sell to people everywhere. Our project stuck out on that level as it consists mostly of renovations. It is harder to sell people what they already have, stating that it will be better than before. That is why one of the first things we did was a big exhibition at the National Museum, where we really broke down all the different components of the project and laid them out with all the urban studies conducted over the last six years, which was a turning point in enabling the local community and residents of Bahrain to understand the project in its full complexity. Soon after, work started on many fronts at the same time and it encouraged people to believe in the project. Similarly, we moved our offices into Muharraq, becoming a fixture in the city where people could approach us. As people became more and more conscious about this, they took ownership of the project - and the anticipation and enthusiasm of people for the project changed significantly.

OD: Did those relationships materialize with some of the inhabitants working on planning for instance?

NS: *We had a very good community liaison officer, Amal Al Saffar, who was the focal point of contact between the project and the inhabitants of Muharraq. One of the other things that forced us to connect even more with the community was the need to upgrade 415 facades of the historical city along the pathway. It was basically doing 15 years of maintenance that had been lacking in the city. For that, we needed to sign 415 single agreements with every one of the owners of these facades, for them to consent that we would be doing those repairs at our own costs, and so on. It took one year to get all of those agreements signed and it was extremely tedious, but also proved a good* *way to meet everyone. This exercise, which started with a legal constraint, really enabled us to connect deeply with the community and to learn who they were, what their fears were regarding the project, and so on. Eventually, all of this fed into our reflection and helped us shape the path.*

OD: Do you think that the inhabitants of Muharraq understand the goals of the project?

NS: *Things are changing for sure. For instance, the 17 public squares along the path were initially only commissioned as a wayfinding system in the city. The architecture team Office Kersten Geers David Van Severen and Bureau Bas Smets came up with the proposal of actually introducing public spaces that were lacking in the city. We immediately understood the added value this could have for the project, and if there was a lack of understanding for public good at first, it was comprehensible given that there had been such a lack of open public space development by the public sector there for such a long time. This notion of what a public space is did not exist when we started, and sometimes, when something is not there and you don't see it, you don't necessarily realize you are missing it.*

People ended up interacting with those public spaces, and if you were to ask them about it now, the replies would be completely different. It was interesting to see that the people had completely forgotten that a year ago it was just barren land with car parks. It was already completely natural that those spaces belonged to them now. I think there is a trend towards community-led interventions in public spaces, which of course is very important, but it is also to understand what power is held within an overall vision, which at a smaller scale, people would not necessarily take into consideration because of more personal considerations towards the city. Taking both into account is the key.

I think that one of the problems with public space in general - not only in those parts of the world - has a lot to do with what your rights in the city should be. The discussion is not often about desire, which on the contrary I think is really important. Public spaces should be places that you just want to be in because they have a certain beauty, a certain quality of shade, temperature and so on...

OD: How was the cultural heritage work on pearling perceived by the inhabitants of Muharraq? Were there any consultations led on that level?

NS: *The construction of the Dars*[3] *was actually a direct request from the pearl singers themselves, who needed a bigger space to perform. Through dialogue with them, we understood that the problem was not so much a functional one, but rather about the place and visibility they had within the city. They wanted to have a presence, and wanted their art form and music to have one too. That's also how the project developed architecturally, by giving them a face and landmark.*

Another challenge was that the social makeup of the city had completely changed since the 1930s: a lot of the original inhabitants had since then moved elsewhere. With the original inhabitants, we did a lot of oral history interviews with many of the house owners, people still living in Bahrain that had all had a relationship with the pearling economy. A huge task of interviewing, recording and archiving these testimonies was conducted.

That said, I find it a bit problematic to frame the project under the understanding of cultural heritage, because that's an equally ever-changing notion. This project has the specific framework of the Pearling Path because of UNESCO's nomination[4] *and funding, but the problem when you start naming and framing things too tightly - which we had at some point - is that there were a lot of initiatives and emphasis on preserving the architectural heritage of the pearling era - coral stone buildings, buildings from the 30s, etc. - while at the same time we got many demolition requests for buildings from the 50/60s, which are also really important to the life of the city. Because so much emphasis had previously been placed on the cultural heritage of the pearling era, people were now wondering why they could not tear apart buildings that were not linked to it. That is why it needs to be communicated more as a general understanding of the city's different historic layers.*

OD: Have you seen a change in terms of population fluxes since initiating the project? How are you hoping to mitigate a potential gentrification phenomenon?

NS: *For sure, and this comes two-fold. On the one hand, at the start of the project, we made sure to our best capability that there were robust urban regulations in place to make sure that once the project was complete, you could not just simply dezone areas or change residential buildings into commercial ones. That is one of the reasons why it was important to establish this framework - to prevent gentrification. Six years ago, we were still receiving lots of demolition requests for old houses, which we obviously halted, and now we are receiving more requests for renovations around the squares of the path and more and more people want to open sidewalk cafés or activities* *of that kind. It is still thankfully at a small scale, with individual requests from private owners, but it is hard to see how gentrification forces will present themselves in the near future to be honest. There is always a risk of falling victim to the success of your own project.*

OD: Was there an institutional will to change Muharraq through this project?

NS: *It is always a sensitive area - what exactly constitutes gentrification... What is important to keep in mind on a project of this scale, is that it needs to guarantee that core elements in the city will be protected. In this case, it is the reason why the public squares were so important, the reason why the architectural heritage is protected, why important monuments were rehabilitated in a very sensitive way. As long as these basic infrastructures are there, what happens beyond that can (and should) have a life of its own. There is always the risk as an architect to try and control every aspect of the project, but I do not think it is necessary. There needs to be a core understanding as to what the basic level of publicness is, which I think we tried to accommodate in the Pearling Path. We have not yet seen big developers coming to inquire about buying entire blocks so far, which is encouraging, but we are wary about those things, as they would break the organic elements that we have tried to protect up until now. But at the same time, if this happens, it will still be the story of the city. Cities change all the time. To a certain extent, I think that we need to accept that and be wary of urban overplanning, which is never truly successful.*

OD: You have mentioned regular re-evaluations of the project. How advanced would you consider the Pearling Path is, and is there an end to it?

NS: *Definitely not. The more you work on it, the more new things appear, other things change... It is a constant engagement for the city. You need to reassess constantly, which is also a bit frustrating. Sometimes I feel optimistic about all the things we have managed to implement, but yesterday I walked the path and told myself that we need ten more years, and are far from done (laughs).*

OD: Have you been, or are you in contact with similar initiatives throughout the region?

NS: *Not really, but we probably should (laughs). I have to admit that there is a bit of a problem in the Gulf, where there are not that many interactions* *in this particular field. We were in communication last year with the team working on the old city of Jeddah in Saudi Arabia, and we shared a lot of our thoughts on what we would have done differently here in Bahrain looking back - which was interesting.*

OD: Do you think the Bahrainis who have left Muharraq might come back at some point?

NS: *I hope so. There is already increased interest in renovating, and what was once considered a liability is now slowly seen as an asset.*

OD: What does the pearl symbolize to you?

NS: *I was giving a tour recently, and someone asked me what the pearls were used for. I told them that they were only used for jewelry, and it is crazy when you think about it - that this whole city was built around them. Around an item of luxury, not a necessity.*

[1] Muharraq is Bahrain's former capital before being replaced by Manama in 1932. It was the hub for all activities related to pearling and hosts the Pearling Path today.

[2] In this context used to refer to a private place (a lounge, or 'salon' in British English and French, or 'saloon' on a ship) where guests are received and entertained.

[3] Traditional music houses in which musicians would still gather today to perform during social gatherings.

[4] Pearl diving is being considered for it and was submitted by Bahrain.

NOUR AL SAYEH-HOLTROP
Is an architect and curator currently working at the Bahrain Authority for Culture and Antiquities (BACA) as Head of Architectural Affairs, where she is responsible for overseeing the planning and implementation of cultural institutions and museums, as well as the creation of an active agenda of exhibitions. She holds a Master's Degree in Architecture from the École Polytechnique Fédérale de Lausanne. Noura was the co-curator of 'Reclaim', Bahrain's first participation at the 12th Venice Architecture Biennale in 2010 awarded with a Golden Lion, and the Deputy Commissioner General for 'Archaeologies of Green', Bahrain's National Pavilion at the Expo Milan 2015, awarded a Silver Medal for Best Architecture and Landscape. Since 2015, she has headed the 'Pearling, Testimony of an Island Economy' UNESCO World Heritage project, which has been awarded the Aga Khan Award for Architecture for the 2019 cycle.

Photo Index and Glossary

Image Index and Photo Attributions

فهرس الصور وإحالات الصور

Image 25 الصورة ٢٥ p. 80 ص

تالين هزبر، ٢٠٢١
نصب في "آلآلئ ترشح"

Talin Hazbar, 2021
Installation "Leaking Pearls" (1)

Image 26 الصورة ٢٦ p. 84 ص

أوليفيه دوبور، ٢٠٢٠
لؤلؤة مستزرعة في محارة في مزرعة السويدي للؤلؤ،
رأس الخيمة، الإمارات العربية المتحدة

Olivier Duport, 2020
Cultured pearl in an oyster at Suwaidi Pearl Farm, Ras Al Khaimah, UAE

Image 27 الصورة ٢٧ p. 87 ص

آلان مارزو، ٢٠٢٠
مقابلة مع عبدالله السويدي في مجلسه ،
رأس الخيمة ، الإمارات العربية المتحدة

Alan Marzo, 2020
Interview with Abdulla Al Suwaidi in his Majlis, Ras Al Khaimah, UAE

Image 28 الصورة ٢٨ p. 89 ص

أوليفيه دوبور، ٢٠٢٠
منظر لجبال الحجر من ميناء الرمس

Olivier Duport, 2020
View on the Al Hajar Mountains from Al Rams harbour

Image 29 الصورة ٢٩ p. 90 ص

أوليفيه دوبور، ٢٠٢٠
مصائد سمك في خور الرمس، الإمارات العربية المتحدة

Olivier Duport, 2020
Fishing installation in Al Rams bay, UAE

Image 30 الصورة ٣٠ p. 97 ص

أوليفيه دوبور، ٢٠٢٠
الرائد علي يقف أمام احدى رحلاته لصيد اللؤلؤ في
جبل علي بالإمارات

Olivier Duport, 2020
"Major Ali" posing in front of one of his pearling embarcations in Jebel Ali, UAE

Image 31 الصورة ٣١ p. 100 ص

أوليفيه دوبور، ٢٠٢٠
محارات خالية من اللؤلؤ

Olivier Duport, 2020
Empty pearl oysters

Image 32 الصورة ٣٢ p. 103 ص

أوليفيه دوبور، ٢٠٢٠
الرائد علي في محمية جبل علي، الإمارات العربية المتحدة

Olivier Duport, 2020
"Major Ali" in the Jebel Ali Wildlife Sanctuary (1), UAE

Image 33 الصورة ٣٣ p. 106 ص

حسن الحجيري، ٢٠٢١
لقطة مقتطفة من الفيلم ذي الشاشتين "ذلك الوقت الذي لم
ننتظر فيه" (٢٠١٩) لحسن الحجيري. نُشرت بموافقة الفنان.

Hasan Hujairi, 2021
Still from 2-channel video "About the Time We Didn't Wait" (2019) by Hasan Hujairi.

Image 34 الصورة ٣٤ p. 107 ص

حسن الحجيري، ٢٠٢١
صورة مقربة لبعض تفاصيل تدوين الموسيقى وتصميم الرقص
لعمل "تدوين محادث: تصميم رقص للدار المتخيل رقم ١" (٢٠١٩)
لحسن الحجيري. نُشرت بموافقة الفنان.

Hasan Hujairi, 2021
Extracted detail from music/choreographic score "Conversational Score: Choreography for Imaginary Dār #1" (2019) by Hasan Hujairi.

p. 108 ص **Image 35 الصورة ٣٥**

حسن الحجيري، ٢٠٢١
صورة مقربة لبعض تفاصيل البيانات المستقرأة توضح الجزئيات المترددة (في الأعلى) وجهارة الجزئيات (في الأسفل) كجزء من التسجيلات التي ستُستعمل في تطوير ماكينة فشل الفجري. مصدر الصوت المستعمل من تسجيلات ميدانية لموسيقى فن الفجري قام بها حسن الحجيري. نُشرت بموافقة الفنان.

Hasan Hujairi, 2021
Detail from extrapolated data source showing frequency partials (above) and amplitude-fil-tered partials (below) to be used as part of the training data. The source of the audio used is field recordings by Hasan Hujairi with Fijiri singers in Bahrain.

p. 109 ص **Image 36 الصورة ٣٦**

حسن الحجيري، ٢٠٢١
لقطة مقتطفة من الفيلم الصامت "تناظر الثلاثون عام" والذي تصاحبه موسيقى تصويرية حية (٢٠١٩) لحسن الحجيري. نُشرت بموافقة الفنان.

Hasan Hujairi, 2021
Still from silent film with accompanying live score "30 Year Palindrome" (2019) by Hasan Hujairi.

p. 113 ص **Image 37 الصورة ٣٧**

أوليفيه دوبور، ٢٠٢٠
مركز زوار مسار اللؤلؤ في المحرق، البحرين

Olivier Duport, 2020
Pearling Path Visitor Center in Muharraq (1), Bahrain

p. 116 ص **Image 38 الصورة ٣٨**

أوليفيه دوبور، ٢٠٢٠
مركز زوار مسار اللؤلؤ في المحرق، البحرين

Olivier Duport, 2020
Pearling Path Visitor Center in Muharraq (2), Bahrain

p. 131 ص **Image 39 الصورة ٣٩**

أوليفيه دوبور، ٢٠٢٠
سفينة صيد اللؤلؤ في ميناء المحرق بالبحرين

Olivier Duport, 2020
Pearling boat in Muharraq harbour, Bahrain

p. 132 ص **Image 40 الصورة ٤٠**

بول مطر، ١٩٧٩
سالم العلان (في اليمين) في دار، الكويت

Paul Mattar, 1979
Salem Allan (right) in a Dar, Kuwait

p. 133 ص **Image 41 الصورة ٤١**

بول مطر، ١٩٧٨
أداء موسيقى الفنون البحرية الشعبية في دار، الكويت

Paul Mattar, 1978
Traditional pearl diving music being performed in a Dar (1), Kuwait

p. 134 ص **Image 42 الصورة ٤٢**

بول مطر، ١٩٧٩
سالم العلان، الكويت

Paul Mattar, 1979
Salem Allan, Kuwait

p. 134 ص **Image 43 الصورة ٤٣**

بول مطر، ١٩٧٩
طاقم يؤدون الموسيقى على متن سفينة، الكويت

Paul Mattar, 1979
Diving crew performing on the deck of a boat (1), Kuwait

p. 135 ص **Image 44 الصورة ٤٤**

بول مطر، ١٩٧٩
طاقم يؤدون الموسيقى على متن سفينة ، الكويت

Paul Mattar, 1979
Diving crew performing on the deck of a boat (2), Kuwait

p. 135 ص **Image 45 الصورة ٤٥**

بول مطر، ١٩٧٩
طاقم يؤدون الموسيقى على متن سفينة ، الكويت

Paul Mattar, 1979
Diving crew performing on the deck of a boat (3), Kuwait

Image 46 الصورة ٤٦ p. 136 ص

أوليفيه دوبور، ٢٠٢٠
آلات موسيقية في انتظار عازفيها في دار في المحرق بالبحرين

Olivier Duport, 2020
Instruments awaiting their musicians in a Dar in Muharraq, Bahrain

Image 47 الصورة ٤٧ p. 137 ص

آلان مارزو، ٢٠٢٠
موسيقيون يقدمون عرضاً موسيقياً في دار في المحرق بالبحرين

Alan Marzo, 2020
Musicians performing in a Dar in Muharraq, Bahrain

Image 48 الصورة ٤٨ p. 138 ص

بول مطر، ١٩٧٨
أداء موسيقى الفنون البحرية الشعبية في دار ، الكويت

Paul Mattar, 1978
Traditional pearl diving music being performed in a Dar (2), Kuwait

Image 49 الصورة ٤٩ p. 146 ص

باس برينسن، ٢٠١٩
الساحات العامة لمسار اللؤلؤ في المحرق ، البحرين

Bas Princen, 2019
Pearling Path public squares in Muharraq, Bahrain

Image 50 الصورة ٥٠ p. 156 ص

أوليفيه دوبور، ٢٠٢٠
الرائد علي في محمية جبل علي

Olivier Duport, 2020
"Major Ali" in the Jebel Ali Wildlife Sanctuary (2), UAE

Image 51 الصورة ٥١ p. 159 ص

أوليفيه دوبور، ٢٠٢٠
مقابلة مع الرائد علي في مجموعة الإمارات للبيئة البحرية في جبل علي بالإمارات

Olivier Duport, 2020
Interview with "Major Ali" at the Emirates Marine Environmental Group in Jebel Ali (1), UAE

Image 52 الصورة ٥٢ p. 163 ص

أوليفيه دوبور، ٢٠٢٠
مقابلة مع الرائد علي في مجموعة الإمارات للبيئة البحرية في جبل علي بالإمارات

Olivier Duport, 2020
Interview with "Major Ali" at the Emirates Marine Environmental Group in Jebel Ali (2), UAE

Image 53 الصورة ٥٣ p. 169 ص

أوليفيه دوبور، ٢٠٢٠
عملية عد اللؤلؤ في رأس الخيمة ، الإمارات العربية المتحدة

Olivier Duport, 2020
Pearl counting, Ras Al Khaimah, UAE

Image 54 الصورة ٥٤ p. 170 ص

أوليفيه دوبور، ٢٠٢٠
مزرعة السويدي للؤلؤ في رأس الخيمة ، الإمارات العربية المتحدة

Olivier Duport, 2020
Suwaidi Pearl Farm in Ras Al Khaimah, UAE

Image 55 الصورة ٥٥ p. 173 ص

أوليفيه دوبور، ٢٠٢٠
إستخراج المحار المستزرع من المياه في مزارع السويدي ، رأس الخيمة ، الإمارات العربية المتحدة

Olivier Duport, 2020
Cultured oysters are being taken out of the water in Suwaidi Farms, Ras al Khaimah, UAE

Image 56 الصورة ٥٦ p. 176 ص

تالين هزبر، ٢٠٢١
نصب في "لآلئ ترشح"

Talin Hazbar, 2021
Installation "Leaking Pearls" (2)

p. 183 **Image 57** **الصورة ٥٧**
ص

بول مطر، ١٩٧٩
طاقم يؤدون الموسيقى على متن سفينة ، الكويت

Paul Mattar, 1979
Diving crew performing on the deck of a boat (3), Kuwait

p. 187 **Image 58** **الصورة ٥٨**
ص

هنري هاني، ٢٠٢٠
عقد من اللؤلؤ الطبيعي

Henry Hänni, 2020
Natural pearl (pinctada radiata) necklace

p. 187 **Image 59** **الصورة ٥٩**
ص

هنري هاني، ٢٠٢٠
عقد من اللؤلؤ الطبيعي (أشعة)

Henry Hänni, 2020
Natural pearl (pinctada radiata) necklace (X-Ray)

p. 188 **Image 60** **الصورة ٦٠**
ص

هنري هاني، ٢٠٢٠
لؤلؤ مستنبت مجوف

Henry Hänni, 2020
Cultured pearl hollow (1)

p. 188 **Image 61** **الصورة ٦١**
ص

بول سلر، ١٩٧٩
طاقم يؤدون الموسيقي على متن سفينة ، الكويت

Henry Hänni, 2020
Cultured pearl hollow (2)

p. 196 **Image 62** **الصورة ٦٢**
ص

جورج كونز وتشارلز ستيفنسون، ١٩٠٨
عقد اللآلئ

George Kunz & Charles Stevenson, 1908
Pearl Stringing

p. 205 **Image 63** **الصورة ٦٣**
ص

آرنولد هيم، ١٩٢٤
سفينة صيد اللؤلؤ على ضفاف شواطئ البحرين

Arnold Heim, 1924
Pearling boat along the Bahraini coastline

p. 204 **Image 64** **الصورة ٦٤**
ص

آرنولد هيم، ١٩٢٤
تفريغ سفينة صيد اللؤلؤ عند الواجهة البحرية في مدينة الدمام ، المملكة العربية السعودية

Arnold Heim, 1924
Unloading of a pearling ship on Demmam's seafront, Saudi Arabia

p. 219 **Image 65** **الصورة ٦٥**
ص

بول مطر، ١٩٧٩
صورة لأبو صالح (٣/٢)

Paul Mattar, 1979
Abou Saleh portrait (1)

p. 223 **Image 66** **الصورة ٦٦**
ص

بورج لونو، ١٩٨١
سفينة صيد اللؤلؤ ، البحرين

Georges Luneau, 1981
Pearling boat (2), Bahrain

Glossary

AGHÂNÎ AL-GHAWS	'Pearl Diving Songs'	أغاني غوص اللؤلؤ	**أغاني الغوص**
AL-BANOOSH	Traditional small pearl diving boat	قارب صيد صغير تقليدي للغطس	**البانوش**
AL-GHAUS AL-BAARED	'Cold Diving', the earliest diving season	أول موسم للغوص	**الغوص البارد**
AL-GHAUS AL-KABIR	'Great Diving', the principal diving season	موسم الغوص الرئيسي	**الغوص البارد**
ASÂS	'Base', handclapping technique	تقنية التصفيق	**أساس**
UZZAL	Independent diver	غواص مستقل	**عزال**
BAGHLAH	Largest type of dhow with decks and a crew up to 100 men used for ocean sailings	أكبر نوع من المراكب الشراعية مع طوابق وطاقم يصل إلى 100 رجل يستخدم للإبحار في المحيط	**بغلة**
BARWAH	Agreement between a captain and a diver	اتفاق بين قبطان وغواص	**بروة**
BOOM	Large pearling boat	قارب كبير لصيد اللؤلؤ	**بوم**
CHOUNA	Boat coating process	عملية طلاء القارب	**شونة**
DACHA	Day on which the pearl divers leave for the sea	اليوم الذي يغادر فيه غواصو اللؤلؤ إلى البحر	**دشّة**
DAAJIN	Traditional basket used by the divers to hold their catch	سلة تقليدية يستخدمها الغواصون لحمل صيدهم	**ديّين**
DÂR	Small hut along the beach where sailors met to chat, drink tea and coffee, and foremost to make music and sing.	كوخ صغير على طول الشاطئ حيث يجتمع البحارة للدردشة وشرب الشاي والقهوة ، و الاهم من ذلك لعزف الموسيقى والغناء	**دار**
DĪWĀNIYA	Kuwaiti equivalent of the Dâr, those spaces also played a social and commercial role as a meeting place.	المعادل الكويتي للدار. بالإضافة إلى كونها كوخ ، لعبت هذه المساحات أيضًا دورًا اجتماعيًا وتجاريًا كمكان للاجتماع	**ديوانية**
FANN AL BAHAR	'The Art of the Sea', used to refer to sailors' songs	كانت تستخدم للإشارة إلى أغاني البحارة	**فن البحر**
FIJIRI	'Until Dawn', generic term for leisure pearl divers' songs	حتى الفجر ، مصطلح عام لأغاني غواصي اللؤلؤ	**الفجيري**
FITAAM	Wooden nose clamp used by pearl divers	مشبك أنف خشبي يستخدمه غواصو اللؤلؤ	**فطام**

قائمة المصطلحات

GHOWS	Pearl diving journey	رحلة غوص اللؤلؤ	**غوص**
GHAASAH	Divers	الغواصون	**الغاصة**
QLAATAH	Share of the sailors	نصيب البحارة	**قلاطة**
GOFAL	Day on which the pearl divers return from the sea	اليوم الذي يعود فيه غواصو اللؤلؤ من البحر	**قفال**
HADDADI	Genre of the Fijiri suite mainly sung at night	نوع الموسيقى الفجيرية تغنى بشكل رئيسي في الليل	**حدادي**
HAMHAMA	Bass vocal drone technique and the most distinctive of the sailors choir	تقنية باس فوكل بدون طيار وأكثر ما يميز جوقة البحارة	**همهمة**
JHÂL	Typical clay water jars used as instruments	جرار ماء طينية نموذجية تستخدم كآلة موسيقية	**جحال**
JALBOOT	Traditional pearl diving boat	قارب غوص اللؤلؤ التقليدي	**جالبوت**
JIB	Small sail	شراع صغير	**جب**
KHABAT	Small finger leather caps used by the divers	قبعات جلدية صغيرة للأصابع يستخدمها الغواصون	**خبط**
KHATM	Balance of wages due to a diver at the end of the pearling season	تسوية أجور الغواصين في نهاية موسم صيد اللؤلؤ	**ختم**
KHRAB	Rigging	تزوير	**خراب**
MAJLIS	Arabic term meaning "council" which can also refer to a social place used for commerce and gatherings	مصطلح باللغة العربية يشير إلى "مجلس" ويمكن أن يشير أيضًا إلى مكان اجتماعي يستخدم للتجارة والتجمعات	**مجلس**
MASHREQ	The eastern part of the Arab world	الجزء الشرقي من الوطن العربي	**مشرق**
NAHHÂM	Lead singer in pearl diving music	المغني الرئيسي في موسيقى غوص اللؤلؤ	**نهام**
NAHMA	'Animal Sound/Voice of The Whale', Used to refer to pearl divers' songs	صوت الحيوان / صوت الحوت ، يستخدم للإشارة إلى أغاني غواصين اللؤلؤ	**نهمة**
NAKHUDA	Pearling boat Captain	قبطان قارب اللؤلؤ	**نوخذة**
RAKBAH	The beginning of the 'Great diving'	بداية "الغوص العظيم"	**ركبة**

RAZIF	Grade above the Cabin Boy	درجة فوق صبي المقصورة	**رازف**
SALAF	An advance, given to a diver about ten days before the start of the season	سلفة تعطى للغواص قبل عشرة أيام من بداية الموسم	**سلف**
SANBOUK	Traditional pearl diving boat	قارب غوص اللؤلؤ التقليدي	**سنبوك**
SEYB	Puller	مجتذب	**سيب**
SAFANIYA	Honours at sea for sailors	التكريم في البحر للبحارة	**سفنيّة**
SHARBAKA	'Intricacy', handclapping technique	"التعقيد" ، تقنية التصفيق	**شربكة**
SHIMAL	A wind in the Persian Gulf	رياح في الخليج الفارسي	**شمال**
TABAB	Cabin boy	صبي المقصورة	**تبّاب**
TABAKH	Boat cook	طباخ القارب	**طباخ**
TABL	Cylindrical drum (Instrument)	طبلة أسطوانية (آلة موسيقية)	**طبل**
TAKSIIRA	A boat maoeuvre, consisting in partially lifting the anchor to explore the surroundings of a pearling bed.	مناورة قارب تتكون من رفع المرساة جزئيًا لاستكشاف محيط سرير اللؤلؤ.	**تقصيرة**
TÂR	Frame drum (Instrument)	أسطوانة الإطار (أداة)	**طارة**
TAWWAASHI	Pearl merchants	تجار اللؤلؤ	**طواشي**
TWAYSÂT	Small metal cymbals (Instrument)	الصنج المعدنية الصغيرة (آلة موسيقية)	**طويسات**
ZUHAYRÎ	Type of lively lyric in pearl divers' songs	نوع من الأغاني الحية من أغاني غواصين اللؤلؤ	**زهيري**

image 39

image 40

image 41

image 42, 43

image 44

image 45

image 46

image 47

imagc 48

تعليق الصور
و قائمة المصطلحات

أوليفييه: هل سبق لك أو هل كنت على اتصال أية بمبادرات مماثلة في أي من أنحاء المنطقة؟

نورة: لم يحدث، وإن كان ربما ينبغي أن يحدث ذلك (تضحك). يجب أن أعترف أن هناك مشكلة صغيرة في الخليج، حيث لا توجد تفاعلات كثيرة في هذا المجال بالذات. تواصلنا العام الماضي مع الفريق الذي يعمل في مدينة جدة القديمة في المملكة العربية السعودية، وتشاركنا الكثير من أفكارنا حول ما كنا سنفعله بشكل مختلف هنا في البحرين - وهو أمر مثير للاهتمام.

أوليفييه: هل تعتقد أن البحرينيين الذين غادروا المحرق قد يعودون في وقت ما؟

نورة: اتمنى ذلك. هناك فعليًا اهتمام متزايد بالإحياء، وما كان يُنظر إليه قبلًا أنه عبء يُنظر إليه حاليًا ببطء باعتباره ثروة.

أوليفييه: ما الذي يمثله اللؤلؤ بالنسبة لك؟

نورة: كنت أقوم بجولة مؤخرًا، وسألني أحدهم فيم تستخدم اللآلئ. أجبتهم أنهم كانوا يستخدمونها فقط في المجوهرات، يدركك الجنون عندما تفكر في الأمر - أن هذه المدينة بأكملها قد بنيت حولهم. حول عنصر من عناصر الرفاهية وليس من أجل ضرورة من الضروريات.

الناس حاليًا عن أسباب عدم قيامهم بإزالة المباني غير ذات الصلة به. لهذا يجب التواصل أكثر بأن الأمر يتعلق بفهم عام لطبقات المدينة التاريخية المختلفة.

أوليفييه : هل رأيت تغييراً فيما يتعلق بالتدفقات السكانية منذ بداية المشروع؟ كيف تأملين في التلطيف من ظاهرة الإحلال الطبقي المديني (الجنترة) المحتملة؟

نورة: بالتأكيد، يحدث ذلك في شقين. من ناحية، في بداية المشروع، بذلنا كل مافي وسعنا لوضع لوائح مدنية محكمة للتأكد من أنه بمجرد اكتمال المشروع، لن يكون من الممكن بسهولة إزالة مناطق أو تغيير المباني السكنية إلى أخرى تجارية. هذا هو أحد الأسباب التي أعطت أهمية لإنشاء هذا الإطار - كي نحمي أنفسنا من ظاهرة الجنترة. حتى ست سنوات مضت، كنا ما نزال نتلقى الكثير من طلبات إزالة المنازل القديمة، التي أوقفناها كما هو واضح، ونتلقى حاليًا المزيد من طلبات التجديد حول ساحات الطريق وعدد متزايد من الناس يريدون فتح مقاهي على الرصيف أو أنشطة مماثلة .. لحسن الحظ لازال النطاق صغيراً، كونها طلبات فردية من ملاك أعمال خاصة، لكن من الصعب أن نعرف كيف ستقدم القوى الساعية لتغيير الطبيعة السكانية للأحياء نفسها في المستقبل القريب إن أردنا أن نكون صرحاء. هناك دائماً خطر الوقوع كضحية لنجاح مشروعك الخاص.

أوليفييه : هل كانت هناك إرادة مؤسسية لتغيير المحرق من خلال هذا المشروع؟

نورة: تلك منطقة حساسة دائمًا - ما هي الجنترة تحديداً... الشيء المهم الذي يجب مراعاته في مشروع بهذا الحجم، هو الحاجة إلى ضمان حماية جوهر من الأشياء في المدينة. في هذه الحالة، فهذا هو سبب أهمية الميادين العامة، وسبب حماية التراث المعماري، وسبب إعادة تأهيل المعالم الهامة تأهيلًا حساسًا للغاية. طالما أن هذه البنى التحتية الأساسية موجودة، فإن ما يحدث بعد ذلك يمكن (ويجب) أن يكون له حياة خاصة به. هناك دائمًا مخاطرة باعتباري مهندسة معمارية تحاول التحكم في كل جانب من جوانب المشروع، لكنني لا أعتقد أن ذلك ضروري. من الضروري وجود فهم جوهري حول ما هو المستوى الأساسي من العمومية، والذي أعتقد أننا حاولنا التوائم معه في طريق اللؤلؤ. لم نر حتى الآن مطورين كبار يأتون للاستفسار عن شراء وحدات مجمعة كاملة، وهو أمر مشجع، لكننا سنمون من تلك الأمور لأنها ستكسر العناصر العضوية التي حاولنا حمايتها حتى الآن. لكن في الوقت نفسه - إذا حدث هذا ، فستظل قصة المدينة. تتغير المدن طوال الوقت. إلى حد ما، أعتقد أننا بحاجة إلى قبول ذلك وأن نكون حذرين من التخطيط الحضري المفرط، والذي لا ينجح أبدًا.

أوليفييه : لقد أشرت إلى عمليات إعادة تقييم منتظمة للمشروع. ما مدى تقدم طريق اللؤلؤ، وهل توجد نهاية له؟

نورة: بالطبع لا. كلما اشتغلت، كلما ظهرت أشياء جديدة، وتغيرت أشياء أخرى ... إنه انهماك في عمل دائم لأجل المدينة. أنت تحتاج إلى إعادة تقييم مستمرة، وهو أمر محبط قليلًا أيضًا. أحيانًا أشعر بالتفاؤل حيال كل ما تمكنا من تنفيذه، لكني بالأمس سرت في الطريق وحدثت نفسي أننا بحاجة إلى عشر سنوات أخرى، وأننا ما زلنا بعيدين عن الإنتهاء من كل شيء (تضحك).

هناك لوقت طويل. هذه الفكرة عن طبيعة الفضاء العام لم تكن موجودة عندما بدأنا، وأحيانًا، عندما يغيب شيئًا ما ولا تراه، فأنت بالضرورة لا تدرك أنك تفتقده. انتهى الأمر بالناس بالتفاعل مع تلك الفضاءات العامة، وإذا سألتهم عنها الآن، فستختلف الإجابات تمامًا. كان من المثير للاهتمام أن نرى أن الناس قد نسوا تمامًا أنه منذ عام مضى كانت هذه الفضاءات أرضًا قاحلة بها مواقف للسيارات. كان من الطبيعي تمامًا أن تكون تلك المساحات ملكًا لهم الآن. أعتقد أن هناك اتجاهًا نحو تدخلات يقودها المجتمع في الأماكن العامة، وهو أمر مهم جدًا بالطبع، ولكن من المهم أيضًا فهم طبيعة القوة الموجودة داخل الرؤية الشاملة، والتي لن يأخذها الناس بالضرورة في الاعتبار على نطاق أصغر بسبب اعتبارات أكثر شخصية تجاه المدينة. أخذ كلاهما في الاعتبار هو المفتاح.

عمومًا أعتقد أن إحدى مشكلات الفضاء العام -ليس فقط في تلك الأجزاء من العالم- لها صلة كبيرة بما يجب أن تكون عليه حقوقك في المدينة. لا تدور المناقشة غالبًا حول الرغبة، التي أعتقد، على العكس من الشائع، أنها مهمة حقًا. يجب أن تكون الفضاءات العامة هي الأماكن التي لا ترغب سوى أن تكون فيها لأنها تتمتع بجمال معين ونوعية معينة من الظل ودرجة الحرارة وما إلى ذلك ...

أوليفييه: كيف كان تصور سكان المحرق لوظيفة التراث الثقافي فيما يخص صيد اللؤلؤ؟ هل أجريت أية مشاورات على هذا المستوى؟

نورة: كان تشييد الدور في الواقع طلبًا مباشرًا من مغني اللؤلؤ أنفسهم، الذين كانوا بحاجة إلى مساحة أكبر للأداء. ,من خلال الحوار معهم، أدركنا أن المسألة لا تتعلق بدرجة كبيرة بإشكالية وظيفية، بل تتعلق بالمكان وفرص الظهور التي كانوا يحظون بها داخل المدينة. لقد أرادوا أن يكون لهم حضورًا، وأرادوا أن يكون لشكلهم الفني وموسيقاهم حضور أيضًا. هذه أيضًا هي الطريقة التي تطور بها المشروع من الناحية المعمارية، من خلال منحهم وجهاً وطابعًا.

كان التحدي الآخر هو أن التركيب الاجتماعي للمدينة قد تغير تمامًا منذ ثلاثينيات القرن العشرين - منذ ذلك الحين انتقل الكثير من السكان الأصليين إلى مكان آخر. فيما يخص السكان الأصليين، أجرينا الكثير من مقابلات التاريخ الشفوي مع كثير من مالكي المنازل، الذين ما يزالون يعيشون في البحرين وكان لهم جميعًا علاقة باقتصاد صيد اللؤلؤ. قمنا بمهمة هائلة تتمثل في إجراء المقابلات وتسجيلها وأرشفتها.

خلاصة القول، أجد أنه من الصعب بعض الشيء حصر المشروع في إطار فهم التراث الثقافي، لأنه مفهوم دائم التغير. لهذا المشروع إطار عمل محدد فيما يخص طريق اللؤلؤ نظرا لترشيح اليونسكو وتمويلها له، ولكن المشكلة أنه عندما تبدأ في تعيين الأشياء وتأطيرها بإحكام شديد - وهو ما قمنا به في مرحلة ما - ظهرت الكثير من المبادرات ويتم التوكيد على الحفاظ على التراث المعماري لعصر اللؤلؤ - المباني الحجرية المرجانية، والمباني من الثلاثينيات، وما إلى ذلك - في الوقت ذاته الذي تلقينا فيه العديد من طلبات الهدم للمباني من الخمسينيات والستينيات، والتي تعد كذلك شديدة الأهمية لحياة المدينة. ونظرًا لأنه جرى ابراز التراث الثقافي لعصر اللؤلؤ في السابق إبرازا كبيرًا، فقد تساءل

لأنه في الوقت الذي لم تبدأ فيه أي من أعمال البناء بعد، توقع الناس الكثير ولكنهم لم يروا الكثير يحدث على الأرض، في حين حدث تنفيذًا فوريًا للإجراءات، مما جعلهم يشعرون وكأنهم يخسرون كل شيء.

بدأنا على الفور في التواصل، على الرغم من مشقة صعوبة المشروع لمثل هذا الإجراء. لا يتمتع الأمر بصورة قوية، خصوصًا في هذا الجزء من العالم- حيث يمكنك رؤية مشاريع عقارية كبيرة رأي العين تنفق عليها أموال طائلة وصور لطيفة يجري ترويجها للناس في كل مكان. عند هذا المستوى صار مشروعنا عالقًا لأنه يقتصر في الغالب على التجديدات. من الصعب أن تبيع للناس ما هو لديهم بالفعل، وذلك بدعوى أنه سيكون أفضل من ذي قبل. ولهذا السبب كان أحد الأشياء الأولى التي قمنا بها هو إقامة معرض كبير في المتحف الوطني، حيث قمنا بالفعل بتفكيك جميع المكونات المختلفة للمشروع ووضعناها مع جميع الدراسات الحضرية التي أجريت على مدار السنوات الست الماضية، وهو ما مثل نقطة تحول في تمكين المجتمع المحلي وسكان البحرين من فهم المشروع بكامل تعقيداته. بعد فترة وجيزة، بدأ العمل على العديد من الجبهات في نفس الوقت وجرى تشجيع الناس على أن يثقوا بالمشروع. وكذلك، نقلنا مكاتبنا إلى المحرق، وأصبح وجودنا في المدينة راسخًا حيث يستطيع الناس الوصول إلينا. وعندما أصبح الناس أكثر إنتباهًا لمشروعنا، أخذوا المشروع على عاتقهم- وتغيرت توقعات الناس للمشروع وحماسهم له على نحو كبير.

أوليفييه: هل أثمرت تلك العلاقات مع عمل بعض السكان في التخطيط على سبيل المثال..؟

نورة: كان لدينا مسؤول اتصال اجتماعي جيد جدًا، أمل الصفار. كانت أمل نقطة الاتصال المحورية بين المشروع وسكان المحرق. أحد الأمور الأخرى التي دفعتنا إلى التواصل بشكل أكبر مع المجتمع هو الحاجة إلى تحسين واجهة ٤١٥ مبنى من واجهات مباني المدينة التاريخية على طول الطريق. في الأساس، كان الأمر هو إصلاح آثار ١٥ عاماً من الصيانة الغائبة عن المدينة. لذلك، احتجنا إلى توقيع ٤١٥ اتفاقية فردية مع مالكي هذه الواجهات، لكي يوافقوا على أن نقوم بهذه الإصلاحات على نفقتنا الخاصة، وما إلى ذلك. استغرق توقيع كل هذه الاتفاقيات عامًا واحدًا وكان أمرًا رتيباً للغاية، ولكنه أثبت أيضًا أنه طريقة جيدة لمقابلة الجميع. هذه التجربة، التي بدأت باعتبارها ضرورة قانونية، مكّنتنا بحق من التواصل بعمق مع المجتمع ومعرفة من يكون أفراده، وما هي مخاوفهم بشأن المشروع، وما إلى ذلك. في الختام، غذى كل هذا أفكارنا وساعدنا في رسم الطريق.

أوليفييه: هل تعتقدين أن سكان المحرق يفهمون أهداف المشروع؟

نورة: الأمور تتغير بالتأكيد. على سبيل المثال، فالسبعة عشر ميداناً الموجودين على الطريق تم التكليف بهم بداية كنظام للإرشاد للطرق. توصل فريق الهندسة المعمارية مكتب كريستين غيرز ديفيد فان سيفيرن ومكتب باس سميتس إلى اقتراح إدخال الساحات العامة التي كانت تفتقر إليها المدينة. لقد فهمنا على الفور القيمة المضافة لهذا المشروع، وما إذا كان هناك قصور في فهم الصالح العام بدايةً، كان الأمر مفهوماً بالنظر إلى وجود قصور كهذا في تطوير المساحات العامة المفتوحة على يد القطاع العام

image 49

أوليفييه: هل يمكنك أن تصفين بإيجاز طريق اللؤلؤ؟

نورة السايح:
طريق اللؤلؤ أحد مواقع التراث العالمي. بدأ الفكرة في عام ٢٠٠٩، بمبادرة من الشيخة مي بنت محمد آل خليفة وتحت رعايتها، حيث أرادت تسجيل مدينة المحرق في قائمة التراث العالمي، كون المحرق واحدة من أكثر المدن الإسلامية احتفاظاً بطابعها الأصلي على الجانب العربي من الخليج الفارسي. وبسبب القيمة العالمية المتميزة للمحرق نظرًا لتراثها في صيد اللؤلؤ ولدت فكرة رسم طريق متداخل مع الهيكل العمراني التاريخي للمحرق، طريق يروي تاريخ وإرث صيد اللؤلؤ في المدينة. يربط الطريق بين سبعة عشر عقارًا في مدينة المحرق التاريخية - بدءًا من قلعة بو ماهر على الساحل التاريخي، التي ستنطلق منها قوارب الداو وأساطيل صيد اللؤلؤ، ثم يتجه إلى صف من العقارات الأكثر تواضعًا التي قد لا تكون بالضرورة الأكثر تميزاً في مدينة المحرق، لكنها مهمة في السردية التاريخية عن صيد اللؤلؤ. من بيوت غواصي اللؤلؤ إلى بيوت القباطنة والتجار ومجالسهم ، إلخ ... من خلال هذه البيوت المختلفة تُروى قصة صيد اللؤلؤ كاملة في المحرق. ما هو مثير للاهتمام حقًا في هذا المشروع هو أنه عبارة عن تداخل السرد مع نسيج المباني.

أوليفييه:ما هي صلتك بالمشروع؟

نورة: أنا مهندسة معمارية، وبدأت في إدارة المشروع في أواخر عام ٢٠١٥. دوري فضفاض نوعا ما، بمعنى أنه -لحسن الحظ- ينبع في جانب كبير منه من المبادرة الذاتية. عندما توليت المهمة، كانت فترة مثيرة للشغف حيث فتح باب التمويل للمشروع للتو وصار من الممكن تحويل خطة الإدارة إلى واقع. كمهندسة معمارية، كان أمرا مثيراً للاهتمام - حيث تغير المشروع كثيرًا، وفي مشاريع إعادة التأهيل الحضري طويلة الأجل، يعد هذا أحد الأشياء الرئيسية التي يجب على المرء أن يأخذها في الاعتبار، لأن تنفيذها يستغرق وقتًا طويلًا. إنها ضرورة حيوية أن تعيد النظر في الموقف وأن تقيمه باستمرار، ذلك إلى جانب التحقق مما إذا كانت الخطة الأولية لا تزال صالحة أو تحتاج إلى إعادة تشكيل فيما يتعلق بمدينة تتغير باستمرار.

أوليفييه:هل كانت هناك نقطة تحول في المشروع؟ لقد قضيت ست سنوات تقريبًا في المشروع، على أية حال ...

نورة: ست سنوات فعلاً؟ (تضحک). تمضي السنوات سريعًا ... أعتقد أن التفاعل مع المجتمع هو أحد أهم جوانب المشروع، وهو ما أجده ضروري. وسواء أعجبك ذلك أم لم يعجبك، ففي هذا النوع من المشاريع المصممة من أجل المجتمع ... يكون المجتمع لاعب أساسي. كان احد العناصر شديدة الأهمية للمشروع هو تقديم اجراءات حضرية محددة تأخذ في الاعتبار الطبيعة التاريخية للمدينة ونسيجها، وهي إجراءات لم تكن موجودة من قبل. لقد كان عملاً شديد الرتابة ذلك الذي نفذه زميلي غسان الشمالي، وهو، كما هو الحال في أجزاء كثيرة من العالم ، يجلب الكثير من الإحباطات للسكان المحليين - في ظل عدم وجود نظام تعويض عن الخسارة النهائية للقيمة التي قد تحدث خلال هذه المرحلة. على المدى الطويل، نحن على ثقة تامة من أن القيمة ستزداد بسبب خصوصية المشروع ونوعية الحياة التي يشجعها. لكن تلك الفترة كانت صعبة على وجه الخصوص،

الحفاظ على التراث:
حوار مع نورا السايح

أوليفييه دوبورت/ فلي

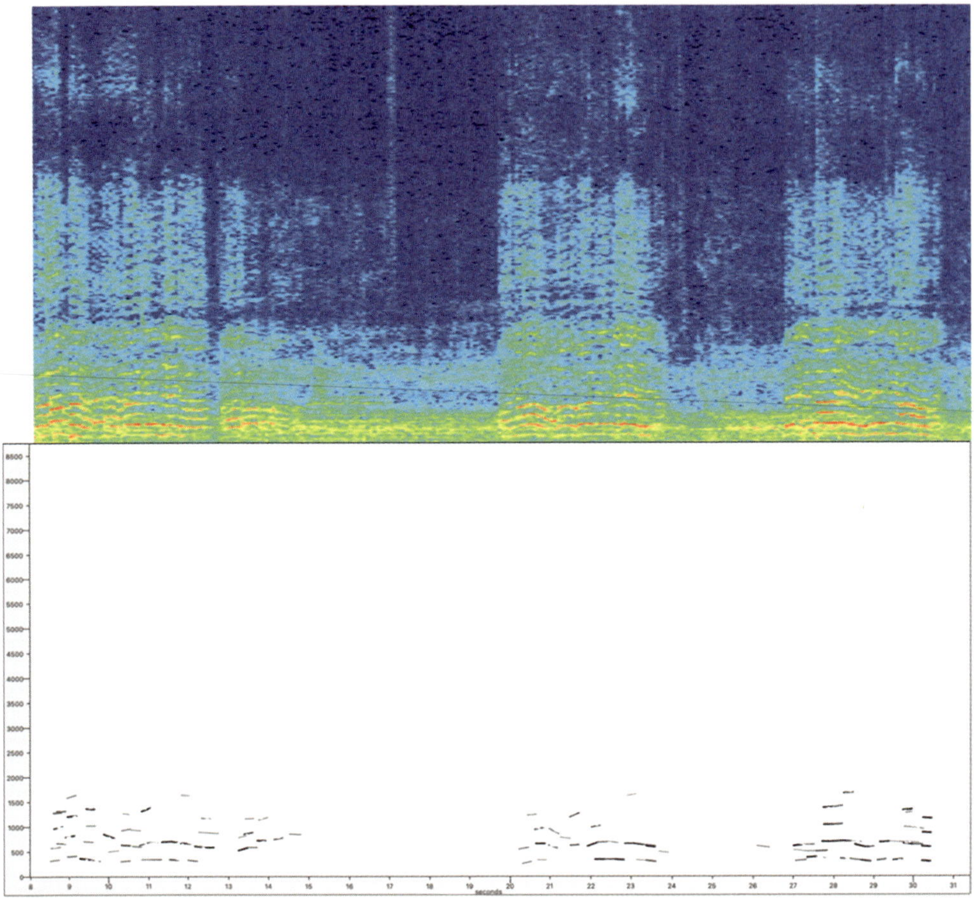

image 35

حسن الحجيري

فنان وملحن وكاتب بحريني مولود في عام ١٩٨٢. يستكشف عمل الحجيري عادة مفهوم الدخيل، ومواجهة البنى التأريخية العليا وطبيعة تركيب السرديات داخل الزمن. يحمل الحجيري درجة الدكتوراة في الفنون الموسيقية في التأليف الموسيقي من جامعة سيول الوطنية بكوريا الجنوبية، حيث بحث في رسالته إعادة توجيه السردية المرتبطة بتقليد المؤلف الموسيقي المارق لتصبح أكثر استيعاباً لمؤلفين عملوا خارج التقليد الموسيقي الكلاسيكي الغربي. يحمل الحجيري كذلك درجة الماجيستير في جامعة هيتوتسوباشي بطوكيو في التاريخ الاقتصادي والاقتصاديات الإقليمية، وقد كتب رسالته عن دلالة فهم منطقة الخليج على ساحليها داخل سياق التأريخ البروديلي.

إن العمل الذي اقترحه في هذا المشروع الذي بين يديكم متعلق بفكرة أكبر أعمل فيها من فترة إلا وهي تشريح مفهوم الفشل. أصناف الفشل التي تهمني على وجه التحديد هي تلك التي من صنع يدي: هي المنبثقة من الغربة التي أشعر بها من خلال فن الفجري (وبالرغم من كل محاولتي لحل تلك المعضلة)، هي الناتجة عن عدم قدرتي على الاندماج في في الفجري جسدياً، وهي أيضاً من الحالات القائمة التي تفاقم شعوري بالفشل بكل ما يخص فن الفجري.

ولكي أنجز عملي في اطار هذا المشروع، قمت بتطوير برنامج يعمل ك»ماكينة فشل" باستعمال وسط /Max MSP. الافتراضية المعتمدة في "ماكينة الفشل" هي البحث في الخواص الفيزيائية للأصوات الكامنة في فن الفجري، والتوصل إلى ما قد يكون ماهية مصادر كل فشلي في التعامل مع فن الفجري. من ناحية عملية، خطوات العمل تتضمن البحث عن الضروب (كما هي معروفة في علم العروض)، المساحات الطيفية التي تتخلل لحظات الايقاع، والتفاصيل المتعارف عليها التي قد تحللها العملية البرمجية بطريقتها الخاصة. أتوقع من هذا المشروع نتيجة مليئة بالأخطاء الحسابية تبالغ من تراكم كل محاولاتي الفاشلة في الماضي فيما يخص فن الفجري، وسيترجم كل ذلك إلى نبضات صوتية غير مسموعة في فن الفجري أساساً. النتيجة إذاً ستكون مقطوعة موسيقية ذات طبيعة توليدية لا نهاية لها مبنية على الأخطاء الحسابية والتحليلية، والتي قد يراها المتلقي كصورة سالبة أو المساحات الأثيرية غير المسموعة الكامنة في فن الفجري. في فترة البحث التي اتخذتها لتطوير هذا العمل، كنت أحاول النظر في مفهوم ما يقارب البصمة الوراثية في الأصوات المؤرشفة والأصوات الميدانية. أتمنى أن أطور هذا "الماكينة" لتبدأ بتخزين ومحاولة فهم (بشكل خاطئ) الكلمات المستعملة في فن الفجري لتترتّب عليها موسيقى جديدة قد يقال عنها فشلت في فهم فن الفجري.

نهايةً، "ماكينة فشل الفجري" تمثل حواراً ذاتياً عليّ الشروع به. المشروع بشكل عام فرصة لي للتحاور مع كل تجاربي السابقة المتعلقة بموضوع فن الفجري وثقافات صناعة اللؤلؤ، وقد يمثل نقطة تحول في مسار عملي الفني والموسيقي. آأمل ألا تكون هيستوغرافيا فن الفجري وثقافات صناعة اللؤلؤ نقطة نهاية المشروع، بل أساساً يسمح لأعمال جديدة وتصورات مستقبلية مغايرة، وبأن هذا العمل نموذجاً لذلك. من ناحية صوتية، أتساءل كيف سيبدو "فجري الفشل"، وهل سيكون خارجاً تماماً عن السياق الأصلي، أو هل ستكون موسيقى الفجري-الفرانكنشتاينية نتيجة لفشلها شيئاً جديداً له معنى وقيمة. أما الآن، كل ما باستطاعتي فعله هو التأمل في طبيعة قرارات ماكينة فجري الفشل وتصور نتائجها المحتملة.

image 36

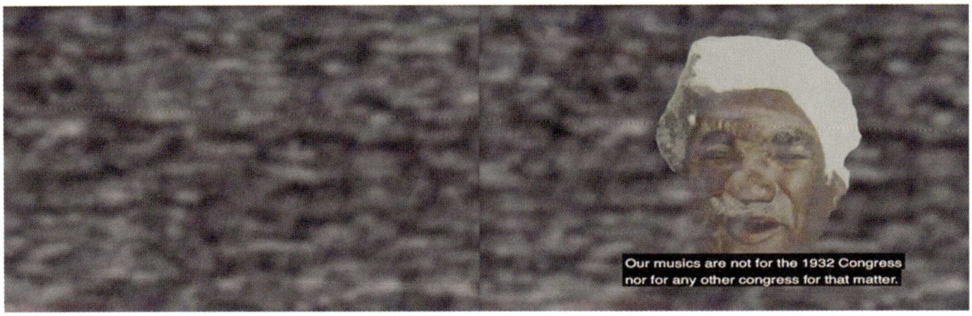

image 33

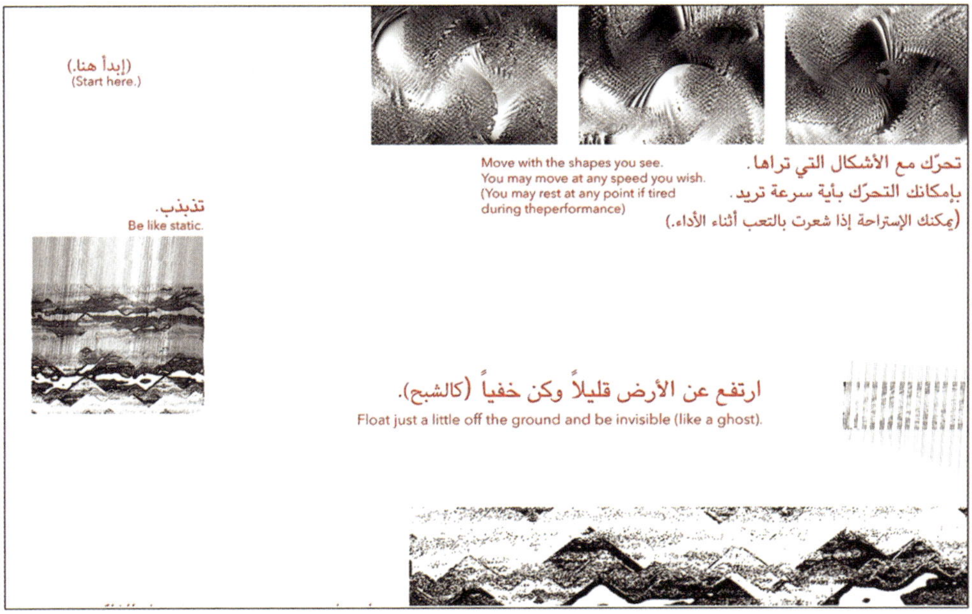

image 34

على مر العشرة سنوات الأخيرة، تناوَلت مجموعة كبيرة من المشاريع الفنية التي عملت فيها ثقافة اللؤلؤ إلى حدود متفاوتة. بعض تلك المشاريع كانت بقيادة فنانين زائرين إلى البحرين، بعضها بتحفيز من مؤسسات ثقافية معينة، وبعضها كانت مشاريعي الشخصية فيما يرتبط بتجاربي في الموسيقى والفن البصري. كان من أوائل المشاريع التي شاركت فيها في عام ٢٠١١م، حيث زار فنان معروف من منطقتنا البحرين ليحاول تلبيس نص تاريخي صيغة فن الفجري (والتي في بعض الأحيان توصف وبشكل ليس بالصورة التامة بموسيقى الغوص للؤلؤ). أثّرت تلك التجربة في نظرتي تجاه الاحتمالات الكامنة في استعمال ذلك الفن التراثي المميز في اطارات فنية متنوعة. بيد أن تلك التجربة بينت لي وجه الاستغلالية من حيث استخدام تلك الثقافة في مشاريع أخرى. شعرت نتيجة اشتغالي بذلك المشروع الأول بالخزي لأني اعتقدت بأنني مكّنت ذلك الفنان المعروف من استغلال ثقافة تراثية مميزة وممارسيها. دفعني ذلك الشعور إلى تفادي أولئك الموسيقيين الشعبيين الذين عملت معهم لأنني خجلت من كيف استغلهم ذلك الفنان الزائر. لم أستطع اللقاء مع الموسيقيين الذين عملت معهم سابقاً إلا بعد مرور عشرة سنوات حينما زارت البحرين فنانة من الخارج كانت تفكر بالعمل معهم في مشروعها الفني القادم.

في أعمالي الشخصية المرتبطة بمجالي فن الفجري وتاريخ صناعة اللؤلؤ في البحرين، وجدت نفسي أعالج تلك الأمور من زاوية مغايرة للزوايا التي عمل فيها الآخرون. بالرغم من زخم الاحتفاء بفن الفجري - خاصة فيما يتعلق في السرد المتداول رسمياً - بأنه يمثل موسيقانا الوطنية في البحرين، دوما ما تركت تلك الموسيقى في قرارة نفسي مزيجا من الانطباعات التي تدور حول فكرة واحدة: الغُربة. استغرق تقبلي لتلك الغربة التي شعرتها ازاء فن الفجري سنين عديدة، وأيضاً لأتقبّل بأنني لست ملاماً لتلك الانطباعات التي تحملتها سابقاً.

الغربة هي من أشد المشاعر التي أكنّها فيما يتعلق بفن الفجري وعلاقتها بثقافات صناعة اللؤلؤ. بالرغم من دراستي لهذا اللون من الموسيقى لما يزيد عن عقد من الزمن، وجدت بأنه من المستحيل عليّ أن أدرك بشكل تام كل تعقيداتها ذلك لأنها مرصّعة بالعديد من التفاصيل اللاموسيقية كالسلوكيات واللغة والثقافة والرقص التي هي خارج نطاق درايتي. تفسيري الخاص لعدم قدرتي على الادراك التام لفن الفجري هو نتيجة عدم تفاعلي جسدياً مع تلك الموسيقى وكل ما يدور حولها من اللاموسيقى. أفهم الآن بعد كل تلك السنين بأن فن الفجري يتطلب نوعاً من المعرفة الجسدية الناتجة عن الممارسة. كما أنني أعتقد بأن الغربة التي أشعر بها تجاه الفجري نتيجة كوني من عائلة لا تمارسها، وقد لاحظت بأن فن الفجري هنا في البحرين لا يمارسها سوى ذكور عوائل معينة يتناقلونه فيما بينهم شفهياً وبشكل خاص. أما أكبر مصدر للغربة التي أشعر بها هو تركيب الحزن الجماعي والعار الجماعي المرتبط بصناعة اللؤلؤ وثقافاتها لأنها تاريخها مبني على الاستغلالية والعبودية، إلا أن اليوم هناك احتفاء بثقافات صناعة اللؤلؤ من دون الاشارة إلى السواد الذي يشوب ذلك التاريخ. كل تلك المفارقات، بالنسبة لي شخصياً، مهمة ولكنها عموماً غير متدارسة علنياً.

لكل تلك الأسباب التي تم ذكرها، وفي طيات عملي على مشروع فني جديد حول فن الفجري والثقافات المرتبطة بصناعة اللؤلؤ، هناك حاجة ملحّة لهيكل فكري يدخل في انشاء العمل نفسه. وبالرغم من هذا التعميم غير المنصف، أجد بأنه هناك أساليب محدودة اتخذت لحد الآن حسب علمي فيما يتعلق بفن الفجري وثقافات صناعة اللؤلؤ. أخذ بعض الفنانين فن الفجري خارج سياقه ليلبسونه حلة ترفيهيه، وقد اتخذ آخرون موقف التعريف بناحيه ضيقة من تاريخ فن الفجري واعادة تفسير نواح معينة بشكل حر لبناء أعمال مكونة تركّب مشاهداً جديدة على مشاهد قديمة والعكس صحيح، وقد يقوم بعض الفنانين بأعمال موسيقية ذات طابع الانصهار والتلاقي (Fusion-Encounter)، وهناك آخرون يحولون استعمالهم لفن الفجري وثقافات صناعة اللؤلؤ إلى مجرد استعراض انثروبولوجي فحسب. بغض النظر عن تحفظاتي لكل تلك الأساليب التي ذكرتها، إلا أن كل تلك الأعمال لها الحق في وجودها ولكل منها مزاياها الخاصة. أنا لم أتوصل بعد إلى نهج بديل في أعمالي لمعالجة فن الفجري، ولكني أعتقد أحيانا بأن ذلك البحث عن البديل هو ما يهمني وما تدور حوله تجاربي الفنية.

آلة الفشل

الفجيري

علي صقر السويدي (الرائد علي)

رائد متقاعد من البحرية الإماراتية خدم في حرب الكويت وعمل كبحار منذ عمر الخامسة. اليوم، يحتل الرائد علي موقع رئيس جمعية الإمارات للبيئة البحرية وهو أحد صيادين اللؤلؤ المعدودين النشطين حالياً في البلاد. ولد الرائد علي في ١٩٥٧ في دبي، ومارس صيد اللؤلؤ منذ حداثة سنه وقد كرس حياته لنقل هذا التراث إلى أجيال أصغر. باعتباره ناشط بيئي حقيقي، وعبر التأثر بتجربته مع جاك كوستو، أنشأ الرائد علي محمية جبل علي البحرية جنوب دبي في عام ٢٠١٨ والتي ترحب بالأطفال والباحثين في فصل الصيف لتثقفهم بشأن صيد اللؤلؤ والتقاليد المرتبطة به.

[١] جاك-إيف كوستو كان ضابط بحري فرنسي ومستكشف وناشط في الحفاظ على البيئة وصانع أفلام ومخترع وعالم ومصور فوتوغرافي ومؤلف وباحث درس البحر وكافة أشكال الحياة في الماء.

[٢] تقليدياً يربط حزام من الأثقال بخاصرة الغوامين ليتيح لهم غوص أسرع بمجهود أقل.

[٣] ملحوظة من المحرر: لم يتم التحقق من الرقم.

أوليفييه:هل تخطط للتوقف عن الغوص؟

الرائد علي:
أبداً! البحر حياتي، إن لم أذهب للبحر، سأموت، مثل سمكة (يضحك). حينما كنت صغيراً كانوا يدعونني بالصبي الإنجليزي لأني كنت أذهب للشاطئ يومياً مما يجعل شعري أخف!

أوليفييه: برأيك ماذا يحمل المستقبل لصيد اللؤلؤ في الخليج؟

الرائد علي:
أرى مستقبل مشرق أمامنا. إنه يعود. في البحرين لديهم ١٠٠٠ قارب يقومون بصيد اللؤلؤ وفي الشهر الماضي أطلقوا قوارب كبيرة. إنه أسطول مهم وهم يجنون أموال طيبة من وراء الأمر. اللؤلؤ طبيعي وهم يبيعونه في الأسواق التي تكبر في المقابل. هذا ما أريد فعله في الأمارات العربية المتحدة حتى لا يتعين علينا أن نعتمد حصرياً على البترول بل أن نجد شيئاً آخر ليزيد دخل بلادنا.

أوليفييه هل لاحظت تأثير التغير المناخي على مهاد اللؤلؤ واللآلئ؟ طبقاً لفهمي فإن مياه دافئة تعني المزيد من الطحالب مما قد يؤثر على المحار...

الرائد علي:
حسناً لقد أجريت بحث لثلاثة أعوام في أبو ظبي بالقرب من الجزر سألت فيه العجائز عن أين كانوا يجدون اللآلئ. كانوا يجدونها في كل مكان من قبل -لآلئ كبيرة. الآن كلها صغيرة، والمحار أيضاً، بسبب الطحالب والملوحة. الملوحة تقلل من العوالق ولا يأكل المحار بما يكفي كنتيجة لذلك. نأمل أن نفعل شيئاً لنساعدهم..

أوليفييه: بمساعدة التكنولوجيا والعلم؟

الرائد علي:
حلمي هو أن أقوم برحلة بحثية. أتعرف من علمني كل هذا؟ كوستو. في مصر أعطاني كتابه وبقيت معه لحوالي ١٥ يوماً. علمني كل شيء. قبل أن يموت قال لي «عليك أن تجري بحثاً لدراسة البيئة في الخليج» وأنا أود بالقيام بدراسة ضخمة حول الخليج. آمل أن يحدث ذلك.

الرائد علي:
نعم وبالأخص خلال حرب الخليج، لأن في أثناء الصراع تسرب الكثير من التبرول في كل ناحية من البيئة المحيطة. كان أمراً شنيعاً للمشاهدة، كانت الحيوانات تموت. لهذا أنشأت الجمعية البيئية. كان مصب اهتمامنا الأول هو تنظيف البحر وإثارة حساسية الناس بحيث لا يلقون بالقمامة في البكر. بدأنا في الاهتمام بالنظام البيئي البحري والحمدلله نجحنا في تغيير العديد من الأشياء. قبلها كان الناس يفكرون في البحر باعتباره سلة مهملات وكانوا يلقون بالكثير من القمامة فيه. الآن هذه الأفعال ممنوعة وتغيرت العقليات. الآن نعلم أهمية الاعتناء بالسلاحف والقروش والدرافيل. على سبيل المثال، لم يكن في دبي سابقاً أي سلاحف، الآن لدينا ٥٢ سلحفاة ولدت على هذا الشاطئ لأني أعتني بهم. في برامجنا التعليمية للأطفال يأتون ليروا البيض، وعندما يفقس البيض وتخرج السلاحف يطلقونهم في البرية. هذا الذي يحدث مذهل! لقد أهديت حياتي للبيئة ولتعليم تراثنا. عمري الآن ٦٣ ومازلت أغطس وأصور وأساعد لأني لا أدخن ولا أشرب (كحول) وآكل أطعمة طبيعية. (يضحك)

أوليفييه: ثقافة صيد اللؤلؤ هي بلا شك ثقافة خليجية. ما هي علاقتك بالغواصين من بلدان أخرى؟

الرائد علي:
لدينا علاقة طيبة خاصة مع البحرين. لديهم مياه نقية في قاع البحر وهذا هو سبب نمو المحار أفضل هناك، بسبب قلة الملوحة وكثرة نمو عوالق البحر التي تغذيهم. كنا نذهب إلى البحرين والكويت لنغطس هناك وهم يأتون إلينا، إنه بحر مفتوح.

أوليفييه: وماذا بشأن التوتر الحالي في الخليج مع قطر: هل يؤثر على عملك أم أن البحر شيء آخر؟

الرائد علي:
إنه يؤثر على عملنا بالطبع، لكن أعتقد مع توقيع الاتفاقية سننتهي من هذه المشكلة. الخليج وواحد وهو مترابط ببعضه البعض وحتى مع إيران.

أوليفييه: ابالحديث عن إيران، هل تقع أغلب مهاد اللؤلؤ في الجانب العربي من الخليج أم أن بإمكانك أن تجد بعضها في الجانب الشمالي؟

الرائد علي:
بإمكانك أن تجد البعض على الناحية الأخرى لأن لديهم بضعة جزر. مياه الخليج ضحلة لكن هناك تتسم بالعمق مما يجعلها مشكلة بالنسبة لتنمو المحار. لكن في بعض الجزر -مثل كيش وأبو موسى وطنب- تحظى هذه الجزر بالمحار ولآلئ جيدة جداً الخليج على هذه الناحية مختلف قليلاً.

image 51

أوليفييه: لكن صيد اللؤلؤ الطبيعي يؤثر على مهاد المحار بالنظر إلى أن نسبة ١٪ فقط من المحار يحتوي على لؤلؤ. كيف تضمن أن يظل هذا التقليد مستداماً من الناحية البيئية؟

الرائد علي:
الآن مع الأشعة السينية يمكنك أن تعلم إن كانت المحارة تحتوي على لؤلؤة قبل أن تفتحها. يمكنك تكرار هذه العملية آلاف المرات دون أن تدمر مهاد المحار بأكثر من اللازم. هذا وإلا سينتهي بنا الحال إلى مشكلة صيد جائر كما حدث في الماضي. هذا النمط من التفكير غير مستدام.

أوليفييه: هل تعتقد أن لآلئ المزارع تؤثر على طريقة تصور اللآلئ الطبيعية كذلك؟

الرائد علي:
نعم لكن في النهاية سيدرك الناس الفارق بين الاثنين. الآن يعود الناس ثانية إلى اللآلئ الطبيعية.

أوليفييه: لقد ذكرت أنك خدمت في الحرب. هل ألهمك هذا الأمر لتصبح أكثر نشاطاً في الناحية المستدامة من الحياة؟

أوليفيية: أنت تستخدم مشبك للأنف، وسلة للمحار...

الرائد علي:
كذلك الأوزان[٢]...

أوليفيية: وتنزل سريعاً - ما هو العمق الذي تصل إليه؟

الرائد علي:
كان جدي يغوص حتى عمق ٤٠ متراً. أنا أصل إلى ١٠، في أقصى الأحوال ١٥ متراً، لا أكثر لأن هذه هي أفضل لتجد المحار. بعضهم مليء بها بحيث يمكنك أن تملأ في دقيقتين. أحياناً يمكنك أن تجد بعضهم هنا وهناك وقد يستغرقك الأمر ٣ أو ٤ دقائق لتملأ سلتك.

أوليفيية: لابد وأن الأمر مرهق. كم غطسة تغطسها في اليوم الواحد.

الرائد علي:
في الماضي كانوا يغطسون ٢٠٠ غطسة في اليوم. بالنسبة لنا الأمر مختلف، نحن نغطس بغرض المرح لذلك نغطس ربما ١٠ أو ١٥ غطسة على الأكثر في اليوم.

أوليفيية: هل لديك طاقم للغطس؟

الرائد علي:
أغطس مع فريقي المكون عشرة أشخاص لأنهم تدربوا على صيد اللؤلؤ. نحتاج إلى المجموعة حيث يقوم جزء منها بالغطس بينما يساعد الجزء الآخر. لكل غطاس مساعٍ. هذا أيضاً للتحكم القيادة ومساعدة القبطان. صيد اللؤلؤ هو عمل جماعي لا يملك أبداً. أحياناً نغطس لمدة شهران ولا يرغب أحد في العودة إلى البيت.

أوليفيية: ما رأيك في لؤلؤ المزارع؟

الرائد علي:
لا أحبه على الإطلاق لأنه يدمر ثقافتنا. حينما ظهرت اللآلئ الصناعية في السوق إنهار اللؤلؤ. كنا لنعاني لو لم يظهر البترول بعدها بقليل. كنا لنموت. أركز على اللآلئ الطبيعية وأحاول زيادة التوعية بها. اللآلئ المزروعة رخيصة وليست جيدة. إن وضعتهم بين أسنانك يمكنك كسرها! أحب اللآلئ الطبيعية وأود لو حصلت على المزيد من هذا النوع. لقد أجريت بحثاً لتنمية المزيد من المحار الطبيعي وآمل في أن أرى المزيد من هذا النوع في المستقبل.

أوليفييه: كيف تنقل هذا التراث؟ لقد أخبرتني أنك تصطحب أطفال معك على القارب أحياناً، هل تعلمهم؟

الرائد علي:
في الصيف، حينما لا يكون هناك دوام مدرسي نستقبل الأولاد هنا. في البداية كان ابني، بعدها بدأ يأتي بأصدقائه. لكن قبل صيد اللؤلؤ يجب أن تتعلم السباحة حسب القواعد ويجب أن تكون في حالة جسدية طيبة. أيضاً لا يسمح بالهواتف للأطفال، كذلك نمنع الأشياء السيئة مثل الوجبات السريعة والبيبسي. حينما يأتون هنا يصبحون تعساء للأيام الثلاثة الأولى بسبب كل هذه المحظورات وتغيير حياتهم. خطوة بخطوة، بعد أسبوع تقريباً، يبدأون في الإعجاب بالأمر والمبيت على القارب. يغسلون أوجههم في البحر ويأكلون التمر والسمك والأرز، هذا كل شيء. بعد عشرين يوم لا يريدون المغادرة. أعتقد أن هذا بسبب الجذور التي يحتفظون بها من جهة أجدادهم. إنه أمر مذهل حينما تشهد مهارتهم تطور باضطراد بينما تعلمهم كيفية الغناء. يغنون على الدوام لجعل أعمالهم أيسر، بالضبط كما في الماضي. هذا جيد، أتمنى أن يستمر هذا الأمر في المستقبل. لدي ٢٠٠٠ طفل يفعلون ذلك سنوياً وبالطبع الفتيات من المجتمع المحلي مرحب بهن.

أوليفييه: الغناء عنصر مركزي في صيد اللؤلؤ، هل تغني؟

الرائد علي:
بالطبع، حينما نبدأ رحلة الصيد نقول «هونها يا رب» لكل شيء نفعله في القارب لدينا أغنية أخرى. العديد من الأغنيات الجيدة تمنح الشجاعة والحماس اللازمين للطاقم للعمل خاصة حينما تحمل المرساة ثقيلة الوزن.

أوليفييه: هناك الكثير من الشعر المرتبط بموسيقى غواصي اللؤلؤ، ما الذي يعنيه اللؤلؤ بالنسبة لك؟

الرائد علي:
نعتقد أن اللؤلؤ -مثلما يعتقد الهنود أيضاً- يساعد دوران الدم. في بومباي اعتادوا على ارتداء الكثير من اللآلئ لتحسين دوران الدم. إنه أفضل شيء يمكنك ارتداءه خاصة بالنسبة للنساء. لا تحتاج للذهب أو الماس، التقط لؤلؤة وارتديها كما هي. هذا هو أفضل شيء بشأن اللآلئ، حياتهم طويلة ويحتفظون بقيمتهم للأبد.

أوليفييه: هل لازلت تغطس على الطريقة التقليدية؟

الرائد محمود :
أنظر، بالنسبة لصيد اللؤلؤ، لا يوجد لديك الكثير من الأشياء لتحمي نفسك، لا نظارة ماء، لا شيء. إن أسرعت، أحياناً تهاجمك القروش. عادة تهاجم القروش فقط إن كنت تحمل طعاماً أو أسماك وهناك فقط بضعة هجمات على غواصين أبلغ عنها في الماضي. إنهم جزء من البحر وكصياد لؤلؤ عليك أن تحيا معهم. البحر ينتمي إلى سلالات أخرى. حينما ندخل علينا أن نلتزم الأدب، كأنك تذهب إلى بيت أحدهم. شخصياً أحمل تاريخ كبير من الغوص، هناك حوالي ١٠ آلاف غطسة في بدني.

أوليفييه دوبور: هلا قدمت نفسك؟

الرائد علي:
أنا الرائد علي، رئيس مجموعة الإمارات للبيئة البحرية. بدأت في التعامل مع البيئة والتقاليد منذ زمن طويل. في ١٩٧١، بدأت في الغوص بسبب القصص الكثيرة التي بلغتني عن جدي ووالدي وأردت أن أعرف ماذا يوجد في أعماق البحر. أردت أن أرى اللؤلؤ.

حينما بدأت الغوص فتحت الآلاف من المحار دون أن أجد شيئاً! أخبرني جدي حينها «حينما تعمل في البحر عليك أن تكون صبوراً.»

بعدها بقليل وجد أول اللآلئ في حياتي، لآلئ جميلة. هكذا بدأت رحلتي في صيد اللؤلؤ. أدعوهن «الوصل» وهو اسم دبي القديمة اليوم. كنت أصطحب أصدقائي وكنا نذهب إلى الجزر المجاورة بالمركب، تلك التي تبعد حوالي ١٥ ساعة، وهناك بدأنا الغوص للحصول على اللؤلؤ.

أوليفييه: كم كان عمرك حين غطست للمرة الأولى؟

الرائد علي:
كان عمري ١٨ حين بدأت.

أوليفييه: هل شجعك الغوص على أن تصبح رئيساً لمجموعة الإمارات للبيئة البحرية وأن تحافظ على البيئة؟

الرائد علي:
حسناً، أنت تعلم أن كوستو كان أبونا الروحي. ذهبت في عام ٨٨ إلى مصر في وقابلته في شرم الشيخ. لقد ألهمني الاعتناء بالبيئة، وبعد عودتي من الرحلة أنشأت جمعية الغوص الإماراتية. بعد حرب الخليج، في ١٩٩٥ أنشأت مجموعة الإمارات للبيئة البحرية. أثناء الحرب كنت في البحرية وحاربت، وكان ذلك قدراً بالفعل. بعدها بدأت في الاهتمام بالبيئة وبتقاليد صيد اللؤلؤ في الإمارات.

أوليفييه: أنت من أواخر الغواصين المتبقين. كيف تنظر إلى التطور في الخمسين سنة الأخيرة؟

الرائد علي:
قبل خمسين عاماً توقف صيد اللؤلؤ بسبب وصول البترول والأموال المرتبطة به. الغوص صعب كما تعلم، ومنذ ذلك الوقت ظللت أفكر بشأن المستقبل. البترول ليس مصدر مستدام على الدوام وأسعاره متقلبة. في يوم ما سينفد، ولهذا أخطط لتعليم الأطفال (الغوص). حينما ينفد سيظل باستطاعتنا الغوص لصيد اللؤلؤ ولهذا أريد أن أصنع جيلاً جديداً من صيادين اللؤلؤ.

image 52

طريق الغواص:
«الرائد علي»

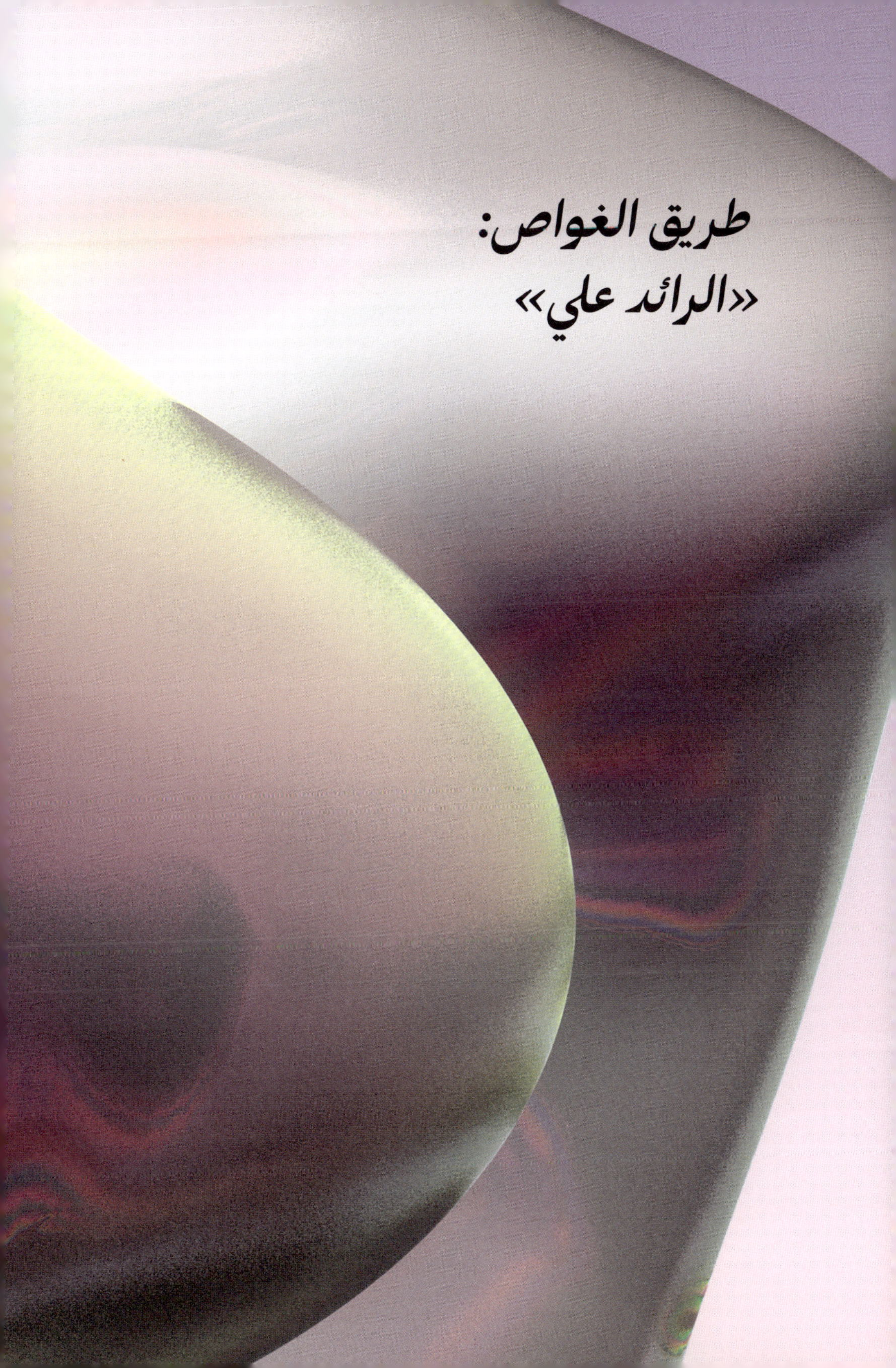

عبدالله سويدي

حفيد محمد بن عبدالله السويدي، صائد لؤلؤ شهير من سلالة جلبهار الشهيرة في رأس الخيمة، وأحد صيادي اللؤلؤ النادرين المتبقين في الإمارات العربية المتحدة ذلك بخلاف كونه مؤسس «لآلئ السويدي،» مزرعة اللؤلؤ الوحيدة في منطقة الخليج بأسرها. بعد أن حصل على شهادته في العلوم السياسية من الجامعة الأمريكية بواشنطن، التحق السويدي بالخدمة الدبلوماسية وخدم في اليابان ثم أستراليا قبل أن يعود إلى الإمارات. هناك، رأس السويدي عدة مشاريع لمصلحة وزارة الشؤون الاجتماعية قبل أن يبدأ في مشروع زراعة اللؤلؤ وتجارته في رأس الخيمة في ٢٠٠٥. كرئيس للمزرعة الوحيدة من نوعها في المنطقة، يدفع السويدي باستمرار بمبادرات جديدة متمحورة حول حفظ التراث المحلي بالتوازي مع تطبيق التكنولوجيا وإجراء الأبحاث كلما تيسر.

[١] حينما كان الخليج تحت السيطرة البريطانية.

[٢] قرية ساحلية صغيرة بجوار راس الخيمة في شمال الإمارات العربية المتحدة.

[٣] الاسم السابق لرأس الخيمة والذي يعني حرفياً «لؤلؤة.»

[٤] عملية زراعة المحار.

قمة الأهمية. من الملهم استكشاف المشاعر الداخلية للغواصين والطاقم بأكمله في سبيل عمل المزيد وإيجاد هذه الجواهر الجميلة التي هي اللؤلؤ لإعالة أنفسهم في وقت لا تتوفر فيه موارد أخرى. كل الشعر والقصص تتمحور منطقياً حول تحدي إيجاد اللؤلؤ الثمين المختبئ في مكان ما في البحر المجاور.

أوليفييه: هل تقتعد أنك ستتوقف عن الغوص أبداً؟

عبدالله: وحده الموت سيوقفني عن الغوص. لهذا أتمنى لو مت في عمر لا أعتمد فيه على آخرين. أعتقد أنه سيكون في السادسة والثمانين من العمر وآمل أن ينعم علي الله بذلك. الغوص مفيد للصحة ويسمح لك بالانفصال عن العالم. يمكنك أن تخلق عالمك الخاص في الأعماق دون اضطرابات العالم الحديث الصاخب المزدحم. في أثناء حظر التجول لم استطع تحمل فكرة البقاء على اليابسة. كانت المزرعة مغلقة أمام استقبال الزوار لكن العمل لم يتوقف. داومت على الغوص معتنياً بالمحار، نظفتهم والشبك وعلمت أننا سنجني المحار حينما ينتهي وباء كورونا.

أوليفييه: هل ترى عالم الأعماق كملجأ؟

عبدالله: ليس ذلك فقط. الضغط الي يقع علينا في حياتنا يختفي مع الضغط الذي تختبره بينما تتدلى إلى أعماق البحر. كل التوتر يتم تنفيسه واللحظة التي تستقر فيها في القاع هي لحظة إعادة البدء -إعادة البدء إلى إعدادات المصنع- في كل مرة تعود كشخص مختلف. لهذا تريد أن تفعلها المرة بعد المرة سواءاً كنت غواص تقليدي أو غواص سكوبا. الغوص راحة عظيمة. إن أخذت زجاجة معك ستطلق كل التوتر قبل أن تمتلئ مجدداً. الشيء ذاته يحدث للبشر، لكنك تتخلص من كل السلبية في أثناء العملية. الطاقة مختلفة تماماً في قاع البحر عن تلك الموجودة على اليابسة. عليك أن تحذر.

أوليفييه: لم تمر بحادث من قبل أثناء الغوص؟

عبدالله: أبداً. كنت خائفاً من العديد من الأشياء لكن لم أؤذ نفسي من قبل. سمعي مازال جيد على الرغم من أن نظري ضعف لأنني اعتدت الغوص بلا نظارات. اليوم أفعلها للحفاظ على نفسي، لذلك أغوص عدة مرات فقط لحوالي ١٥ دقيقة على عمق يبلغ ١٠ أمتار. فعلها جدي لأيام لأنهم كانوا يحتاجون الأمر للبقاء. العديد من الناس يظنون أن حبس أنفاسك هو ذاته مثل حبس أنفاسك على اليابسة. الأمر ليس كذلك. بمجرد أن تبلغ الأعماق لديك هواء أكثر لتتنفسه.

أوليفييه: هل تظن أن أطفالك سيكون بإمكانهم حمل هذا التراث؟

عبدالله: لم أجبر على اتباع خطى جدي. بحث ومازلت أبحث عنه بنفسي. لابد أن أطفالي رأوا ما فعلته وبالمثل سيكون لديهم الخيار إما أن يكملوا عملي أو أن يسلكوا طريق آخر. كيف حافظنا على آلاف السنين من الكتابة واللآلئ في الخليج على مر الزمن؟ هناك سبب لذلك.

أوليفييه: هل تمكنت من اقناع منتقديك بهذا الحل؟

عبدالله: *هذه المحادثة لن تنتهي وليس لدي الوقت لها. أنا الآن في سابعة والأربعين من العمر وأفضل أن أركز على تنمية ما أقوم به.*

أوليفييه: في رأيك لماذا يتغيب الدعم المؤسسي لمبادرتك بالمقارنة بتقاليد أخرى مهمة في المنطقة مثل تدريب الصقور وسباقات الإبل؟

عبدالله: *الأولويات. صيد اللؤلؤ ليس واحداً منها. الصقور لديها العديد من المحبين وأعدادهم تنمو باستمرار. أما صيد اللؤلؤ فلا، وهذا الفصل -من التاريخ- تم اعتباره منتهياً. لا أقبل ذلك وأنوي أن أثبت وجهة نظري عبر إنشاء مشروعي القادم والذي سيكون أكاديمية لصيد اللؤلؤ حيث سيتعلم الناس كيف يغوصون بالطرق التقليدية -أي بلا مساعدة- والطرق الحديثة أي الغوص باستخدام الرئة المائية. هذا ما أفعله حالياً في أغلب أيامي وأعلم أن صيد اللؤلؤ سيصبح أولوية مرة أخرى.*

أوليفييه: لقد ذكرت الاستدامة التجارية، لكن ماذا عن الاستدامة البيئية؟ هل مازالت تستثمر في البحث عن التطورات المتعلقة بذلك؟

عبدالله: *بدأت العمل في صيد اللؤلؤ في ٢٠٠٣. كان البذر الأول[٤] في ٢٠٠٥ ووجدت لؤلؤتنا الأولى بعدها بثلاثة أشهر. بالنسبة لي وللمراقبين الأجانب، كان هذا الأمر لا يقل عن كونه معجزة. لم نستطيع التصديق. حاولنا المرة تلو المرة، وبدأ الغطاء الخارجي للؤلؤة الأولى يتكون من الشهر الأول! لذلك من ٢٠٠٥ إلى ٢٠١٨ اقتصر الأمر على الاختبار والاختبار والاختبار. رحلة طويلة من جمع المعلومات لنفسي لإرضاء حاجتي للمعرفة.*

ترى، يستبطن مشروعي فهماً عميقاً للبيئة المحيطة. درجة الحرارة، الأوكسجين وملوحة الماء كلها عوامل حاسمة. التوقف عن البحث والتطوير سيقتل المشروع. الأمر بالغ الأهمية. يوماً ما، أريد أن افتتح مختبر البحث خاصتي لأشارك هذا البحث مع علماء الأحياء البحرية وعلماء الجواهر من جميع أنحاء العالم لإجراء التجارب والأبحاث معي. أنا متأكد أنهم سيكونون مندهشين مما سيروه. لا نستطيع فعل أي شيء مع التحديات البيئية الفعلية لأنها عالمية، لكن بإمكاننا التفكير في أفكار بسيطة مبنية على الموارد الطبيعية للتغلب على الكوارث الطبيعية.

أوليفييه: كيف تخطط لنقل موسيقى صيادين اللؤلؤ كجزء من تراث أكبر صيد اللؤلؤ في مشاريعك؟

عبدالله: *لم أفكر في هذا الأمر قبل أن أقابلك اليوم. نحن لسنا مثاليين وهناك دائماً شيء ما غائب. مع مشاركة المعرفة يمكننا تجسير هذه الفجوة. تبين أن الموسيقى شديدة الأهمية لأنها تغذي النشاط على القارب بينما نحن وحيدون في عرض البحر. الارتباط بالعائلات والتعود على الخوف وعدم اليقين في مثل هذه الرحلات، الأمل في إيجاد لؤلؤة تغطي تكاليف الموسم كله أو قضاء أيام طويلة في انتظار الريح لتدفع الأشرعة، كثير من الأشياء تتعلق بهذه الموسيقى. كلمات هذه الألحان المستقاة من الشعر العربي هي في*

image 53

image 54

يحدث في الماضي. كانوا يحصدون البحار كما تحصد الأرض والآن من بين ٧٤ ألف غواص في الخليج، حفنة فقط ظلت نشطة. النوع الثاني من اللآلئ هو لآلئ المزارع الذي اخترعه مزارع اللؤلؤ الياباني ميكيموتو في ١٩٠٥ والذي جرب بذر جسد غريب داخل المحارة وبهذا أصبحت اللآلئ تحصد بتدخل بشري. اليوم ٩٥٪ من اللآلئ المباعة حول العالم هي لآلئ مزروعة. من يمكنه أن يتحمل تكلفة اللآلئ الطبيعية اليوم؟ لا أحد. الجرام الواحد يباع على أقل بألفي دولار وقد يرتفع إلى ٤ آلاف دولار اعتماداً على النوع والحجم واللمعة وشكل اللؤلؤة. أخيراً هناك اللآلئ المصنعة المصنوعة من الزجاج أو عناصر كيميائية والتي تبدو وكأنها لؤلؤة دون أن تكون كذلك. اللآلئ المصنعة ليست لآلئ مزروعة لكن استخدام هذا المفهوم خلق خلطاً دفع أسعار اللؤلؤ الطبيعي إلى أعلى فيما حط من سعر اللآلئ المزروعة إلى مستوى اللآلئ المصنعة. أعرف هذه الاستراتيجية وهي ليست بالأمر الجديد. هكذا كان الحال منذ اختراع اللآلئ المزروعة.

الحل هو تقديم اللآلئ العربية الطبيعية والمزروعة بأسعار مقبولة بالنسبة للجمهور. هذا هو التحدي الرئيسي الخاص بي في سبيل جعل هذا الإرث مستداماً. لنتمكن من ذلك علينا أن نركز على كل الناس، ليس فقط الأغنياء والمشاهير. أريد أن أثبت أن خليجنا الجميل مازال ينتج أفضل اللآلئ. أن أقدم بديلاً. لؤلؤ مزروعة في ذات المحارة التي تنتمي جينياً إلى اللؤلؤ الطبيعي. لتفعل ذلك، ننسلها في ذات المنطقة والبيئة التي تنمو فيها اللآلئ الطبيعية. هذه هي طريقة مزج التراث والحداثة وطريقة جعل الأمر مشروعاً مستداماً.

الحقيقية. بلغ اللؤلؤ هذا المكان بعد آلاف السنين والخطر قائم الآن بقطعه عن الأجيال الجديدة. فهمت أن اللؤلؤ قد ينتهي وينسى مع أغانيه وقصائده وقصصه. وقد أكون الشخص الذي سيمنح قبلة الحياة للؤلؤ ويحيي تراثه.

أوليفييه: هل تعتقد أن الأمر ينجح؟ هل الأجيال الأصغر تتلقى هذه الرسالة وهل أنت متصل بأناس آخرون في سبيلهم لتحقيق ذات الهدف؟

عبدالله: *إجابتي البسيطة هي التالي، في الموانئ الإنجليزي في عام١٩٠٦[١] ذهب ٧٤ ألف رجل إلى موسم صيد اللؤلؤ في الخليج بأكمله ابتداءً بقريتي المحببة الرمس[٢] وحتى الكويت. اليوم في الإمارات العربية المتحدة هناك على الأقصى صيادين أو ثلاثة متبقين. كان هناك أكثر لكنهم يموتون وأنا على الأرجح الأصغر بعمري البالغ ٤٧ عاماً. هذا هو التحدي الأكبر، كيف تمرر هذا الأمر للجيل المقبل. المزرعة تظهر التراث وقصة صيادين اللؤلؤ لنجذب الناس ونشارك هذه المعرفة. اللؤلؤ هو أحد الجواهر العظيمة التي بإمكانها أن توحدنا.*

أوليفييه: ما الذي تعتقد أنه أكبر تحدي يواجهك في تمرير هذا الإرث للأجيال الأصغر؟

عبدالله: *على الأرجح فإن التراث والحداثة كانا في صدام في الماضي. أما اليوم فهما يكملان بعضهما البعض. لا يمكن أن نعيش دون الحداثة ودون التراث العظيم الذي نحوزه. الحفاظ عليه وصيانته يتطلب معادلة بيئية معقدة. انتاج لآلئ طبيعياً أو عبر زراعة وبذر المحار هو علامة بيئية إيجابية. أن نفشل في ذلك يعني أن النظام البيئي غير نظيف مما يفسر لم لا يتمكن المحار من الاستمرار بها. بالنسبة لي التحدي الأكبر في المستقبل هو كيفية الحفاظ على البيئة. قمامة أقل في البحر، لا مخلفات كيميائية، الحد من العوامل التي تؤدي إلى التلوث - مثل السفن الكبيرة التي تسافر في الخليج وتلقي بمخلفاتها هناك- كل هذه الأفكار لحماية البحر من المعاناة والتي ستؤثر علينا جميعاً حتماً في يوم من الأيام. الحفاظ على البيئة والمضي قدماً هو ما فعلته في نطاق محدود وآمل أن ألهم آخرين ليفعلوا مثلي وربما أفضل. جلفار[٣] كانت واحدة من مراكز تجارة اللؤلؤ في العالم. حاولت الحفاظ عليها وتقديمها للعالم. لنرى كيف ستتمكن كل من أبو ظبي ودبي من المضي قدماً بتقديم هذا الإرث الجميل. أؤمن أنه في يوم ما سنحتفل بهذه الثقافة المتفردة.*

أوليفييه: اللآلئ المزروعة تعتبر قضية كبرى في الخليج حيث أثر اختراعهم على السوق بشكل هائل. هل قوبلت مبادرتك الخاصة بمزرعة اللؤلؤ بالمقاومة أو النقد؟

عبدالله: *قطعاً واجهتني العديد من التحديات فيما يتعلق بشرح عملي للناس. لاقيت هجمات من الإعلام لكن هذه الهجمات لم تكن مؤيدة بحجج حيث قدمت أنا حججي وأنا أعلم لماذا أصنع ما أصنع. أسألهم: إن كنتم تحتفون باللؤلؤ الطبيعي وتريدون الحفاظ عليه، ماذا تريدون أن تصنعوا بشأن الأمر وكيف ستتحركون قدماً بذلك الخصوص؟ لا أتلقى إجابة ولا يريد أحد فعل أي شيء.*

هناك أناس تلاعبوا بأسماء وتعريفات ثقافة اللؤلؤ ليربطوها باللؤلؤ الصناعي وهو أمر مزيف بالكامل. اللآلئ الطبيعية التي يجلبها الغواصون من أعماق البحار نسبة الحصول عليها من المحار تبلغ ١٪. فمن كل مائة محارة واحدة فقط ستجلب لك لؤلؤ. في هذه الحالة فستقتل ١٠٠ محارة لينتهي بك الأمر للحصول على لؤلؤة واحدة وهذا ما كان

أوليفييه دوبور: هلا قدمت نفسك؟

عبدالله سويدي:
أنا صائد لؤلؤ شغوف ومتصل بالماضي وبالتراث العظيم لصيد اللؤلؤ. أرى نفسي أنتمي للأزمنة القديمة لا الحديثة. لا أرتدي ساعة، ولا أتوافق مع العلامات التجارية الشهيرة. أنا من كانه جدي، صائد لؤلؤ. حينما أرى الطريقة التي نعيش بها حياتنا اليوم أجدها مختلفة بالكلية عن الحياة القديمة. وهذه الحياة القديمة هي شغفي.

أوليفييه: لقد أنشأت مزرعة لؤلؤ هنا في رأس الخيمة وهي الوحيدة من نوعها في الخليج، هل بإمكانك أن تخبرنا المزيد عنها؟

عبدالله: *لقد غصت في سبيل الحصول على اللؤلؤ على مدار الخمسة وعشرين عاماً الماضية. فكرت كثيراً وكان لدي الكثير من الأفكار لجذب الناس ليروا أهمية تاريخنا. الندرة وشح اللآلئ الطبيعية دفعاني للتفكير في استعمال التكنولوجيا والبحث للحفاظ على تراث أجدادنا. الناس مدفوعون الآن بالدفاع على البيئة ومهمومون بحفظها. هذا المكون حديث ويمكنه أن يساعد في الحفاظ على تراث صيد اللؤلؤ.*

لقد فعلت ذلك لأن جيلي كان الجيل الأخير الذي شهد ورأى أناساً يغوصون للحصول على اللؤلؤ حتى نهاية الأربعينات من القرن الماضي. ابني وجيله لم يروا جدي يغوص كما فعلت في أوائل السبعينات. نحن جيل عالق بين انهيار تراث صيد اللؤلؤ وبعثه المحتمل. هذا فقط إن استطعنا فعل شيء لنقله للأجيال القادمة. لهذا أجد نفسي مسؤولاً عن صنع وذلك ولهذا أنشأت المزرعة.

أوليفييه: هذه مسؤولية كبيرة أن تنقل هذا الموروث إلى الجيل القادم. هل يشاركك آخرون في الخليج الاعتقاد بأهمية تمرير هذا التراث؟

عبدالله: *بالنسبة ليه، صيد اللؤلؤ في الخليج هو بمثابة سحر غير ملموس. لا يهم الجيل، سيظل الخليج مرتبطاً بصيد اللؤلؤ. الصغير أو الكبير، إن سألت أي أحد هنا في الخليج عن من هم بالنظر إلى الهوية سيجيبونك: اللؤلؤ. لكن إن سألتهم كيف حدث ذلك، لن يتمكنوا من الإجابة، لكنهم سيظلوا حاملين لهذه التركة السحرية. لم؟ لأن بطريقة ما يتم تمرير هذه التركة من جيل إلى جيل حيث تضم كل عائلة إما غواص أو شيال أو بحار أو مغني أو طباخ أو قبطان أو ملاح أو تاجر لؤلؤ. هذا الأمر شكل الحياة في الخليج اجتماعياً واقتصادياً بل وحتى سياسياً.*

إن عدت في التاريخ سترى الرحالة الإغريق والرومان والفرس والعرب من أمثال ابن بطوطة والمسعودي والإدريسي كلهم مروا من هنا وتحدثوا عن هذه المنطقة وتبعهم البرتغاليون والطليان والفرنسيون والبريطانيون. فهم العالم كله جمال اللؤلؤ الأنيقة التي جائت بهم جميعاً حتى الخليج. كنا معولمين من قبل أن يشير الناس للأمر بوصفه «عولمة» نحن موصولون بالعالم، وهذا بفضل سحر اللؤلؤ. لو سألت الكثير من الناس في الخليج إن كانوا قد رأوا لؤلؤ، سيجيبك الكثير بالإيجاب لكن الحقيقة أنهم لا يعرفون اللآلئ العربية

image 55

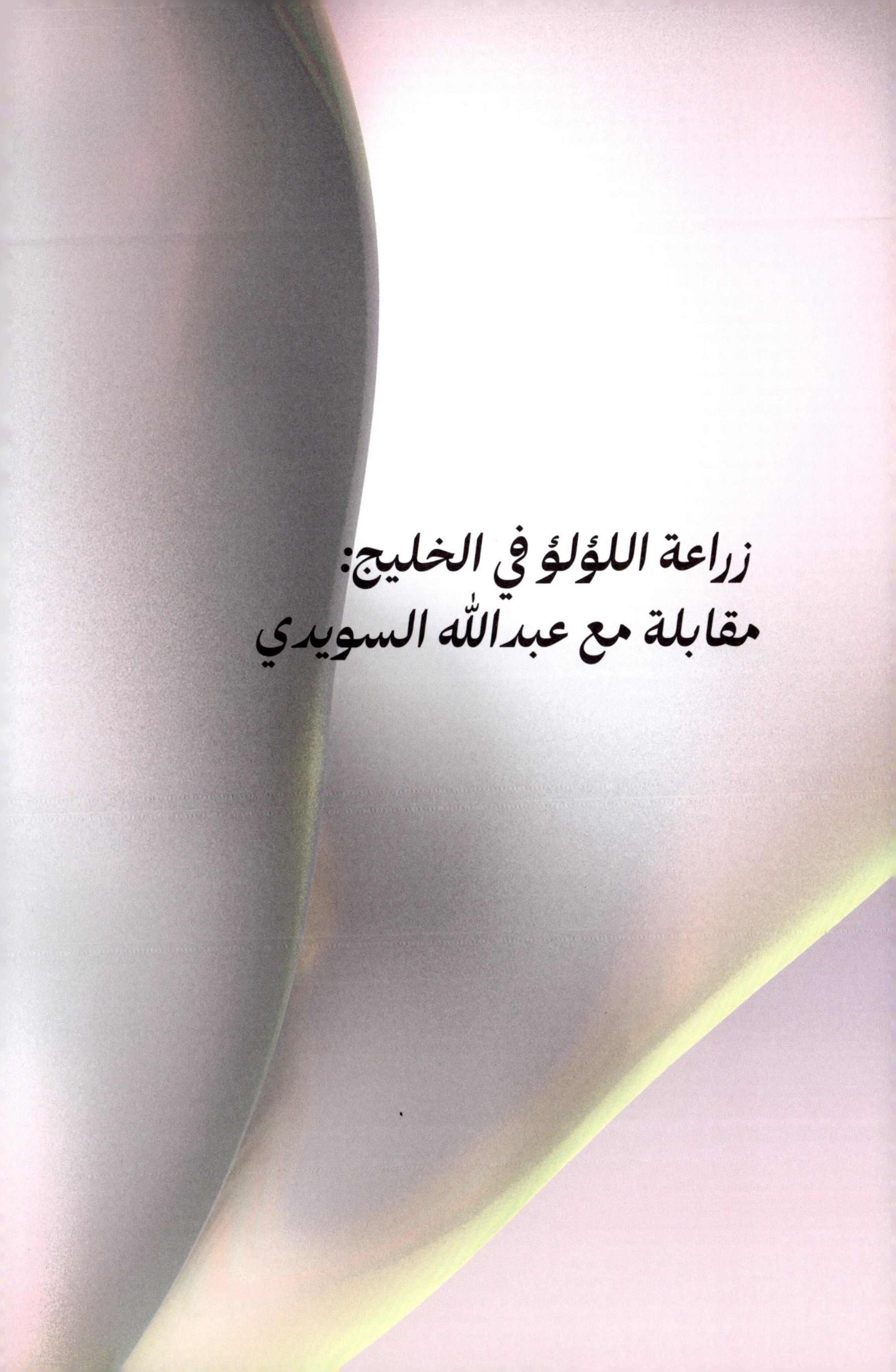

زراعة اللؤلؤ في الخليج:
مقابلة مع عبدالله السويدي

image 56

تالين هزبر

ترتبط أعمال تالين هزبر ارتباطا وثيقاً بالبيئة المحيطة بها وبنيتها المتشابكة والمعقدة. من خلال عملها، يمكن ملاحظة الطابع المؤقت وعدم الديمومة في إنشاء هياكل تسمح للنمو الطبيعي ضمن مجموعة معينة من الثوابت. يأتي الاهتمام بالطبيعة والهياكل سريعة الزوال على قدرتها على العمل والتصرف على المستوى المجهري والكلي في وقت واحد. ترتكز تالين هزبر على إعادة تعريف فكرة القوالب والأنظمة. باستخدام القوالب القابلة للتشكل، يمكننا تحقيق هياكل متماسكة ومتجاوبة لبيئتها.

وتعتزم هزبر استخدام دراستها ومواضيعها البحثية للمساهمة في إعادة تعريف المواد التجريبية. ويتمثل الهدف في عرض المجالات المتداخلة في الجوانب البيئية والتاريخية والاجتماعية لتشكيل روابط أوثق وفهم أفضل للعناصر الملموسة وغير الملموسة التي تساهم وتنشأ في بيئاتنا.

بالنظر إلى الأنظمة والحدود غير المرئية المحيطة، تتشكل سلسلة من التساؤلات: ماذا يعني أن تكون مضيفًا، وماذا يعني أن تكون ضيفًا؟ ما هي الحالة الانتقالية التي يصبح ويتحول فيها المرء من حالة إلى أخرى؟ ما هي علاقتنا بالبيئة التي هي دائمًا في حالة تغير مستمر؟ إلى أي مدى يمكننا أن نستقر ونعتمد على الأسس غير المرئية وغير الملموسة؟

أدت النظم البيئية البحرية دورا مهما في التنمية الاجتماعية، الاقتصادية والثقافية في المجتمع المحلي. كان صيد الأسماك والغوص بحثا عن اللؤلؤ المصدر الرئيسي لكسب الرزق للكثيرين. الاعتماد على صيد اللؤلؤ في الخليج العربي أعاد تشكيل المنطقة وتحويلها قبل الطفرة النفطية حيث ترتبط قصص النضال والفخر والاقتصاد ارتباطًا وثيقًا بالبحر ككل ومغاصات اللؤلؤ على وجه الخصوص. حيث طور الصيادون وغواصو اللؤلؤ أنظمتهم الخاصة في المحيط . و بالرغم من معرفة أن البحر محيط غير مدرك و سريع التقلب، حرصوا على وضع أنظمه والإبحار والغوص بشتى الطرق و الأدوات لفهم المحيط بما يحتويه من تقلبات فنشأ ترابط ملموس بين ثروة شبه الجزيرة العربية و المجتمعات المحلية.

التركيب الجيولوجي لقاع البحر ودرجة الحرارة وعمق المياه ما هي إلا عوامل أساسية تسهم في تحديد مغاصات اللؤلؤ من جهة.. حيث تم تحديد وتسجيل مغاصات اللؤلؤ من حيث جودة لآلئها، وكثافة المحار الذي تم جمعه خلال مواسم الغوص. وتتمثل النقطة المحورية والرئيسية لوجه التشابه بين مغاصات اللؤلؤ الطبيعية ومهنة الغوص: حيث المحار ونمو اللؤلؤ يعتمدان على صحة النظام البيئي البحري ككل. ويعتمد الصيادون والغواصون على الصلات القوية والنظام المترابط بين أفراد الطاقم لنجاح موسم الغوص. في كلتا الحالتين، الاعتماد على النظم وعلى العوامل والافراد حاضرين دائمًا...

العمل التركيبي، هو عمل ينظر إلى الترابط الذي يتكون ضمن النظام العضوي الذي يعتمد على عوامل مختلفة، من خلال وحدات كروية منسوجة معًا لتشكيل هيكل مرن قابل للتغير والتحول. يستكشف الهيكل كيفية تشكله وتفاعله مع المحفزات المختلفة أثناء وجوده في مياه البحر. يؤثر البحر والنظام البيئي على الهيكل المغمور ككل ووحدة البناء على وجه الخصوص. حيث يتشكل الهيكل ثم يستقر داخل بيئته الجديدة ثم يتأقلم في قاع البحر لإعادة تكوين و تسيير الهيكل المنسوج.

إن قيعان البحر غير مرئية وغير ملموسة، على الرغم من كونها في حالة تغير مستمر وتغير دائم، إلا أنها كانت أيضًا في حالة سكون تسمح بالنمو والتجدد. إنها بنية تحتية مرنة، استمرت في الإنتاج والاستجابة بشكل منهجي زمني. الهدف من الهيكل هو دراسة هشاشة وحساسية الوحدة، وآلية التكيف الشاملة للهيكل عبر الزمن. من هيكل منسوج وقابل للتكيف إلى هيكل ثقيل وصلب ومنظم من خلال التراكمات التي سيشهدها على سطحه.

يوفر الهيكل مساحة للتفكير في العلاقات البيئية والاجتماعية. ويرتكز على التحولات التي تؤثر في كونه المضيف والضيف ووجوده ضمن الأنظمة غير مستقرة وغير ثابته. وينظر في تعقيدات الأنظمة والآثار البيئية داخل النظام وتلك التي يشكلها النظام.

فهم الوقت، من خلال وزن المواد المتكونة والمتراكمة، وفهم القيمة من خلال التحولات التي تطرأ على سطحه. تهدف القطعة إلى إعادة تخيل مواقع مغاصات اللؤلؤ السابقة، وكيف تم تعريفها وكيف تطورت. لإثارة التساؤلات حول الحدود غير المرئية ضمن فضاء مرن، وقيمة هذه المواقع في البحر المفتوح في وقتنا الحالي.. يطرح الهيكل تساؤلات وجودية؛ كيف نحدد الأنظمة التي نصنعها وكيف تتعايش أنظمتنا داخل أنظمة أكبر وأشمل؟ عندما تختفي مهنة الغوص، ويبقى القاع وعندما يتقلب ويتحول القاع فما الذي يتبقى؟ وما هي صلة القاع بمهنة الغوص؟

سيتم غمر هذا الهيكل المنسوج في مياه البحر. سيبقى ضيفًا تحت الماء ليتحول الى مضيف حتى إشعار آخر.

لآلئ ترشح

تالين هزبر

تشارلز ستانغ

أستاذ في الفكر المسيحي المبكر ومدير مركز دراسة أديان العالم في كلية هارفارد لعلوم الألوهية. يركز نشاطه البحثي والتدريسي على تاريخ المسيحية في سياق عالم البحر الأبيض المتوسط القديم وبخاصة في التنويعات الشرقية للمسيحية. بصورة أكثر دقة فإن أبحاث ستانج تخاطب تطور الزهد والرهبانية والروحانية في المسيحية، والفلسفة القديمة وخاصة الأفلاطونية المحدثة، والتقاليد السريانية المسيحية وتحديداً انتشار التقليد السرياني الشرقية بطول طريق الحرير، والحركات الفلسفية والدينية الأخرى في حوض البحر المتوسط القديمة بما في ذلك الغنوصية والهرمسية والمانوية وأخيراً الفلسفة القارية الحديثة والعلوم اللاهوتية وخاصة في تقاطعها مع الدراسات الدينية. صدر كتابه الأحدث عن مطبعة جامعة هارفرد في عام ٢٠١٦ تحت عنوان «صنونا الإلهي».

[١] آر. إيه. كارتر، بحر اللآلئ: سبعة آلاف سنة من الصناعة التي شكلت الخليج (لندن، ٢٠١٢). أنظر أيضاً آر. إيه. دونكن، ما وراء الثمن: اللآلئ وصيد اللآلئ، أصول عصر الاكتشافات (فيلادلفيا، ١٩٩٨).

[٢] من أجل الاطلاع على مذكرات تتناول صيد اللؤلؤ، أنظر سيف مرزوق الشملان، الغوص على اللؤلؤ في الخليج العربي.. مذكرات كويتية، ترجمة بي. كلارك (لندن ٢٠٢٠).

[٣] أنظر بريان كولس، حكمة تجار اللؤلؤ: مختارات من الباطنية المسيحية السريانية (كلامازو، إم آي، ٢٠٠٨).

[٤] أنظر جويل واكر، «علامات مضيئة: اللؤلؤ والسلطة الملكية في إيران وأوراسيا في العصور القديمة المتأخرة،» في نيكولا دي كوسمو ومايكل ماس (تحرير) إمبراطوريات أوراسية في العصور المتأخرة القديمة: روما والصين وإيران والسهوب (كامبريدج، ٢٠١٨) ٢٥٣-٢٦٧.

الأخمينيون هي الإمبراطورية الفارسية الأولى والتي تحكمت في قمة تمددها في منطقة تمتد من أوروبا الشرقية وحتى وادي إندوس. أما الإمبراطورية البارثية فقد حكمت منطقة أصغر من تلك التي حكمها الأخمينيون الذين ادعوا أنهم ورثتهم. على ناحية أخرى، فقد صمدت الإمبراطورية الساسانية، والتي تدعى أحياناً بالإمبراطورية الفارسية الجديدة، لفترة هي الأطول بين الإمبراطوريات الثلاثة وكانت الأخيرة في الترتيب قبل وصول الإسلام في منتصف القرن السابع.

[٥] الصغد كانت حضارة إيرانية قديمة واقعة في وسط آسيا. عرف الصغديين كتجار ينقلون البضائع بين فارس في الغرب والصين في الشرق.

[٦] (١٣: ٤٥-٤٦)

[٧] السريانية هي لهجة من الآرامية ظهرت في القرون الأولى بعد الميلاد، ربما في الرها، وأصبحت لغة أدبية وطقوسية أساسية للمسيحيين في الشرق الأوسط بين القرنين الرابع والثامن. في العصور القديمة المتأخرة، تكونت المجتمعات المسيحية المتحدثة بالسريانية من الأناضول وحتى الصين.

[٨] الترانيم الخمسة «عن اللؤلؤة» هم الترانيم من ٨١ حتى ٨٥. أنظر ترجمة جيفري ويكس (واشنطن دي سي: الجامعة الكاثوليكية في أمريكا، ٢٠١٥)، الصفحات ٣٧٧ – ٣٩٢.

[٩] لمختارات عن التقليد الروحي الذي أدى إلى هذا «العصر الذهبي،» أنظر سيباستيان بروك، الآباء السريان: عن الصلاة والحياة الروحية (كلامازو، إم آي: مطبوعات السيسترسية، ١٩٨٧).

[١٠] مطران فولوكولمسك ألفييف، «البحث عن اللؤلؤة الروحانية: مار اسحق السرياني وأعماله،» في مار اسحق السرياني وتراثه الروحي: محاضر من مؤتمر آباء الكنيسة الدولي، موسكو، ٢٠١٣ (يونكرز، نيويورك، مطبعة سان فلاديمير العلمية، ٢٠١٥)، ١٣.

[١١] الجزء الثاني، موعظة؛ ٣٤:٤، مقتبس في المرجع السابق.

[١٢] مقتبس في كولس، حكمة تجار اللؤلؤ، ١.

[١٣] موعظة ٤٨ من «المواعظ التقشفية لمار اسحق السرياني، مترجمة على يد دير التجلي المقدس (بوسطن: دير التجلي المقدس، ١٩٨٤).

[١٤] مقتبس في كولس، حكمة تجار اللؤلؤ، ١.

[١٥] المرجع السابق.

[١٦] أنظر ماريو قزاح، عبد الرحي أبو حسين، سيف شاهين الموريخي، هيا آل ثاني (تحرير)، مختارات من الكتاب السريان من قطر القرن السابع (بيسكاتاواي، نيوجيرسي: مطبعة جورجياس، ٢٠١٥)؛ ومجموعة الدراسات المصاحبة، الكتاب السريان في قطر في القرن السابع (بيسكاتاواي، نيوجيرسي: مطبعة جورجياس، ٢٠١٤).

image 57

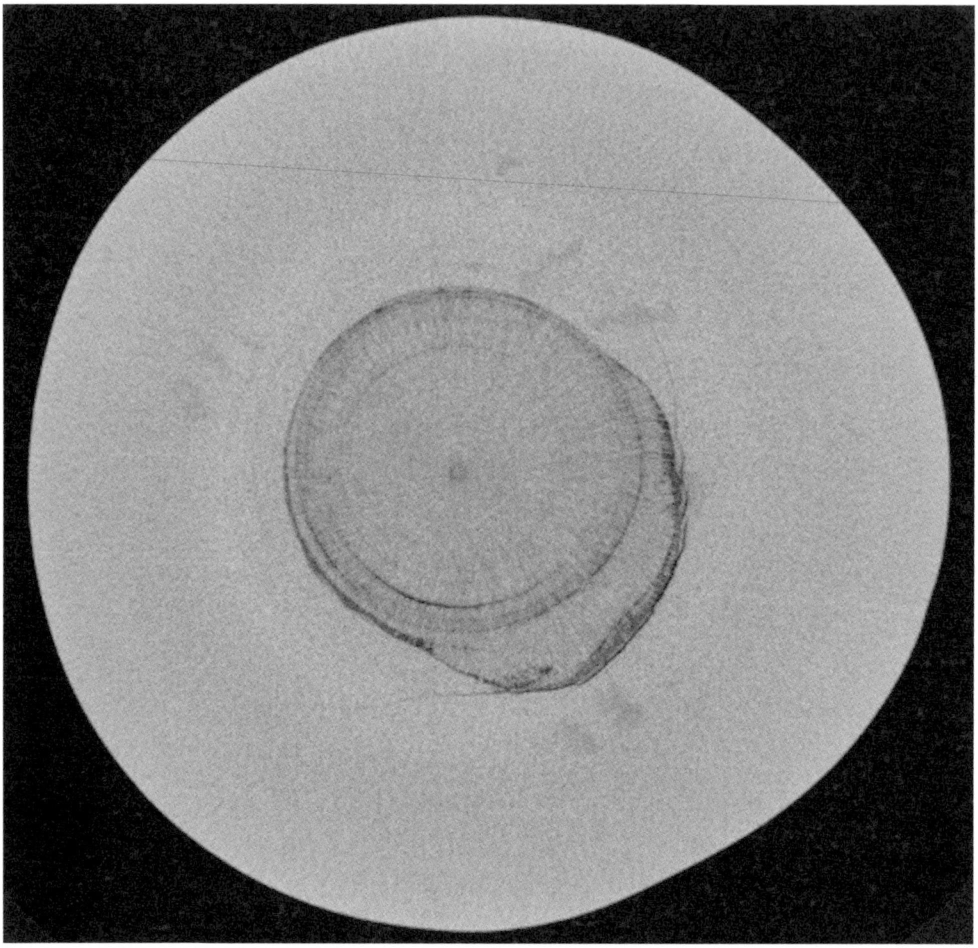

image 20

يسوع المسيح.»[13] اللؤلؤة مازالت تعرف باعتبارها يسوع المسيح، لكن الصحراء استبدلت بالراهب نفسه، أو ربما ما هو أفضل، فالراهب نفسه يتم الكشف عنه باعتباره صحراء حقيقية، مكان أجرد حقاً، والذي في تجرده من أي شيء تكمن لؤلؤة خفية في مكان ما. لغز المسيح المجسد لن يمكن إيجاده في مكان غريب أو مهجور، بل بالداخل. يقترح إسحاق أن الاتحاد الروحي يمكن إيجاده عبر الالتفات للداخل لنجد أن المسيح يعيش بالفعل بالداخل بانتظار من يجده، كما تنتظر اللؤلؤة أن يجدها الغواص.

اسحق ليس وحيداً: باطنيين أخر من ذات العصر يتحدثون عن صيد اللؤلؤ باعتباره مجازاً عن الحياة الروحية. كتب يوحنا المبجل في القرن الثامن: «هذه اللآلئ الثمينة تجمع وتحفظ بين كنوز عقله على يد التاجر المنشغل بالصلاة، والغواص العنيد أسير الرغبة للبحر الذي يغسله.»[13] يتحدث معاصره يوسف الرائي عن جهود الراهب المتوحد باعتبارها «عمل التاجر المستمر حتى يحل وقت وقوع اللؤلؤة ذات القيمة العظيمة في يديه.»[15] على الرغم من انجذاب اسحق لصيادي اللؤلؤ فإن هذين الكاتبين، ربما بوحي من مثل المسيح، عادا إلى تاجر اللآلئ الخليجي ليفهما عباداتهم وتقواهم، زهدهم وروحانيتهم.

لقد قدمت زوجاً من العيون يمكن باستخدامها أن نتأمل في « اللؤلؤة العظيمة القيمة» ومعانيها المختلفة في العصور المديمة. في عيون الملوك الفرس، التي كانت اللآلئ بالنسبة لهم رمزاً للقوة الإمبراطورية والثروة والتأثير، يختفي الغواصون أنفسهم فيما يتبادل الملوك والأمراء غنيمتهم الثمينة. في عيون المسيحيين القدماء، التي كانت اللآلئ بالنسبة لهم رموزاً لأسرار الإيمان وتحديداً سر تجسد المسيح، يعاود صياد اللؤلؤ الظهور لكنه يفهم الآن كقالب للراهب والمتصوف. في أي من الحالتين لا نفهم بشكل أفضل للأسف من كانوا أولئك الغواصين وكيف فهموا هم مهنتهم الشاقة وكنوزها. لأداء هذه المهمة، علينا أن نتجه من العصور القديمة وإلى الحداثة، ونستمع ليس فقط للكلمات التي حفظها النخب المتعلمة ولكن لكلمات وإيقاعات أغنيات الصيادين أنفسهم.

***

في الختام، أود أن أثير سؤالاً يتعلق بمكان أولئك المسيحيين القدماء في تاريخ الخليج (أو بيت قطراية، كما يدعونه)، بما في ذلك تراثها المميز في صيد اللؤلؤ. لعقود قام علماء الآثار بعمل هام في الكشف عن البقايا المادية لهذه المجتمعات. كذلك استمر المؤرخون في جمع الأدلة والشهادات الوثائقية الخاصة بمسيحيي الخليج كاسين العظام لحماً إن جاز التعبير. على ناحية أخرى يعمل علماء النصوص على جمع وتحرير وترجمة مدونة بيت قطراية من الأدب الرهباني والروحاني.[16] يتيح بحثهم هذا القصة لجمهور أوسع بما في ذلك مواطني الخليج المعاصر والمقيمين فيه.

لماذا قد يكون ذلك الأمر مهماً؟ أولاً وقبل أي شيء، لأن هذا التاريخ يجب أن يحتضن باعتباره جزءاً من تراث الخليج الخاص وكشهادة على ماضيه التاريخي التعددي وكمصدر للتفكير في التعددية في الحاضر والمستقبل. كان الخليج في أوقات وطناً للديانات الإبراهيمية الثلاثة. من بين الديانات الثلاثة، يتباهى التاريخ المسيحي في الخليج بواحد من أعظم علماء العقيدة المترهبنين المتصوفة في الألفية الأولى، اسحق النينوي. ما الذي سيعنيه الأمر للخليج لو اعترف باسحق وتراثه الأوسع باعتباره له؟ ما الذي سيعنيه الأمر بالنسبة للخليج بالاعتراف بهذه المدونة المسيحية بكاملها والمجتمعات التي انتجتها باعتبارها تخصه؟ كما يعترف اليونانيون، الذين يدينون بالمسيحية الآن، بهوميروس وأفلاطون كجزء من تراثهم، وكما يعترف المصريين، الذين يدينون بالإسلام، بالفراعنة وحضارتهم كجزء من تراثهم؛ لما لا يعترف الخليج كذلك باسحق وتقاليده المسيحية كجزء من تراثه؟ أن يتم الاعتراف بهذا التاريخ قد يعني أن نرى أولئك الرهبان والباطنيين في الخليج كجزء من تاريخ أوسع للتنوع والتعددية في المنطقة. تاريخ غير مفاجئ في الحقيقة بالنظر إلى أن الخليج من بين أشياء أخرى، هو سلسلة من الموانئ حيث لم يتم تبادل المنتجات فقط بل الأفكار كذلك وبهذا فهو مكان لا يمارس فيه الرهبان فقط التبشير بل التجار أيضاً.

وأخيراً، إن كنا بصدد تحديد وضع هذا التقليد المسيحي الباطني في الخليج بإنصاف، ماذا سنرى أو نفهم بشأنه كنا مما كنا قد فشلنا من قبل في رؤيته أو فهمه؟ في حالة اسحق، فالاعتراف به كابن للخليج سيشجعنا لنقرأ لاهوته الباطني عبر طورة صائد اللؤلؤ. ولكن ماذا لو قرأنا اسحق وكتاب مسيحيين آخرين من الخليج بعين على السياق التضاريسي الأوسع الذي نشأوا فيه، بالبحث عن لغة الرياح والبحار، والواحات والصحاري، والموانئ والتجارة؟ بعبارة أخرى، هل أخطأ القراء الغربيون لاسحق في فهم جوانب مهمة من كتاباته لأننا انتزعناه من سياقه الثقافي؟ ما الذي قد يعني أن نرى اسحق والتقليد الباطني السرياني الذي يعتبر اسحق أشهر ممثليه عبر الأعين المميزة للتجربة الخليجية؟ ما الذي يعنيه أن نراه عبر أعين اللؤلؤ؟

وبلاد الرافدين وفارس.[٧] يخبرنا التقليد أن الرهبانية أتت إلى الخليج من مصر، ويدعى الرجل الذي يقال أنه أحضرها شرقاً من مصر مار أوكين (توفي ٣٦٣ م.) تقول القصة أنه كان هناك صياد لؤلؤ في القرن الرابع يعيش على جزيرة في السويس، يغوص لاصطياد اللؤلؤ ويوزع عوائد غوصه على الفقراء. سافر الصياد إلى الصحراء الغربية وهناك التقى واحد من مؤسسي الرهبانية المصرية المشهورين، راهب يدعى الأنبا باخوم (٢٩٢ - ٣٤٨ م.). كلفه الأنبا باخوم بأن يأخذ معه سبعين من رهبانه ويذهب ليؤسس مجتمعاً في شمال بلاد الرافدين. بغض النظر عن صحة القصة أو عدمها، نعرف أن الأديرة من عينة الدير الذي أسسه مار أوكين انتشرت في بلاد الرافدين، نزولاً مع دجلة والفرات وصولاً إلى الخليج حيث أقيموا بمحاذاة الساحل الشرقي. من البداية الأولى إذن يرتبط تاريخ الرهبانية في الخليج بصيد اللؤلؤ. سيزداد هذا الرابط قوة حينما يألف مسيحيو الخليج الصنعة أكثر، وسيتجه بعض الكتاب إلى صيد اللؤلؤ كمجاز عن جهودهم الروحانية الخاصة.

أحد الخصائص المميزة للمسيحية السريانية هي تقليدها الخاص بصياغة العلوم اللاهوتية في صورة شعرية. في نفس الوقت الذي كان فيه مار أوكين، صياد اللؤلؤ السابق، يقدم الرهبانية للمشرق كان إفرام السرياني، الشاعر اللاهوتي المحتفى به، يكتب سلسلة من خمس ترانيم تتناول رمزية اللؤلؤ.[٨] يقول إفرام أنه في الوقت الذي تكفي فيه الأحجار الكريمة لتمثيل الملائكة، فقط اللآلئ تستحق أن ترمز للمسيح ذاته. في هذا السياق فإن ثقب اللؤلؤة بمخرز لتسلك في عقد أو قرط يصبح بالنسبة له رمزاً للصلب. على الرغم من أن إفرام لم ير أبداً صيادي اللؤلؤ أثناء عملهم لكنه تخيل نفسه غواصاً. عند نقطةٍ ما، يمسك إفرام بلؤلؤة ويسائلها عن خفاياها، تتحدث إليه وتقول أنه مثل دهشة الغواص الذي حصل عليها، وهي ابنة البحر، من أعماق البحر غير المتناهية ومثل المسيحي الذي يجب عليه ألا يتجرأ على محاولة معرفة طبيعة الرب الذي تمتد أعماقه أبعد من أي قدرة على الفهم. في هذه الحالة، تصبح اللؤلؤة شاهدة على جوهر الرب غير القابل للمعرفة وعمقه غير المتناهي.

اشتهرت المسيحية السريانية بتراثها الباطني الغني. فهم الباطنيين أنفسهم باعتبارهم صيادي وتجار اللؤلؤ، موظفين الحرفة العتيقة كمجاز قوي لبحثهم في هذا العالم عن الطهارة والاستنارة والاتحاد بالإله. استمر ما يسمى بالعصر الذهبي للباطنية المسيحية السريانية من القرن السادس وحتى القرن التاسع الميلادي [٩] وبلغ ذروته في القرن السابع مع اسحق النينوي. لم يولد اسحق في نينوى ولم يربى بها، بل ولد في بيت قطراية (قطر في العصر الحالي)، لكن هناك تقليد قديم في المسيحية يقضي بنسبة الأساقفة إلى أبرشياتهم، وفي حالتنا هذه؛ رسم اسحق اسقفاً لنينوى (الموصل في العصر الحالي) في عام ٦٧٦ م. وهو السبب وراء تسميته باسحق النينوي. كان اسحق راهباً ومعلماً ببيت قطراية لأعوام عديدة، لكنه لم يكن سعيداً بالمنصب. بعد خمسة أشهر فقط، تخلى اسحق عن أبرشياته وتقاعد في جبال خوزستان المطلة على الساحل الشمالي للخليج حيث عاش حياة هادئة.

نعرف أقل القليل عن حياة اسحق، لكننا نعلم أنه ولد وتربى في الخليج في مكان يرى البحر، وكما لاحظ أحد الباحثين فإن كتابات اسحق مليئة بالإحالات إلى البحر: «إنه يتكلم عن السفن، القباطنة والبحارة، عن عواصف البحر والرياح، عن الغواصين والمحار المجموع من أعماق البحر.»[١٠] كان اسحق ابنا لشاطئ البحر، ونتيجة لذلك فقد أصبحت تجارة اللؤلؤ وصيده مجازات شجية لمسعاه الرهباني نحو القداسة. كتب اسحق، «لو وجد الغواص داخل كل محارة لؤلؤة، لأصبح أي رجل غنياً سريعاً. وإذا وجد الغواص اللؤلؤة على الفور ولم تغالبه الأمواج ولم يقابل القروش، لم يكن ليضطر لحبس نفسه لحد الاختناق، ولم يكن ليحرم من الهواء الطلق المتاح لكل الناس ولم يكن ليهبط إلى قاع البحر، إذن لفاضت اللآلئ بأكثر من مرات سطوع البرق.»[١١] لكن الغواص لا يجد لؤلؤة في كل محارة بالطبع. عليه أن يبحث وأن يجلو من أجل لؤلؤة واحدة بين عدة محارات. سيتعين عليه أن ينأى بنفسه عن صحبته وأن يعاني فيما يدرب نفسه وجسده. بذلك يصبح صياد اللؤلؤ رمزاً للراهب والصوفي، ويصبح البحر وأخطاره رمزاً للعالم وعوالقه التي قد تطيح بسعيه. بعبارة أخرى، يرى اسحق معاناة صياد اللؤلؤ كمعادل لمعاناته لتحقيق الطهارة والتنور والاتحاد.

في موضع آخر، يجعل اسحق تشبيه الغواص والراهب أكثر وضوحاً، «يغوص الغواص عارياً في البحر ليجد لؤلؤة؛ والراهب الحكيم يمر عارياً على منازل الصحراء ليجد اللؤلؤة، يسوع المسيح ذاته.» [١٢]

في تنويع على ذات المقولة يقول اسحق أن «السباح يغوص عارياً في البحر حتى يجد لؤلؤة، والراهب الحكيم، مجرداً من كل شيء، يرتحل عبر الحياة حتى يجد داخله اللؤلؤة،

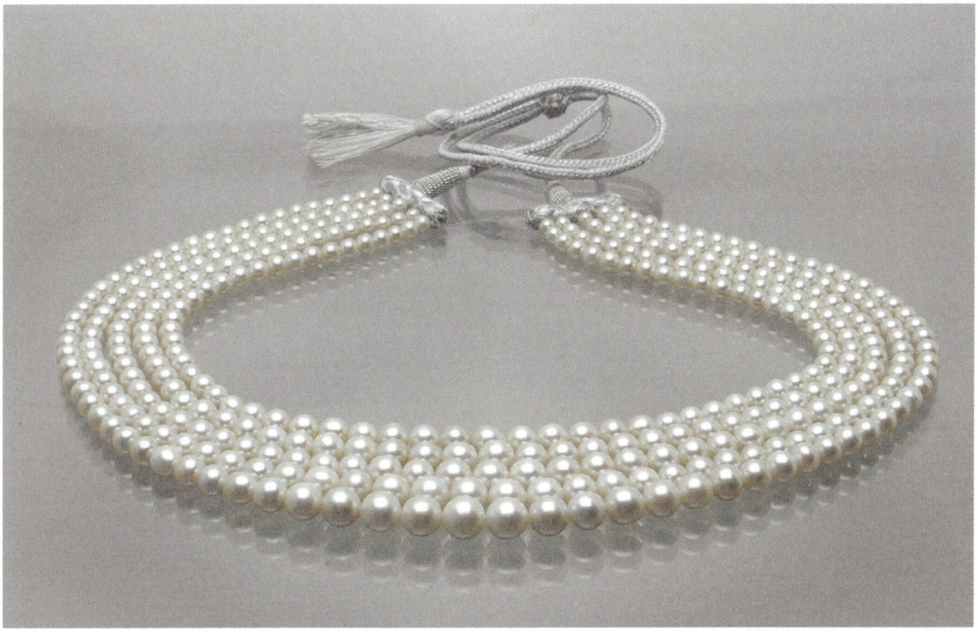

image 58

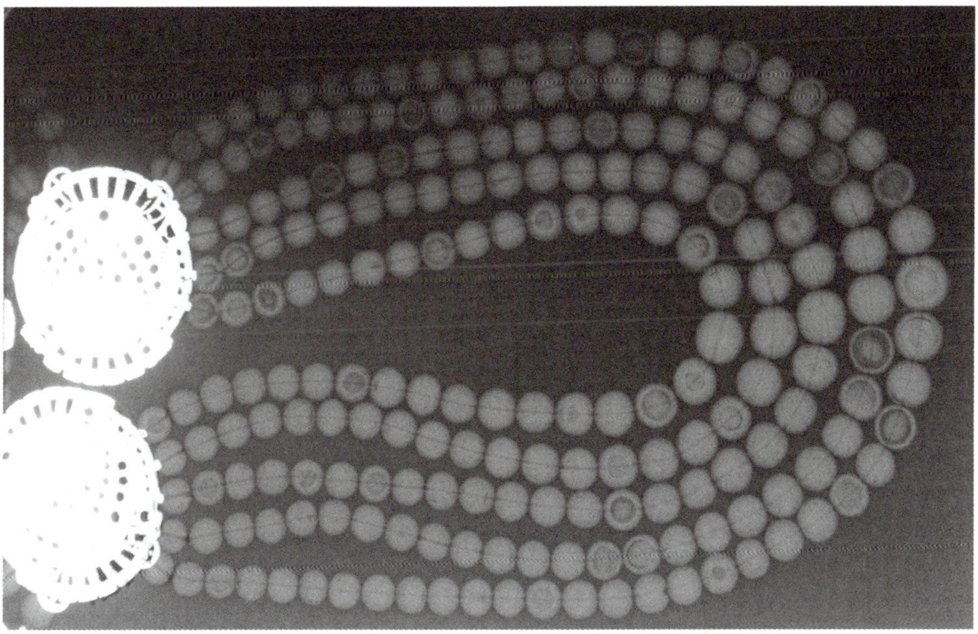

image 59

image 60

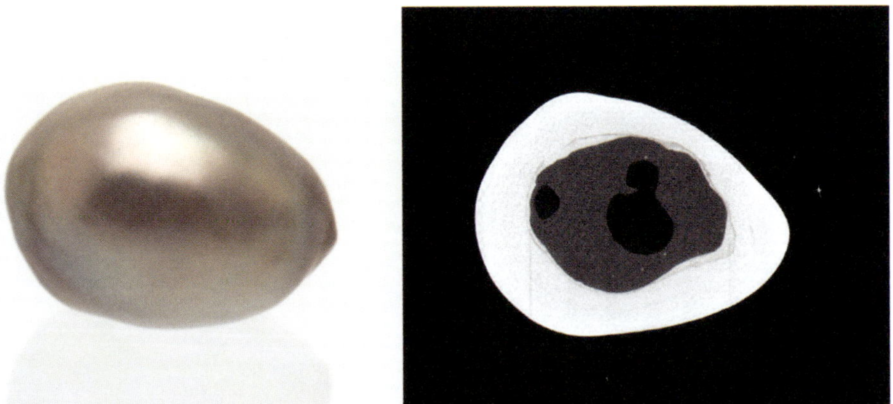

image 61

أي شيء بشأن اللؤلؤ يأسر الخيال البشري؟ أهي فكرة أن كرة كاملة الاستدارة تنبت من قلب صدفة شائهة ومهلهلة لحيوان رخوي؟ أن شيئاً بهذا الجمال يأتي مما يبدو وكأنه قمامة عديمة الشكل؟ أم أنه يدين بجماله إلى شائبة، حبة رمل يرسي فوقها المحار سطح أبيض بلون اللبن؟ أعيننا منجذبة إلى هذا السطح، المنير والعتم في آن بطريقةٍ ما؛ يبرق بالنور لكنه ضبابي بالنسبة إلى أبصارنا. جزءٌ منه رملي وجزءٌ آخر بحري، أرضي ومائي في الوقت نفسه؛ حادثة من الطبيعة، لكنها حادثة تبدو وكأنها تتقن الطبيعة؛ كتناقض، كمفارقة، وكلغز.

يغوص الناس في سبيل اللؤلؤ منذ العصر الحجري الحديث.[١] كان الخليج العربي وساحل جنوب الهند موقعا الغوص الأبرز في العالم القديم حتى القرن السادس عشر حينما أغرقت لآلئ العالم الجديد السوق العالمي. بعد اختراع زراعة اللؤلؤ في اليابان في أواخر القرن التاسع عشر، بدأت الممارسة التقليدية لصيد اللؤلؤ في الاتجاه إلى الأفول.

صيد اللؤلؤ عمل صعب وشاق وفي العصور القديمة عادة ما وقع عبء هذا العمل على العبيد وعمال السخرة. للأسف، فقدت أصواتهم عبر الأجيال ومعها الموسيقى التي لعبوها والأغاني التي غنوها.[٢] في العالم القديم، نعرف اللآلئ، وأحياناً صيادوها، من أناس بعيدين عن العمل الشاق الخاص بحصادها: أولاً، من سجلات النبلاء والملوك الذين تزينوا بها، وثانياً، من الكتاب المسيحيين القدامى الذين أضحت اللآلئ وغواصوها مجازاً مهماً بالنسبة لهم للعقيدة والروحانية.[٣]

في العالم القديم، لم يقدر أحد اللآلئ أكثر مما فعل الفرس: كانت السلعة المفضلة بين ملوكهم عبر الأسر المختلفة بما في ذلك عهود الأخمينيين (٥٥٠ - ٣٣٠ ق.م.) والبارثيين (٢٤٧ ق.م - ٢٢٤ م.) والساسانيين (٢٢٤ - ٦٢٤ م.).[٤] قبل أن يموت الملك الساساني بيروز (حكم من ٤٥٩ إلى ٤٨٤ م.) في المعركة ضد الهياطلة، يقال أنه وضع جانباً قرطه اللؤلؤي الضخم الشهير حتى لا يحوزه أحد الهون كغنيمة. بعدما علم الرومان بهزيمته عرضوا على الهون مبالغ طائلة لأجل القرط: يقول البعض أن الهون لم يجدوه أبداً ويقول اخرون أنهم باعوه لابن بيروز عوضاً عن الرومان. كان الرومان تواقون للحصول على القرط لأن بحلول القرن الرابع الميلادي كان اللؤلؤ مرادفاً لثروة ملك الفرس التي كانت مضرباً للأمثال. كان القرط ليكون جائزة للإمبراطور الروماني ليتباهى بهذا الرمز للسلطة الفارسية حيث لم يرتدي الملك الفارسي اللآلئ بنفسه فقط بل أهدى المجوهرات والأحزمة المزينة باللؤلؤ للنبلاء والنبيلات في بلاطه كعلامة على الحظوة والرفعة لقاء ولائهم للتاج.

تسربت الأناقة الفارسية إلى الجيران، حيث لم يقتصر الأمر على الرومان فقط بل امتد إلى العرب والأرمن والصغديين[٥] من بين آخرين غمرتهم الصيحة الجديدة وارتباطاتها بالثراء والقوة الأسطوريين. كانت تجارة اللؤلؤ الدولية، والتي كانت قد بدأت بالفعل بحلول القرن الأول قبل الميلاد، منتشرة ومهيمن عليها باضطراد من قبل الساسانيين بين القرنين الثالث والسابع الميلادي. يعزى الفضل إلى أحد الملوك الساسانيين، أردشير (حكم بين سنة ٢٢٤ و٢٤٠ م.)، في إنشاء عدد من المدن على الخليج الفارسي لترويج التجارة البحرية وخاصة في اللؤلؤ. في تلك القرون ذاتها، أصبح الخليج وطناً لعدد من المجتمعات المسيحية والتي مثل لها اللؤلؤ ونشاط صيده معنى خاص.

في إنجيل متى، يقدم المسيح مثلاً من أمثلة عديدة حول مملكة السماء قائلاً: «أَيْضًا يُشْبِهُ مَلَكُوتُ السَّمَاوَاتِ إِنْسَانًا تَاجِرًا يَطْلُبُ لآلِئَ حَسَنَةً، فَلَمَّا وَجَدَ لُؤْلُؤَةً وَاحِدَةً كَثِيرَةَ الثَّمَنِ، مَضَى وَبَاعَ كُلَّ مَا كَانَ لَهُ وَاشْتَرَاهَا.»[٦] كما في أغلب أمثلة المسيح، لا يبدو المعنى واضحاً على الفور. السؤال الذي يعتلج داخل أغلب القراء هو التالي: ما هي هذه اللؤلؤة الواحدة كثيرة الثمن؟ أياً تكن، المطلب واضح: لتدخل مملكة السماء عليك أن تكون كالتاجر الذي يبيع كل ما يملك في سبيل الحصول على هذه اللؤلؤة الواحدة. حينما وصل المسيحيون إلى الخليج في القرن الرابع، واجهت تأملاتهم حول خفايا اللؤلؤ الواقع القاسي لأولئك الذين يغوصون للحصول عليه والمتاجرون فيه. دبت الحياة في أوصال مثال المسيح بطرق جديدة حيث أوَّل أولئك المسيحيين غواصي اللؤلؤ في ضوء تقليدهم الديني الخاص وفي المقابل أعادوا تأويل تقليدهم الديني على ضوء ذلك العالم الجديد.

لدينا أدلة على وجود المسيحيين في الخليج تبدأ من القرن الرابع وتنتهي إلى القرن التاسع. المسيحيون المهاجرون إلى الخليج لم يكونوا من المسيحيين المتحدثين باليونانية من الغرب وإنما المسيحيين المتحدثين بالسريانية من سوريا

لؤلؤة القيمة العظمى

تشارلز إم. ستانج

أوليفييه: كيف تميزون اللآلئ الطبيعية من تلك المزروعة؟

طلال: *٪ من اللآلئ التي نراها لا تحتاج إلى اختبار. لكن عندما يتعلق الأمر بمنتج نهائي، مثل القلادة على سبيل المثال، فأنت بحاجة إلى التحقق من طبيعة اللؤلؤ لصالح المستهلك ولصالح نفسك كبائع، لتكون في الجانب الآمن - من خلال استلام وثيقة تفيد بأن اللآلئ طبيعية. يضمن هذا أن العميل لن يعود إليك في المستقبل بمزاعم حول طبيعة اللآلئ. فيما يخص نسبة ٢٠٪ المتبقية من اللآلئ، فأنت تحتاج إلى آلات متطورة لتمييزها عن بعضها.*

أوليفييه:هل ترتدي اللؤلؤ؟

طلال: *لا ، أنا لا أرتدي أي شيء - لا ساعة ، لا خواتم ، لا شيء. أنا خال تمامًا (يضحك).*

أوليفييه: ذكرت أنك تعلم هذه الموسيقى لأطفالك. كيف تتأكد من أن هذا الإرث ينتقل من جيل إلى آخر؟

طلال: *بالنسبة لجيل أطفالنا، من الصعب عليهم تعلمها أكثر مما كان عليه الحال بالنسبة لجيلنا، لأن لديهم اليوم مشتتات للإنتباه لم تكن لدينا في الماضي. عليك أن تقنع الأجيال الجديدة بطريقة أخرى. تعلمهم العزف على الطبول أولًا كي يتمكنوا من اكتشاف العالم والعمل في صيد اللؤلؤ يعتبر وسيلة جيدة لذلك. لا يمكنك إجبار الأطفال على فعل شيء - يجب أن ينبع من داخله.*

طلال مطر

أستاذ الفكر المسيحي المبكر ومدير مركز دراسة أديان العالم في مدرسة اللاهوت بجامعة هارفارد. يركز بحثه وتدريسه على تاريخ المسيحية في سياق عالم البحر الأبيض المتوسط القديم ، وخاصة الأنواع الشرقية للمسيحية. وبشكل أكثر تحديدًا ، تتناول أبحاثه: تطور الزهد والرهبنة والتصوف في المسيحية. الفلسفة القديمة ، وخاصة الأفلاطونية الحديثة ؛ التقليد السرياني المسيحي ، ولا سيما انتشار التقاليد السورية الشرقية على طول طريق الحرير ؛ الحركات الفلسفية والدينية الأخرى في البحر الأبيض المتوسط القديم ، بما في ذلك الغنوصية ، الهرمسية ، والمانوية ؛ والفلسفة واللاهوت القاريان الحديثان ، خاصة أنهما يتقاطعان مع دراسة الدين. أحدث كتبه هو Our Divine Double (مطبعة جامعة هارفارد ، ٢٠١٦).

أوليفييه: هل سبق أن أردت أن تحتفظ لنفسك بأي من الآلئ؟

طلال: *احتفظت دائمًا ببعضها لنفسي. أرى بصورة متكررة لآلئ أشعر أنني لم أر مثلها في حياتي من قبل، حتى الصغيرة منها. في بعض الأحيان يكون لها شكلًا أو لونًا فريدًا، وإذا بعتها فلن تكون سعيدًا بالثمن الذي تحصل عليه، لذا من الأفضل أن تحتفظ بها لنفسك (يضحك).*

أوليفييه: بالعودة إلى اللآلئ المزروعة، ما رأيك فيها؟

طلال: *لا أرى اللؤلؤ المزروع لؤلؤًا. إذا كنت تستطيع قيادة رولز رويس، فهل ستقود سيارة فورد؟ أنك حتى لن تنظر إليها. اللآلئ المزروعة لا تستهويني إطلاقًا وحتى خلال المؤتمرات أو عروض الأحجار الكريمة لا تجذبني. لدي الشيء الثمين، فلماذا أزعج نفسي بشيء مصنوع؟ في السابق، كانت اللآلئ المزروعة هي منافسنا ولكن حاليًا بسبب الصين وفيتنام والفلبين وقيامهم بالزراعة الجماعية، انخفضت قيمة اللؤلؤ المستزرع إلى ما يقرب من الصفر. كان سعر اللآلئ المزروعة التي اخترعها ميكيموتو ٢٠٠ دولار، والآن أصبح سعرها دولارين. لم تعد منافسًا للآلئ الطبيعية حاليًا.*

أوليفييه: كيف تعاملت مع وصول اللؤلؤ المزروع إلى السوق؟

طلال: *أحب أجدادي اللؤلؤ، وقادوا ومعهم كثير من التجار الآخرين الإجراءات لرفع قضية ضد ميكيموتو في محكمة نيويورك. حكمت المحكمة لصالح ميكيموتو، ولكن على الرغم من ذلك، استمر الغوص بحثًا عن اللؤلؤ في البحرين حتى أواخر الخمسينيات من القرن الماضي، حتى عندما وصل اللؤلؤ المزروع إلى السوق في بداية عام ١٩١٦. ببساطة لم يعره الناس اهتمامًا. جاء التأثير الرئيس على الصناعة من جراء اكتشاف النفط. اعتاد معظم الغواصين على العمل لمدة أربعة أشهر متتالية على قوارب صيد اللؤلؤ، لكن مع النفط أصبح بإمكانهم العمل خلال النهار والعودة إلى أسرهم في المساء. في هذه المرحلة، لم يعد أحد يغوص بحثًا عن اللؤلؤ - باستثناء بعض الأشخاص الذين كانوا يمارسون الغوص كهواية حتى التسعينيات/أوائل الألفية. لكن في الآونة الأخيرة، توسع أسطول الغواصين -رجالًا ونساءً- ووصل عددهم إلى ٢٠٠٠ شخص، وهو رقم كبير!*

أوليفييه: هل تعتقد أن استمرار وفاء البحرين للؤلؤ الطبيعي يمنحك ميزة اليوم؟

طلال: *بالطبع. كما تعلم، يوجد قانون في البحرين يحظر على أي شخص التعامل مع اللؤلؤ المزروع على التراب الوطني. يمكن أن تُسجن أكثر من ١٠ سنوات إذا قبضوا عليك وبحوزتك كميات كبيرة منه. يساعد ذلك كثيرًا، ونحن الدولة الوحيدة في العالم التي لديها مثل هذا الإطار القانوني. إذا قمت باستيراد اللؤلؤ، فيجب أن يتم اختباره واعتماده قبل دخوله فعليًا للبلاد. وإذا تبين أنه مزروع، فسيمنع من دخول البحرين.*

أوليفييه: في رأيك ما الذي يحمله المستقبل لصيد اللؤلؤ ولموسيقاه في العموم؟

طلال: *أعتقد أن هناك طفرة قادمة، حيث أصبحت المنافسة اليوم ضعيفة مقارنة بعدة أعوام مضت. يفقد الماس قيمته في الوقت الحاضر بسبب تلك الاصطناعية وبسبب عمليات الترسيب الكيميائي للبخار (CVDs)، لذلك أعتقد أن المستقبل سيكون مشرقًا للؤلؤ الطبيعي. قبل ١٠٠ عام، أثر اختراع اللؤلؤ المزروع تأثيرًا مدمر على سوق اللؤلؤ. حاليًا الماس الاصطناعي يؤثر على صناعة الماس بنفس الطريقة. وفيما يتعلق بالموسيقى، أرى جيلًا شابًا يهتم اهتمامًا كبيرًا بهذا التقليد وأنا متفائل جدًا بما يخبئه المستقبل، خاصة وأن لدينا الآن من بينهم بعض الموسيقيين المتعلمين الذين يمكنهم قراءة وتدوين الموسيقى. وسيساعدنا هذا في المستقبل على نقل هذه الموسيقى ويسهل تعليمها.*

أوليفييه: أنت تحاول جمع أرشيف لهذه الموسيقى. هل يمكن أن تحدثنا أكثر عن ذلك؟

طلال: *نحن لا نقرأ الموسيقى لذا من الممتع تدوينها. للقيام بذلك، يجب أن تكون سعيد الحظ كذلك لأن لديك ٢٠ شخصًا يعزفون بدون نوتة موسيقية ولا يمكنك التحكم فيها جميعًا. أحيانًا يكون البعض سعيد جدًا ويعزف بصوت أعلى قليلاً، والبعض الآخر يسعل أحيانًا أو يعزف في باستخدام درجات موسيقية أعلى، وقد يكون المغني في مزاج سيء ... يوجد الكثير من العناصر المختلفة التي يجب أخذها في الاعتبار عند التسجيل وهذا هو سبب قيامنا دائمًا بتسجيل ما نقوم بعزفه على شريط. لدي أكثر من ٥٠٠ تسجيل لهذه الموسيقى التي عزفتها من بينها خمس أو ست قطع موسيقية فقط حققت نجاحًا حقيقيًا. البقية كان بها شيء ما غير منضبط.*

أوليفييه: كيف تتم عملية شراء اللؤلؤ من الغواص؟

طلال: *بادئ ذي بدء، عندما يأتي إلى غواص، يجب أن أشتري كل ما لديه. لا يمكن التدقيق في اختياري. إذا لم أخذ سوى الكبار وأفضل ماعنده، فماذا سيفعل بالباقي؟ الغالبية العظمى من اللآلئ التي يحصلون عليها هي لآلئ صغيرة، مما يعني أنها بلا قيمة. عليك أن تقيم كل شيء. وبالطبع ، العامل الرئيس الذي سيزيد السعر هو وجود لآلئ أكبر أو عدم وجودها. قد تشتري خمسة أو ستة جرامات من اللآلئ مقابل لؤلؤة واحدة. إنها أول ما تبحث عنه. وكما نقول هنا: الكل يبحث عن مكسبه، وهذا صحيح بخاصة عندما يتعلق الأمر باللؤلؤ - لأنك إذا لم تشتر عندما يقدم اللؤلؤ إليك، فأنت لا تعرف متى تحصل على فرصة أخرى للشراء. إن عشوائية الطبيعة هي التي تملي التصرف على النقيض من الماس. أيًا كان ما يخرج من البحر فأنت مضطر للتعامل معه.*

أوليفييه: ألا توجد طرق تسعير أو مصادر مرجعية لتلك المبادلات؟

طلال: *لا، ولكن يوجد خمسة عوامل رئيسة يجب الانتباه إليها عندما يتعلق الأمر باللآلئ: الحجم والوزن والشكل واللون واللمعان. يوجد كذلك جزء نفسي بالطبع. فأنا أفضل اللآلئ ذات اللون القشدي، ولكن قد يكون للآخرين أذواق أخرى، ولهذا السبب من المستحيل أن يكون لديك معايير حيث لا توجد لؤلؤتان متشابهتان في العالم، حتى لو أتوا من نفس المحار.*

في السابق لم يكن هناك سوى مكان واحد مفتوح في الليل: الدار. كان هذا هو الترفيه الوحيد في ذلك الوقت.

أوليفييه: لماذا تعزف هذه الموسيقى؟

طلال: *لأننا نحبها! في وقتنا الحاضر، من النادر جدًا رؤية الأشخاص الذين يلعبونها جيدًا. والسبب الآخر هو أننا يجب أن نواصل في المران حتى نحصل على نتيجة معقولة، لأنه عمل مشترك. وفي الواقع، تحتاج المجموعة كلها إلى الغناء بنفس المستوى، والتوقف في نفس الوقت، والعزف بنفس الإيقاع. علاوة على ذلك، نحن لا نقرأ ولا نكتب الموسيقى، لذلك لا يمكن تحقيق النتيجة الصحيحة إلا بتجارب العزف المشترك والمران. وإلا سوف نفقدها. نعزف في كل مكان رغم أن ذلك عادة ما يكون في الدور. بمجرد أن يجتمع أكثر من ١٥ عازفًا، نعزف الفجيري على الفور. نعزف أيضًا أشياء أخرى، ولكننا عادةً ما نبدأ بذلك دائمًا وينبغي أن يعرف كل منا طريقة عزفها.*

أوليفييه: هل تعزف بانتظام؟

طلال: *قبل وباء الكورونا كنت أعزف مرة أسبوعيًا على الأقل. الآن الأمر يعتمد على التعليمات.*

أوليفييه:ما هو الحد الأدنى لعدد الأشخاص المطلوب للعزف؟

طلال: *ما لا يقل عن ١٠ أشخاص إلى ١٥. ومع ذلك، كلما زاد عدد الأشخاص، زادت قوة الموسيقى. إنها مثل كرة القدم، إذا كان لديك ١١ لاعباً، فهذا أفضل من وجود خمسة أو ستة فقط في الملعب (يضحك). لا يمكنك اللعب إذا لم يكتمل فريقك.*

أوليفييه: ما الذي يأسرك أكثر في موسيقى صيد اللؤلؤ؟

طلال: *لا أعرف، لأنه شيء نشعر به ولأننا شهدنا عزف هذه الموسيقى عندما كنا أطفال، على العكس من الأجيال الشابة. في المدرسة كانوا يجيئون بنا كل يوم أربعاء إلى نفس الدار للاستماع إلى هذه الموسيقى. خلق هذا الأمر اتصالاً من نوع ما بالنسبة لنا. يحتاج الشباب إلى التعلم من البداية، ولكن لحسن الحظ، أجاد بعضهم ذلك وحاليًا توسعت مجموعتنا لتشمل ٢٥ لاعبًا جيدًا حقًا.*

أوليفييه:أنت تعمل مع غواصي اللؤلؤ الذين يجلبون لك اللآلئ. هل ما زال البعض يعمل بالطريقة التقليدية؟

طلال: *لا يعمل أحد بتلك الطريقة- ولم يفعلون ذلك؟ لديك معدات تجعل حياتك أسهل، فلماذا تجعلها صعبة مرة أخرى عن قصد؟ يوجد الآن أكثر من ٢٠٠٠ غواص في البحرين ولا تحتاج حتى إلى أي معدات عندما تذهب في المياه الضحلة. في المياه العميقة، يستخدمون معدات الغوص لأن الماء يصبح شديد البرودة كلما غصت أبعد.*

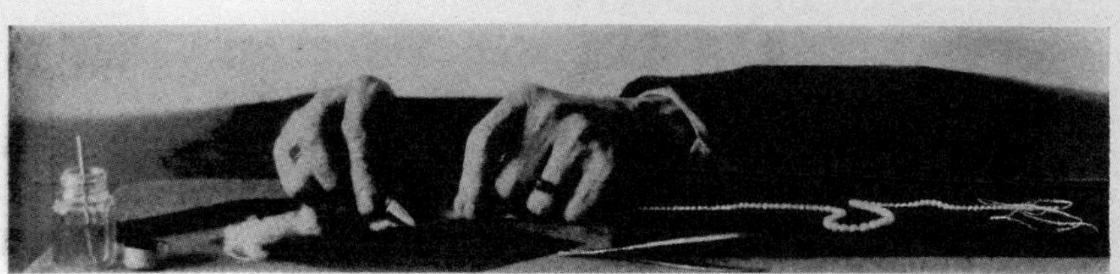

Scraping ends of silk threads for stringing pearl necklace

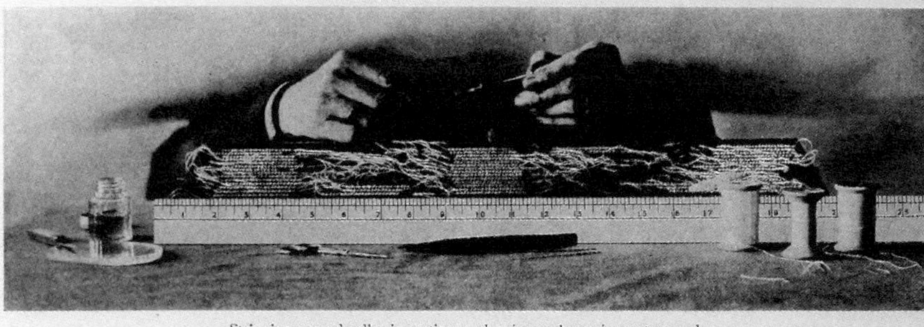

Stringing a pearl collar in sections; cleaning and reaming out a pearl

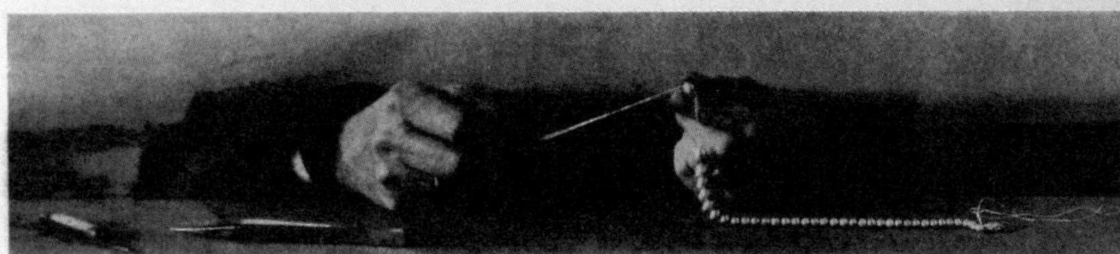

Sliding a pearl along the string in pearl stringing

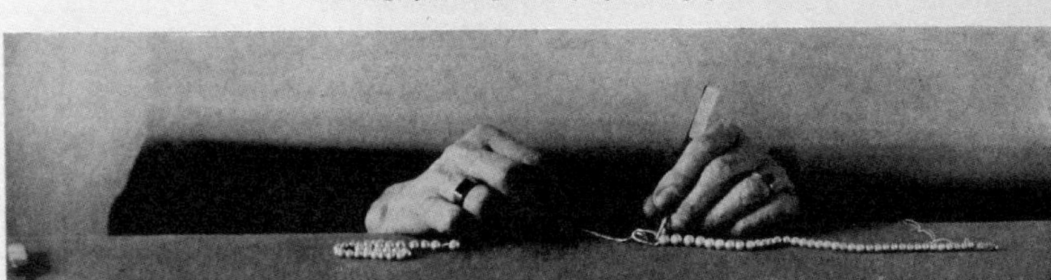

Tying a knot between pearls in pearl stringing

PEARL STRINGING

أوليفييه: هل يمكنك أن تصفين بإيجاز طريق اللؤلؤ؟

طلال مطر:
أنا طلال مطر من عائلة مطر، نعمل في هذا المجال منذ أكثر من ٢٠٠ عام. عملت عائلتي كتجار للؤلؤ - نسميها «طواش» بالعربية. لم نعمل سوى في اللؤلؤ والقلائد. في عام ٢٠٠٤ بدأنا العمل في مجال المجوهرات والآن نعمل في الأمرين: البيع بالجملة وصناعة المجوهرات.

أوليفييه: عائلتك تتاجر في اللؤلؤ من قديم الزمن؟

طلال: *لدي بالفعل رسائل تعود إلى وقت طويل، حتى من باريس من فندق بوي لافاييت، موجهة إلى جدي الأكبر في عام ١٨٨٤.*

أوليفييه: هل يتعاملون مع أشخاص من جميع أنحاء العالم؟

طلال: *معظم المهتمين باللآلئ يأتون إلى البحرين التي كانت معقلًا من معاقل اللؤلؤ. لم يسافروا من قبل، حيث كان الناس يأتون إليهم مباشرة.*

أوليفييه: هل يوجد غواصين لصيد اللؤلؤ في عائلتك؟

طلال: *لا لا، تجار فقط.*

أوليفييه: كيف تصف علاقتك بموسيقى صيد اللؤلؤ؟

طلال: *بما أننا تجار لؤلؤ، فلدينا علاقة بكل ما يرتبط به. يمكن تقسيم موسيقى صيد اللؤلؤ إلى جزأين: موسيقى تعزف على متن السفينة وموسيقى تعزف على اليابسة في غير موسم اللؤلؤ في الدور. لقد ولدنا بموسيقى تُعزف يوميًا منذ زمن جدي. نحن مرتبطون بهذه الموسيقى لأنها تراثنا وثقافتنا في البحرين. ليست شيئًا مستوردًا، إنها ثقافة عائلتنا وأمتنا. لا تنحصر علاقتي الوثيقة بالأمر في موسيقى صيد اللؤلؤ فقط ولكنها تمتد إلى موسيقييها في المنطقة. يعود هذا الارتباط إلى جدي - كان لدينا جميعًا روابط رائعة معهم.*

أوليفييه: كيف تعلمت الموسيقى؟

طلال: *نشأنا نتعلم الإيقاع. كان أبي وجدي كلاهما يعرفانه وتم تمريره عبر الأجيال. حتى أبنائي يتعلمون بسرعة كبيرة، فهو سهل لأنهم معتادون على هذا النوع من الموسيقى. نشعر بذلك، فمن الأسهل بالنسبة لنا تشغيل هذه الموسيقى أكثر من أي موسيقى أخرى في العالم.*

أوليفييه: لقد أشرت إلى تراث مشترك ارتبط بهذه الموسيقى.

طلال: *بالطبع، خاصة في الماضي حيث لم يكن هناك ترفيه آخر ولا مطاعم ولا استراحات.*

تجارة اللؤلؤ والأغنيات:
زيارة لطلال مطر

الدكتور مارك هوبز

كاتب ومؤرخ مقيم في لندن بخبرة تفوق العشرة أعوام في العمل في قطاع التراث الثقافي. عمل هوبز لمؤسسة باركر لانجام لاستشارات التراث ولمجموعة من المؤسسات المرموقة منها: الأكاديمية الملكية للموسيقى، والمكتبة البريطانية والجمعية الملكية للبستنة. في مؤسسة باركر لانجام، عمل هوبز كمستشار تنسيق لمتحف بن جلمود في قطر والذي يسعى إلى رفع الوعي بالمساهمات الاجتماعية والثقافية والاقتصادية الهامة التي قدمتها الشعوب المستعبدة سابقاً في تاريخ الحضارة الإنسانية. نشرت كتابات هوبز في دورية إيربان هيستوري جورنال، ومجلة بابلك دومين ريفيو الإلكترونية، ومجلة ذا باريس ريفيو الأدبية المرموقة.

[١] لوسيا افيال تشيتشارو، "الرومان فضّلوا هذه الجواهر على الماس"، مجلة ناشيونال جيوغرافيك (٢ أبريل ٢٠١٩

[٢] ماركو بولو، "السفر في أراضي قوبلا خان" (لندن، ٢٠٠٥)، ص ٥٣ أنظر بريان كولس، حكمة تجار اللؤلؤ: مختارات من الباطنية المسيحية السريانية (كلامازو، إم آي، ٢٠٠٨).

[٣] جورج فردريك كونز وتشارلز هيو ستيفنسون، "كتاب اللؤلؤ: تاريخ وفن وصناعة ملكة الجواهر"، (نيويورك، ١٩٠٨)، ص.

[٤] ماثيو س. هوبر، "عبيد لسيد واحد: العولمة والاستعباد في شبه الجزيرة العربية في عصر الامبراطوريات (نيوهيفن، ٢٠١٥)، ص ٨٦ الصغد كانت حضارة إيرانية قديمة واقعة في وسط آسيا. عرف الصغديين كتجار ينقلون البضائع بين فارس في الغرب والصين في الشرق.

[٥] تم ترقيم ونشر العديد من سجلات شركة الهند الشرقية وأرشيف مكتب الهند فيما يتعلق بمنطقة الخليج منذ عام ٢٠١٣ م من قبل مكتبة قطر الرقمية (https://qdl.qa) وهي مشروع مشترك بين المكتبة البريطاني ومؤسسة قطر. المصادر التي تشير إلى أرشيفات شركة الهند الشرقية ومكتب الهند مصدرها الفعلي أرشيفات المكتبة البريطانية. نسخ رقمية لكل المصادر متواجدة على موقع https://qdl.qa

[٨] تم التوصل إلى هذا المبلغ والمبالغ المعدّلة حسب تقديرات اليوم باستعمال حاسبة تضخم مؤشر أسعار المستهلك٩ الترانيم الخمسة «عن اللؤلؤة» هم الترانيم من ٨١ حتى ٨٥. أنظر ترجمة جيفري ويكس (واشنطن دي سي: الجامعة الكاثوليكية في أمريكا، ٢٠١٥)، الصفحات ٣٧٧ – ٣٩٢. (www.officialdata.org)

image 47

الضفة العربية من الخليج. في حال مواجهة عبد لمشاكل مثل سوء المعاملة من قبل سيده، بإمكانه تقديم طلب انعتاق عند الحكومة البريطانية. الحكومة البريطانية أعطت العبيد المعتقون شهادات عتق.[١٣]

إن بيانات العتق التي سجلها ممثلو الحكومة البريطانية في الخليج في بداية القرن العشرين تشير بأن أكثرية الذين كانوا يطلبون الانعتاق لم يكونوا عبيداً بالمفهوم العام، بل كانوا من العبيد المتعاقدون. كان من السائد أن يكون غواصو اللؤلؤ مدينين لأرباب عملهم. كان النواخذة يقدمون القروض للغواصين، ذلك لدعم أسرهم لفترة غيابهم مع موسم صيد اللؤلؤ، وأيضاً لدعمهم في فترات توقف
صيد اللؤلؤ. كان نظام الاقتراض يفرض على الغواصين الدين الدائم للنواخذة، مما كان يجبرهم على العودة إلى مصائد اللؤلؤ سنوياً. وفي حال تقلص عوائد اللؤلؤ، وجد غواصو اللؤلؤ - عبيداً وأحراراً - ديونهم تتراكم من عام إلى عام، بالرغم من الجهد الذي كان يبذلونه.

تراجع تجارة اللؤلؤ

كانت محنة غواصي اللؤلؤ في الخليج محفوفة بالمخاطر: كانوا مجبورين للعمل في تجارة مدمرة للصحة، تجارة لا تضمن دخلاً مالياً، تجارة مريبة حتى فيما يتعلق بأبسط الحقوق وأكثرها حرمة إلا وهي الحرية. ازدادت الأوضاع سوءاً في العشرينيات والثلاثينيات من القرن الماضي بسبب الاضطرابات والانحدار السريع في صناعة اللؤلؤ في الخليج.

بلغت قيمة صادرات اللؤلؤ من الخليج ذروتها في السنوات التي سبقت الحرب العالمية الأولى. ارتفعت الصادرات بشكل طفيف بعد الحرب قبل أن تتراجع بشكل حاد في الثلاثينيات. في سبيل المثال، قدّر المسؤولون البريطانيون سوق تصدير اللؤلؤ في البحرين في ، ١٩٢٧ ليكون في حدود ٤٦٦ ألف جنيه إسترليني (٢٨ مليون جنيه إسترليني بالقيمة الحالية). في عام ١٩٣٥ - الفترة ما بين ١٩٢٦ تقلص هذا الرقم إلى ٣٥،٠٠٠ جنيه إسترليني فقط (٢،٥ مليون جنيه إسترليني بالمعايير الحالية)، أي أقل من عُشر قيمته قبل عقد من الزمن. ١٤ اجتمعت عدة عوامل لتدمير صناعة اللؤلؤ في الخليج. أولاً، أدت الحرب العالمية الأولى إلى انخفاض كبير في الطلب العالمي على السلع الكمالية. تم القضاء على الانتعاش الجزئي في أوائل العشرينيات من القرن الماضي سريعًا بسبب الكساد الاقتصادي العالمي الذي أعقب انهيار وول ستريت عام ١٩٢٩ . في غضون ذلك، تم إجراء تحسينات على عملية إنتاج اللؤلؤ المستزرع، التي كان رائدًا فيها رائد الأعمال الياباني كوكيتشي ميكيموتو. كانت هذه التحسينات تعني أنه من عام ١٩١٦ فصاعدًا، أصبح من الممكن إنتاج اللؤلؤ بكميات كبيرة في المزارع البحرية. بحلول أواخر العشرينيات من القرن الماضي، أصبحت اللآلئ
المزروعة «المصنعة» في اليابان والبحار الجنوبية، والتي لا يمكن تمييزها تقريبًا عن اللآلئ الطبيعية وتكلف ثلث قيمتها، متاحة على نطاق واسع.

كان لتراجع صناعة اللؤلؤ تأثيراً كارثياً على سكان الساحل العربي للخليج الذين كانوا يعتمدون بشكل شبه كامل على تجارة اللؤلؤ في معيشتهم. كتب مسؤول بريطاني ملاحظة في عام ١٩١٥ بأنه إذا توقفت تجارة اللؤلؤ، فإن البحرين "ستتقلص إلى حوالي خُمس حجمها الحالي وستتوقف موانئ عُمان المتصالحة [دبي وأبو ظبي]، اللتان لا تملكان أي موارد أخرى، من ناحية عملية في الوجود. ١٥ كتب تشارلز بلجريف في عام ١٩٢٨ : «إن ازدهار البحرين ووجودها يعتمد على صناعة اللؤلؤ".[١٦]

لكن الحظ السعيد كان قاب قوسين أو أدنى. جلبت الثلاثينيات من القرن الماضي تغييرات مهمة إلى منطقة الخليج، ومع ظهور صناعة جديدة - والتي هي النفط - سرعان ما حلت محل صيد اللؤلؤ كمصدر رئيسي للدخل في الخليج. منذ أوائل الثلاثينيات فصاعداً، تم توقيع سلسلة من اتفاقيات امتياز النفط بين شيوخ المنطقة وشركات النفط من بريطانيا وأوروبا والولايات المتحدة:
البحرين في عام ١٩٣٠ ، والكويت في عام ١٩٣٢ ، وقطر في عام ١٩٣٥ ، وأبو ظبي في عام ١٩٣٩ . هذه الامتيازات، وأولى صادرات النفط، جلبت ثروات جديدة إلى منطقة الخليج. كما أنها جلبت تحديثاً دراماتيكياً في أعقابها، ذلك مع وصول مجموعة من الابتكارات الغربية مثل الكهرباء والتبريد والاتصالات السلكية واللاسلكية والسيارات.
ينظر سكان الساحل العربي للخليج اليوم إلى الثلاثينيات من القرن الماضي على أنها فترة بطولية في تاريخهم: فترة من المشقة الشديدة الناجمة عن انهيار صناعة اللؤلؤ، والتضحيات الكبيرة التي قدمها الرواد الأوائل الذين عملوا في الصحراء تحت أشعة الشمس الحارقة بحثاً عن النفط، ورسم الحدود القومية وتأسيس الدول القومية الحديثة.

جنيه استرليني حسب تقدير اليوم.[٧] جاء هذا الارتفاع في الطلب نتيجة تزايد الرخاء الاقتصادي العالمي، خاصة في حالتي أوروبا وأمريكا الشمالية، والتي شهدت اهتماماً جديداً في "الشرق" والسلع التي كانت تتداول على طول طريق الحرير.

إلى جانب قيمة الصادرات، من الممكن تقييم مدى نجاح تجارة اللؤلؤ في الخليج من خلال حجم الأساطيل في كل الموانئ، وعدد العاملين في مفاصل تلك التجارة. في ١٨٣٣ م قدر الملازم جيمس ويلستيد من البحرية الهندية الملكية بأن هناك ٤،٣٠٠ سفينة و ٣٠،٠٠٠ رجل تم توظيفهم في تجارة اللؤلؤ في الخليج.[٨] في عام ١٩٣٠ م، قدّر المستشار البريطاني في البحرين تشالرز بلجريف بأن عدد العاملين في تجارة اللؤلؤ في الخليج يقارب ال ١٠٠،٠٠٠ رجل.[٩]

موسم الصيد

كان الموسم الرئيسي لصيد اللؤلؤ يحدث بين شهري مايو واكتوبر. في كل يوم كانت أعداد هائلة من السفن المجهزة لصيد اللؤلؤ تتجه نحو الضفاف الضحلة من البحر. كان طاقم كل سفينة يتكون من القبطان (النوخذة) ومجموعة من الغواصين والسيبان المتخصصين في اعادة سحب الغواصين إلى ظهر السفينة من قعر البحر. شهد (ولستيد) عملية الغوص للؤلؤ في مياه الخليج. وقد علّق على تلك التجربة بالآتي:

عندما تصل السفينة إلى موقع في البحر يُعتقد بأنها مناسبة لجمع اللؤلؤ بناءاً على حالة قعر البحر، يتم إنزال المرساة وتقسيم الطاقم إلى قسمين: قسم يبقى على السفينة لاستلام المحار ولسحب الغواصين من تحت الماء، وقسم ينزع ملابسه ويقفز في البحر. يستلم كل غواص سلة صغيرة تسع ثمان إلى عشرة محارات والتي تعلّق من الذراع الأيسر؛ ومن ثم يَسدّ كل غواص أنفه بسدّادة المصنوعة من قرن مرن، فيضع قدمه على صخرة مربوطة بحبل، وعندما يشير إلى الآخرين من خلال رفع يده اليمنى، يتم ترك الحبل وينزل الغواص بسرعة إلى قعر البحر. بعدما يجمع الغواص كل ما باستطاعته جمعه من تحت البحر، يسحب الحبل بشده فيتم رفعه بسرعة إلى السطح.[١٠]

كان الغوص للؤلؤ عملية مجهدة بدنياً حيث أن فئة الشباب هم من كان باستطاعتهم العمل في ذلك المجال. كما أن الغوص مجال مُتعب وموسمي، وكان هناك اعتماداً كبيراً على العمالة الوافدة المتنقلة. ولذلك، فإن مجال صيد اللؤلؤ اعتمد إلى حد كبير على ظاهرة العبودية والتي لم تمانعها بريطانيا كلياً بالرغم من اكتساحها لمنطقة الخليج. لم يتم الثبات على تعداد المستعبدين في مجال صيد اللؤلؤ في منطقة الخليج. في عام ١٩٢٩ م، قدّر ضابط بحري رفيع المنصب بأن رُبع الغواصين في الخليج (أي ما يعادل ٢٠،٠٠٠ شخصاً) من المستعبدين.[١١]

إلا أن العدد ٢٠،٠٠٠ لم يُفرّق بين العبيد بمفهومه العرفي والذين أُجبروا على العبودية التعاقدية والذين كانت أعدادهم ضخمة في السنوات الأخيرة من تجارة اللؤلؤ قبيل انهيار عوائد اللؤلؤ. التفريق بين العبودية والعبودية التعاقدية كان صعباً، لا سيما أن خواص كلاهما شديدة التشابه. صعوبة التفريق بين أنواع العبودية السائدة في تلك الفترة تعكس التعقيدات في طبيعة العبودية في شبه الجزيرة العربية. كانت العبودية في المنطقة تختلف كثيراً عن العبودية في المحيط الأطلسي، حيث قامت القوات الاستعمارية الأوروبية، بين القرني السادسة والتاسعة عشر، بنقل الالاف من الرجال والنساء والأطفال من افريقيا إلى الامريكتين للعمل في مزارع قصب السكر والقطن والتبغ. كان للاستعباد في شبه الجزيرة العربية تواجداً منذ قرون طويلة كجزء من شبكة واسعة من طرق التجارة والتي تُعرف أحياناً بعالم المحيط الهندي. تم استعباد الناس من خلال الحروب والغزوات والاستعمار وأيضاً كرد على الطلب للقوى العاملة في مجالات متنوعة كصيد اللؤلؤ وزراعة التمور. في فترات اجتياح المجاعات والكوارث الطبيعية، لم يكن من خارج المألوف بأن يقدم الكثيرون من شبه القارة الآسيوية أنفسهم أو ذويهم إلى العبودية، ذلك لأنه كان سبيلاً من سبل النجاة.[١٢] جاء العبيد من أماكن متعددة. قامت الدولة العثمانية في فترة توسعها في القرون الوسطى باستعباد الأوروبيين من البلقان والقوقاز. افريقيا الشرقية كانت مصدراً آخراً للعبيد، والذين تم نقلهم على طول طرق التجارة البحرية المتأثرة بالرياح الموسمية وعلى طرق التجارة البرية. كان هناك أيضاً فئة من العبيد القادمة من شبه القارة الآسيوية و من جنوب شرق آسيا. أكثر السجلات تفصيلاً في وصف حالة معيشة غواصي اللؤلؤ المستعبدين في الخليج التي كُتبت في بدايات القرن العشرين هي بيانات العتق لمئات الرجال المسجلة في وكالات للحكومة البريطانية في المنطقة. بالرغم من أن الحكومة البريطانية قامت بإلغاء تجارة العبيد، وبالرغم من أنها أخذت خطوات لردع تلك التجارة كلما ظهرت في مكان ما، إلا أنها تغاضت عن الاستعباد المتواجد على

image 64

في كتاباته التاريخية كيفية استخدام الطبقة الاستقراطية في روما للآلئ في الحلي. ١ تُصوّر الرسومات المقدسة لساراسواتي، والتي هي الآلهة الهندوسية المعنية بالعلم والموسيقى والفن والحكمة والمعرفة وهي تمسك قلادة لآلئ. ماركو بولو وصف كيف في القرن الثالث عشر كان الامبراطور المنغولي قوبلاي خان يكافئ مواليه باللؤلؤ وأحجار كريمة أخرى.[٢]

كانت اللالئ التي تم العثور عليها بالقرب من الضفة العربية من الخليج تعتبر أفضلها في العالم. في كتاب هيستوريا ناتوراليس، كتب بليني الأكبر بأن «أجود وأروع» اللؤلؤ هو اللؤلؤ الخليجي.[٣] على مدى مئات السنين، صيد اللؤلؤ كان أكبر نشاط تجاري في الضفة العربية من الخليج، وكان سكان وحكام المنطقة يعتمدون على تلك الصناعة بشكل كبير. في ١٨٦٣ م، في خطاب يوضح مدى أهمية تجارة اللؤلؤ بالنسبة له، قال حاكم قطر الشيخ محمد بن ثاني إلى المكتشف الانجليزي ويليام بالغريف "كلنا مِن أرفعنا مقاماً إلى أنزلنا عبداً لسيد واحد، اللؤلؤ".[٤] كانت تتمحور أكبر مصائد اللؤلؤ حول البحرين، كما أنه كانت هناك أساطيل صغيرة تتخصص في صيد اللؤلؤ تُدار من الكويت والدوحة ودبي وأبوظبي.

من أهم المراجع لفهم مدى أهمية تجارة اللؤلؤ أرشيف شركة الهند الشرقية البريطانية وأرشيف مكتب الحكومة البريطانية في الهند في المكتبة البريطانية في لندن. تم كتابة تلك السجلات لأن بريطانيا هي من كانت فعلياً تتحكم بالخليج وبمياهها في بداية القرن التاسع عشر، وذلك بعد أن استطاعوا اقناع شيوخ الخليج على توقيع مجموعة من المعاهدات. ٥ في عام ١٨٣٣ م قدّرت الحكومة البريطانية قيمة صادرات اللؤلؤ من الخليج بما يقارب ٣٠٠،٠٠٠ جنيه استرليني (أي ما يقارب ٣٦ مليون جنيه استرليني اليوم). في عام ١٨٦٦ م، بلغت تلك القيمة ٤٠٠،٠٠٠ جنيه استرليني (٤٨ مليون جنيه استرليني اليوم). ٦ شهد بداية القرن العشرين ارتفاعاً ملحوظاً في الطلب العالمي للؤلؤ. في تقرير نُشر في ١٩٠٦ م ذُكر أن قيمة سوق اللؤلؤ - سوق يمثل نصف منتوج اللؤلؤ على مستوى العالم - قد ارتفع إلى ١،٤ مليون جنيه استرليني، أي ما يعادل ١٧٠ مليون

أول زيارة لي إلى قطر كانت في عام ٢٠١١ م. كان ذلك في شهر أغسطس وكانت درجة الحرارة تفوق ال ٤٠ درجة مئوية، هواء العصر شديد الحرارة، وتنفسه من المستحيلات. كانت تلك الزيارة أيضاً تصادف شهر رمضان، وكانت الشوارع خالية، المدينة بأسرها مهجورة. وبينما كنا نمرّ بالدوّارات في الطريق إلى الفندق كان سائق سيارة الأجرة يعدد المعالم التي كانت تحيط بنا: سوق واقف، متحف الفن الإسلامي والذي صممه المهندس آي. ام. بي، الديوان الأميري، فندق الشيراتون بشكله الهرمي، وأمامنا، فوضى الآفاق في منطقة ويست باي، والتي تزخر بناطحات سحاب من تصميم مشاهير عالم فن العمارة، كلها تتنافس مع بعضها لجذبالأنظار.

يُعتبر منظر ويست باي في الدوحة من أكثر مناظر الخليج تألقاً - هو رمز سرعة اقتناء دولة قطر للثراء، وذلك نظراً لمخزونها الضخم من الغاز الطبيعي. كنت في قطر للعمل: بشكل خاص كنت أعمل في مشروعي بناء متحفين ضخمين، كلاهما بدعم من ثروات الدولة، وكلاهما حاولا تأطير الدور الذي لعبته ثروة النفط ومن ثم ثروة الغاز الطبيعي في التحولات التي طرأت على تلك الدولة الخليجية الصغيرة. كما أن مشروعي المتحفان بحثا تاريخ قطر قبل اكتشاف النفط في ثلاثينيات القرن الماضي، وكلاهما يشملان موضوع اعتماد المنطقة في السابق على صناعة اللؤلؤ.

إن رواية اعتماد قطر والخليج بشكل عام على مصائد اللؤلؤ غير معروف لمن هو من خارج تلك المنطقة، ولكن تلك الرواية محورية للتراث بالنسبة إلى قطر والبحرين والإمارات العربية المتحدة والكويت - والتي قد تُعتبر دول حديثة التكوين. توجد العديد من المصادر التي تشير إلى اللؤلؤ في الضفة العربية من الخليج: في المشاريع العقارية المرموقة، في المناطق السياحية والتراثية، وفي المتاجر اللؤلؤ المتواجدة بكثرة في الأسواق الشعبية وفي المجمعات التجارية المكيّفة.

من خلال البحث في تاريخ البشرية نجد أن اللؤلؤ دوما ما كان مرتبطاً بالثراء والجمال. السعي وراء السلطة يرافق الثراء، ومع الجمال تأتي مفاهيم الذوق. ذكر بليني الأكبر

image 63

صناعة اللؤلؤ على الساحل العربي الخليجي

الدكتور مارك هوبز

[١] المقاطع الواردة في النص مقتبسة من ترجمة دكتور نايف خرما المنشورة تحت عنوان «أبناء السندباد،» مطبعة حكومة الكويت، ١٩٨٢.

منيرة القديري

فنانة بصرية كويتية ولدت في السنغال وتلقت تعليمها في اليابان. في ٢٠١٠، حصلت القادري على درجة الدكتوراة في الفلسفة في الفن متشابك الوسائط من جامعة طوكيو للفنون، وركز بحثها على جماليات الحزن في الشرق الأوسط النابعة من الشعر والموسيقى والفن والممارسات الشعائرية. يستكشف عمل القادري الهوية الجندرية وثقافات البترول ومستقبلهم المحتمل بالإضافة إلى موروثات الفساد. تقيم القادري حالياً في برلين.

إسماعيل كان موسيقياً معروفاً في الكويت، وأنه من أفضل مزايا المركب.»

تبدو كل هذه القصص وكأنها نوع من الخيال بالنسبة لي، على الرغم من سماعي لذكريات عائلية شديدة الحياة عن حياته لسنوات. ربما كنت شديدة الهوس به، أدرك ذلك الآن بعدما عشت في اليابان لوقت طويل ووجدت نفسي أشارك في معتقد عبادة الأسلاف الشائع رؤيته في الميدان الثقافي الشرق آسيوي. من كان هذا الجد؟ هل شعر بالتشاؤم والغضب والرغبة في الانتقام من العالم الذي تخلى عنه كما تصف لنا العديد من كلمات أغنيات البحر؟ أم كانت تلك فقط محنة رفاقه من غواصي اللؤلؤ فيما بقي هو هناك يغني وينوح على هامش الحدث بينما يقفزون في المحيط مرة تلو المرة، فقط لأنه كان قائد إيقاع حياتهم العملية.

«وكان الاثنان، مثلهما في ذلك مثل البحارة الآخرين، يرقصان حفاة الأقدام، ويذرعان السجادة جيئة وذهاباً، بخطوات متناغمة مع موسيقى ذلك الوحش ذي الشارب الضخم. وهكذا كانا يقطعان السجادة جيئة وذهاباً، وأيديهما متشابكة، بينما كانت أصابع إسماعيل السوداء تعذب أوتار القيثارة، وصوته الأجش يولول. وكلما أصبحا في مواجهة إسماعيل المغني، كانا يتوقفان لحظة ويفرقعان أصابعهما، وأحياناً يهزان بطنيهما وجسميهما حتى الكتفين بطريقة تشبه ما تفعله فتيات مراكش الراقصات. كان شيئاً غريباً.

في بعض الأحيان كان البحارة، في أثناء غنائهم، لا يستطيعون ضبط أعصابهم عند سماعهم إحدى المقطوعات المؤثرة من ذلك المغني الحزين، فينفعلون ويهبون واقفين، ويكونون صفوفاً خلف القبطانين، ويفرقعون أصابعهم، ويهزون أجسامهم بعنف شديد.»

ربما أنا فقط مهتمة بذكورته الطاغية وبفنه، بتخيل هذه الحياة الماضية التي لا تزال تسكن جسدي. لكن بغض النظر عن محاولاتي المضنية لتخيل الأمر، هناك نشاز يحتل مساحتي العقلية سريعاً ودونما رحمة. تعميني لعنة اللؤلؤ الأسود -النفط- عن مخيلتي التاريخية الخاصة. لقد صرت تحور بلا ماضي، بلا تاريخ، بلا ذاكرة. جسدي وعقلي مشوهين، مشوشين، ولن يعودا أبداً كما كانا.

«لابد أن إسماعيل كان يضمن أغانيه بعض الأمور التي تجذب المستمعين إليه، وإلا فكيف يمكنهم أن يتحملوا تلك الأنغام الفظيعة، وذلك الأداء البغيض؟ أعتقد أن عملي ذاك لم يكن لائقاً، فليس من المعقول أن أطلب منه التوقف عن العزف والغناء، بينما كان الجميع يستمتعون بإنشاده. ولكنه كان يبالغ في الأمر أحياناً فيمتد عزفه وغناؤه في الهزيع الأخير من الليل، وكانت الطبول تصاحب القيثارة في بعض الأحيان، وكان هذا أفضل، لأن دوي الطبول كان يطغى على الموسيقى الفظيعة. وغالباً ما كان الرجال يرقصون، ولكنه كان نفس الرقص الرتيب الممل، الذي لا يزيد عن المشي ذهاباً وإياباً والقفز وهز الأكتاف وفرقعة الأصابع، الذي كنت قد شاهدته في خليج المعلا للمرة الأولى. كما لم يشترك في الرقص على ظهر المركب أية فتيات، لأن الفتيات لم يكن يغادرن اليابسة.»

أمتلك بعض اللؤلؤ، ألمسه وأنظر له أحياناً في سبيل محاولة إيجاد بعض الروابط غير المرئية معه. بعضهم غريب ومشوه، غير مرغوب به في السوق الذي لا يطمع سوى في كاملات الاستدارة. ربما قابل بعضهن في أسفاره في البحر. ماذا لو نحتّ هذه الكريات غير المرغوبة ذات البريق الصدفي في شكل حفارات بترول؟ ربما تندمج تشوشاتها بتشوشاتي الخاصة، لتخلق شكلاً متحوراً، شكلاً أقرب لنسخة أحفورية من ذاتي غير الطبيعية.

لطالما كانت حفارات البترول نفسها موضوعاً لافتتاني الخاص لبعض الوقت، حيث تحفر بلا نهاية في قشرة الأرض المغطاة بالذهب والماس بما يشبه الأخطبوطات وكائنات البحر والكائنات الفضائية. لأن سرديتي الخاصة نبذت بشدة على يد اللؤلؤ، وجدت بعض العزاء في هذه الماكينات، حيث جسدت شيئاً يتوافق أكثر مع جيلي الشاذ.

«أما إسماعيل، فقد كان الطلب على موسيقاه كبيراً، ولذاك كان مشغولاً باستمرار في إقامة الحفلات الموسيقية، والعزف في النوادي الليلية العربية، وكان هذا مدعاة سرور غامر لكلينا: له لأن ذلك كان يدر عليه ربحاً وفيراً، ولي لأن في غيابه هدوء المركب وراحة لي.»

ربما باستطاعتي أن أحرر نفسي من أوهامي الموروثة عبر خلق أوهام خاصة بي، مثل حفارات اللؤلؤ، البقية الوحيدة من الماضي والمؤشر الوحيد على مستقبل يخلو من النفط.

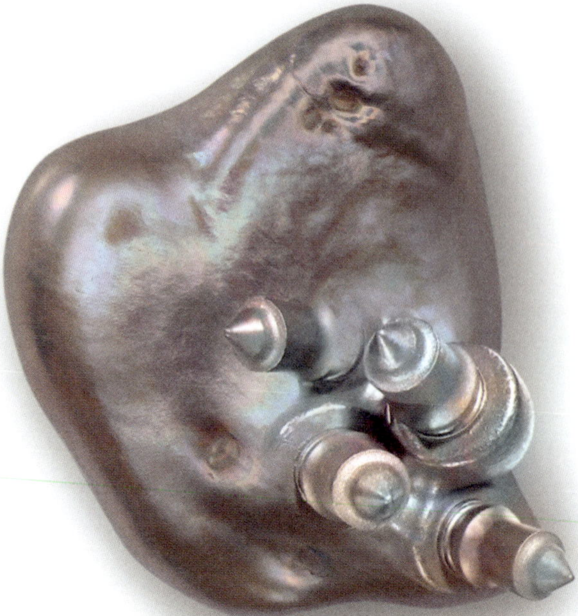

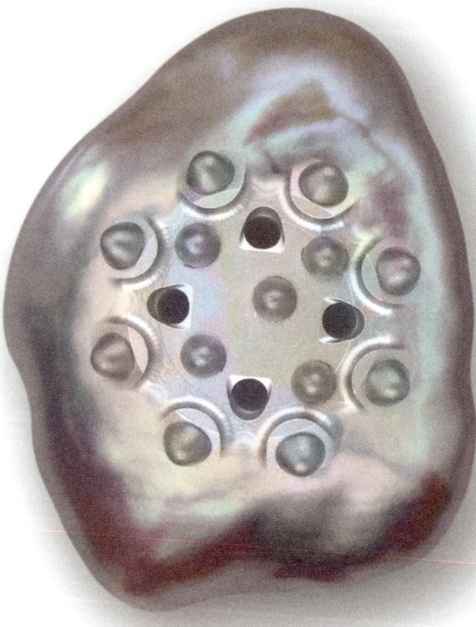

«عدنا إلى الشاطئ في قارب النجاة الطويل. وعلى الطريقة الكويتية التقليدية كان عشرون من البحارة الأشداء يقومون بالتجديف بالمجاديف الطويل وهم يرتدون أفضل ملابسهم ويهزجون بقوة وحماس. لقد كان تجديفهم ممتازاً وكانت أهازيجهم أفضل من أغانيهم. وعندما لم يكونوا يهزجون كانوا يصدرون من أقصى حناجرهم أصواتاً عميقة مدمدمة كأنها هدي سرب من الطائرات قاذفات القنابل القادمة من بعيد.»

نظرياً، يحتوي كتاب «أبناء السندباد» المنشور عام ١٩٤٠ للمستكشف الأسترالي ألان فيليبرز[1] بعض المقاطع عن جدي، مغني مقيم على سفينة صيد لؤلؤ كويتية استقلها من ميناء في اليمن فيما وفر رفاق رحلته الإيقاع والرقص المصاحب لموسيقاه.

«وكان الموسيقي رجلاً عربياً ضخماً ذا عينين ثاقبتين وشارب أسود ضخم، وكان يعزف على القيثارة التي بدت لي كأنها قد جلبت من أوروبا (والتي عرفت فيما بعد أنها كانت قد اشتريت من البصرة). وربما كان عزفه جيداً بحسب المفاهيم الموسيقية العربية التي لم تكن لسوء الحظ، هي نفس مفاهيمي. وقد زاد الطين بله غناؤه المتصل بصوته الأجش المزعج. ومهما كان نوع الغناء الذي كان يؤديه فقد كان من الواضح أنه كان مستساغاً جداً لدى جمهور المستمعين فيري، فقد كان بإمكاني الاستغناء عنه كلية. وقد همس علي في أذني قائلاً بأن ذلك الشخص كان أحد مشاهير الغناء في الكويت. ولكن ذلك الإعلان عن شهرته لم يغير من الأمر شيئاً بالنسبة لي، ولم يجعل غناءه أفضل وقعاً في مسامعي. وكل ما تمنيته حينئذ هو ألا يكون هذ المغني الذي قيل لي أن اسمه إسماعيل، من طاقم المركب الدائم. وقد سرني أن أرى نفراً من البحارة ومعهم رجل قصير القامة، كأنه طباخ، يأتون وهم يحملون طبولاً صغيرة جداً، أسطوانية الشكل، مصنوعة من فخار البصرة، مشدود على منها قطعة من جلد الماعز المسخن. وكان عدد تلك الطبول ستة تقريباً، كما كانت هناك بعض الدفوف الكبيرة الأخرى. وقد أخذ البحارة يتناوبون على قرعها، مستخدمين أصابع الإبهام والأصابع الأمامية الأخرى، فيصدر عن ذلك إيقاع جميل للغاية. وقد أحببت تلك الطبول فقد كانت نغمتها خافتة تهدهد السمع كما كانت تساعد على التخفيف من صخب الموسيقى التي كانت تصدر عن قيثارة إسماعيل.»

لم أقابل جدي، الذي توفي قبل أعوام قليلة من ولادتي، أبداً. كان رجلاً قاسٍ وصعب طبقاً لما سمعته، لم يغني أبداً -على وجه التقريب- جملة واحدة بعد عودته للبيت من البحر، على الرغم من شهادة جدتي بحيازته صوتاً جميلاً يمكن سماعه من على بعد أميال. لكن بالنسبة له، كان الغناء موسيقى للعمل حصراً لمساعدة معنويات ونفسيات رفاقه. كان يعمل لشهور طويلة بينما يركب الأمواج تحت الشمس الحارة.

«لقد كان عملاً شاقاً، بل كاد يكون وحشياً. وكان البحارة يتوقفون من آن لآخر لكي يرقصوا ويغنوا، ضاربين الأرض ضربات منتظمة منسقة بأقدامهم الحافية، ومصفقين بأيديهم الضخمة بحيث كان صوت تصفيقهم يسمع في جميع أرجاء الميناء، بينما كان عريف الملاحين (المقدمي) يدق طبلاً هندياً. لقد كان هذا الرقص أفضل بكثير من أداء يوم الأحد وكان يعمل كدواء مقو للبحارة، يجدد نشاطهم لمتابعة أداء مهامهم الشاقة. فلم يكونوا يقومون بأي عمل من غير مقدمة راقصة، كما أنهم كانوا دائماً يهزجون بشكل موسيقي وهم يعملون.»

لطالما تخيلت حياته، لكني وجدت الأمر مستحيل الاجتياز ذهنياً، كشخص ما-بعد نفطي قطع روابطه مع ماضي اللؤلؤ بفعل قوة غريبة هي البترول. هل خاطروا جميعاً بحياتهم حقاً، ليل ونهار، من أجل لمحة من حلية صغيرة براقة؟ حتى يستطيع ملك ما في بلد بعيد أن يستعرضها على شخصه غير عالم كم شخص عاش وقضى في سبيل استخراجها من البحر؟ هل كان حقيقياً أنهم جميعاً كانوا عبيداً لسيد واحد، اللؤلؤ؟

«وبعد الوليمة، كنا نتناول القهوة ثم ننام. وبعد النوم يحين موعد صلاة الظهر، يتبعها عزف من إسماعيل الموسيقي على قيثارته اللعينة، يقضي على كل ما كنا ننعم به من الهدوء والسكينة. لقد كان عزفاً نشازاً لم تكف ستة أشهر لكي أتعود عليه، فلم يكن فيه من وجهة نظري ما يحببه إلي. فإن المرء أن يتعود على قرب الاسكتلنديين ومزامير السياميين وأجراس أهالي بالي وجاوا. وحتى السواحليون عندما يقرعون صبولهم، فإنهم يصدرون نوعاً من الإيقاع الموسيقي، كما أن مزامير البدو على نغماتها مقبولة إلى ما. إلى أن عزف إسماعيل على قيثارته كان يمزق آذان البشر. فإذا ما شجعه أحد، كان إسماعيل ينطلق بالغناء، وكان هذا شر المصائب. فقد كان أغانيه طويلة رتيبة حزينة بغيضة، يشدو بها بشكل غير طبيعي وبصوت قبيح إلى أبعد الحدود. ومع كل ذلك فقد كان الجميع يقولون بإصرار أن

كريات من النشاز المتحور

منيرة القديري

image 6

[١] أقيمت مجالس العزاء للبحار في البحر مباشرة وفي السفانية. من اسم هذه المنطقة في بحر الخليج يأتي اسم أكبر حقل بترول بحري في العالم اليوم.

[٢] كان نوخذة كويتي مشهور من منطقة الفحاحيل. امتلك عدة سفن لصيد اللؤلؤ وكان قريباً من دوائر السلطة والأسرة الحاكمة في الكويت. مات في ١٩٦٣.

[٣] في ١٩١٧، كان روبيه واحد يساوي ٣١,٤ سنتًا أمريكيًا. الأجر المذكور كان يساوي في حينه ما بين دولارين ونصف وثلاثة دولارات أمريكية.

[٤] في تراتبية أعمال السفينة فالرضيف درجة أعلى من الطباب، خادم السفينة.

[٥] مساعدو الغواصين.

[٦] حوالي ١٥ دولارًا أمريكيًا في ١٩١٧.

[٧] اسم أنصبة مختلف أعضاء طاقم سفينة صيد اللؤلؤ.

[٨] تحريف محلي لكلمة مجداف. أغنية يغنيها النهام أثناء تجديف البحارة وتتخللها زفرات حارة عالية الصوت.

[٩] مشتقة من الفعل خطف. أغنية موقعة تتخللها أصوات الطبول والتصفيق وتغنى مع فرد الشراع للإبحار.

[١٠] في البحرين، الفجيري هو وصلة غنائية تتكون من البحري يتبعه العدساني ثم الحدادي والمخولفي وأخيرًا الحساوي. لكن في الكويت تتجاور الأنواع الخمسة تحت مسمى «أغاني استرخاء البحارة» بينما يستخدم الفجيري لوصف نوع غنائي آخر غير مرتبط بالأنواع الخمسة سابقة الذكر. في البلدين، تشترك هذه الأغنيات في كونها تؤدى خلال أوقات الراحة وليس في أوقات العمل في المراكب.

[١١]أحد الأنواع الفرعية الخمسة من وصلة الفجيري. الحساوي هي الذروة النهائية في ترتيب أغنيات الوصلة الخمسة.

[١٢] عملية تبطين أسفل السفينة منعاً لنفاذ الماء.

[١٣] أغنية تؤدى عند وصول طاقم صيد اللؤلؤ إلى منطقة غنية باللؤلؤ.

بول مطر

أفنان لبناني ولد في حي مصر الجديدة بالقاهرة عام ١٩٤٦. مثل مطر للتليفزيون والمسرح والسينما قبل أن يصبح مؤلف ومخرج حيث أخرج سلسلة من الوثائقيات عبر العالم العربي بتكليف من اليونيسيف لأغراض تعليمية، كما ألف العديد من الأغنيات الشهيرة بالعربية والفرنسية. خلال أسفاره، انكب مطر على دراسة إثنوموسيقية مدققة للأغنيات والأهازيج التراثية في منطقة الخليج وجمعها في كتاب بعنوان «خليج الأغاني» نشرته دار المثلث في بيروت في عام ١٩٨١. حفظت مجموعة تسجيلاته في متحف جنيف الإثنوغرافي. اليوم، يدرس مطر في كلية سان جوزيف في بيروت، ذلك إلى جانب إدارته لمسرح مونو المرموق، بالإضافة إلى كونه مؤسس بيت الفنون والحكي في بيروت والذي يعمل على حفظ تقاليد النقل الشفاهي.

بول: كيف تؤدى «الشونة» [١٣]؟

أبو صالح: *نغني نهمة ونسأل بركة النبي.*

بول: كيف تم التحضير للرحلات؟ الغذاء وما هي أدوات الغوص والمواد اللازمة على متن السفن؟

أبو صالح: *ماذا تريد أن تعرف بالضبط؟ أنت تخلط بين أشياء.كثيرة (يضحك) بالنسبة للطعام، نحمل التمر والأرز بكميات تلائم حجم القارب. السمك كنا نطبخه ونأكله في البحر بعد صيده..يعتنى القبطان بهذا فلن يحضر أحد طعامه إلى السفينة. فهو يلتفت لأدق التفاصيل ويهتم بجميع جوانب الحياة على متن السفينة. من القروض ذات الفائدة إلى «الخراب» (تجهيزات السفينة) وجميع التفاصيل الصغيرة على المركب..وبمجرد بيع اللؤلؤ، يأخذ القبطان حصته تلقائيًا، وهي تساوي خمس الإيرادات الكلية للقارب من كل عملية بيع، بعد خصم جميع النفقات الضرورية للرحلة. توزع الإيرادات المتبقية حسب رتبة كل فرد في الطاقم.*

بول: هل توجد أغانٍ معينة تؤدى أثناء الإحتفال بتجهيز السفينة بالخراب والمرساة؟

أبو صالح: *نعم، نعزف بعض الدواري لهذه المناسبة، وهو نوع يتميز بإيقاع محدد جداً من التصفيق بالأيدي.*

بول: كيف تتابع عملك عند وصولك إلى منطقة اللؤلؤ؟

أبو صالح: *حينما نصل، إذا وجدنا كميات كبيرة من المحار، نغني تكسيرة [١٣] « ونهتف «خايب» («أي استدر»). وهذا من شأنه أن يشير إلى بداية العمل الذي يتكون من رفع واحدة من المراسي التي تعمل على تثبيت القارب أثناء الغطس للسماح للقارب بالدوران وفقًا للتيارات، بقطر من ١٠ إلى ٢٠ مترًا، مما يسمح بالغوص المتكرر في منطقة بها كميات من المحار*

بول: وإذا لم نجدوا كميات من المحار في منطقة اللؤلؤ؟

أبو صالح: *نرفع المرساة ونواصل البحث عن منطقة لؤلؤ آخرى بها كميات أكبر من المحار.*

بول:ولن تقوموا بالغناء في هذه الحالة؟

أبو صالح: *لا، بالطبع كل هذا تصاحبه الأغاني والموسيقى.*

بول:هل يمكنني سماع مقاطع من الأغاني في حال عدم وجود لآلئ؟

أبو صالح: *ماذا تريد؟ آسف، في مرة أخرى، لدي اجتماع في البنك.*
(يغادر فجأة ويتجه إلى البنك).

بول: كيف كان يتفق البحارة والقبطان على موعد بدء رحلة صيد اللؤلؤ؟

أبو صالح: *قبل رحلة صيد اللؤلؤ، وعندما يصبح الطقس أكثر ملاءمة للغوص بحثًا عن اللؤلؤ، كان من الممكن أن تشعر بحالة استثارة حقيقية بين السكان. سيكون الجميع متحمسين ويبدأون في تجهيز أنفسهم لأنهم افتقدوا البحر. كان الناس ينزلون إلى الشوارع بالمئات ويبدؤون الغناء والاحتفال بعودة الموسم وقرب خروج رحلات صيد اللؤلؤ.*

بول: هل تتذكر إحدى الأغاني التي تغنى قبل بداية الموسم؟

أبو صالح: *يعتمد هذا على النوع الذي تريده. ميداف[٨]؟ ختفة[٩]؟ هل هناك شيء تود سماعه حقًا؟*

بول: : لاأعلم، اخبرني!

أبو صالح: *كانوا عادة يؤدون بعض الفجيري[١٠] أو الحساوي[١١] خلال تلك المناسبات. كانوا أيضا يغنون الحدادي للترويح. في بعض رحلات صيد اللؤلؤ، لا توجد فترات راحة ، لذلك لن نكون بالضرورة قادرين على أداء تلك الموسيقى. وهذا هو سبب عزفهم وغنائهم خلال فترات الاحتفال، كتلك التي تسبق بداية الموسم، أو أثناء الرحلات التجارية.*

بول: عندما يحل يوم الرحيل في الرحلات، كيف تستقبلونه؟

أبو صالح: *سيكون الوالدان والعائلة على الرصيف وأغني لهم - ولزوجتي على وجه الخصوص - نهمة، تقول ما معناه «ارحل بسلام، يا نور عيني - في بعادك، لم يغلق جفن عيني - تعدني، أنه عندما أغمض عيني، سأظل جسد بلا روح. اعتني بي كما أعتني بك « ونسختها الأصلية هي:*

وادعتكم بالسلامة يا ضوى عيني
وخلافكم ما غمض جفني على عيني
واعدتني بالوعد لمن حفت عيني
ظليت يا سيدي جسم بليا روح
شد فرمن عقل وظل الجسم مطروح
كل العرب هودت وانا شقي الروح
يا نور عيني مثل ما راعيک راعيني

هذا ماكنا نغنيه عندما نرحل إلى البحر. لقد كان موالًا حزينًا جدا. كنا نضع القارب على بعض جذوع الأشجار الخشبية و ندحرجها على طول الطريق إلى الماء، ثم نجره، كي نستطيع السفر لشهور.

بول: هل تتذكر كيف كانت رحلات صيد اللؤلؤ عندما بدأت في الثامنة من عمرك وكيف كانت في نهاية حياتك المهنية؟

أبو صالح: *خلال رحلتي الأولى لم أكن سوى صبي يعمل في المقصورة، ولذلك لم يعطني القبطان سوي ٨ حتى ١٠ روبيات[٣]. كانت رحلة صيد اللؤلؤ تستغرق أربعة أشهر وعشرة أيام. كان هناك طفلان مثلي على متن المركب، تقدمت ببطء وترقيت في التسلسل الهرمي على متن السفينة، وأصبحت «رضيف»[٤] وحصلت على ربع حصة. ارتقيت ببطء لكن بثبات وانتهى بي المطاف بالفوز بنصف حصة حيث بدأ الناس يدركون أنني أمتلك صوتًا حلوًا. كان عملي على متن السفينة مزدوجًا. كنت «السيب»، أسحب الغواصين من البحر بالحبال، وكنت أغني.*

بول: هل تذهب إلى البحر دائمًا مع نفس الطاقم؟

أبو صالح: *نعم ، دائمًا مع نفس الطاقم. كانوا عضيرتي وعائلتي. في نهاية مسيرتي المهنية، وخلال رحلتي الأخيرة، كان هناك ٥٠ غواصًا و ٤٠ سيبًا[٥] على متن السفينة أي ما مجموعه ٩٠ من أفراد الطاقم. كان أفضل طاقم عرفته على الإطلاق. أبحرت معهم لمدة أربع سنوات قبل أن اعتزل العمل.*

بول: ماذا كنت تعمل قبل موسم صيد اللؤلؤ وبعده؟

أبو صالح: *يا الله، كنا نصطاد، نعمل في الإسكان، أو ننقل المياه من البصرة.اشتغلنا في كل عمل توجد حاجة إليه. وذات يوم أرسل لنا الله النفط مما سمح لنا بالراحة. لقد عينت في الخدمة العمومية ومنذ ذلك الحين ونحن نعمل بها.*

بول: هل كان دخلك خلال موسم صيد اللؤلؤ يكفيك ويكفي عائلتك؟

أبو صالح: *نعم. كان بامكاني كسب ما يصل إلى ٥٠ روبية[٦] (لرحلة بحرية واحدة ولكن كقرض يعطيني إياه القبطان. وهذا يسمح لي بالعيش لمدة أربعة أشهر تقريبًا وبقية الوقت أكون في البحر. ولحسن الحظ، فإن زوجتي مدبرة وليست مسرفة مثلي، وقد تجنبت القمار والممارسات الحمقاء الأخرى. أرسل الله لنا الكثير من النعم ولم يحرمنا شيئًا.*

بول: ألم تكن بحاجة إلى العمل بوظائف أخرى لزيادة دخلك كي تربي أطفالك، أو لتتيح لهم حياة مريحة؟

أبو صالح: *ليس بالضرورة، لكنني عملت في غير موسم صيد اللؤلؤ كعامل بناء وقمت ببعض الوظائف لأشغل نفسي قبل تلقي العروض الأولى للعمل في الرحلات التجارية. في هذه المرحلة ارتفع دخلي ونصيبي إلى واحد ونصف «قلاطة»[٧]. كان الغناء عملاً شاقًا وكان القباطنة يتصارعون من أجل محاولة الحصول على أفضل مطرب عن طريق المزايدة. ولا يقع عليك الاختيار عليك كنهام إلا من أجل صوتك.*

أبو صالح: *نعم قضى حياته في البحر والغوص. ذات مرة تشاجر مع النوخذة وجرح في أثناء المشاجرة. كان يعاني من ألم في صدره وكان يسعل دما. أخبره النوخذة أنه يجب عليه الغوص رغم ذلك لأنه أعطاه مقابل عمله. انتهى به الأمر إلى أن غطس لكن روحه فاضت إلى بارئها. ودفن في السفانية[1].*

بول: هل لديك أطفال؟

أبو صالح: *نعم، لدي سبعة أطفال. يعمل أحدهم في البلدية والآخر مدرسًا للجمباز. لا يفكرون أبدًا في أن يصبحوا بحارة أو في العيش في البحر. ليس من المفترض أن يهتم الأطفال بالبحر أو الغوص بحثًا عن اللؤلؤ. لقد عشت هذه الحياة ثم ربيتهم قدر الإمكان حتى يصلوا إلى حيث هم الآن.*

بول: متى بدأت حياتك في البحر؟

أبو صالح: *كنت في الثامنة من عمري عندما ذهبت إلى البحر للمرة الأولى. سجلوا اسمي على متن قارب صيد اللؤلؤ وتعلمت بالممارسة لعدة سنوات على السفينة. حينئذ عينت تبابًا (صبي بحار) لأنهم اعتبروا أن صوتي جميلًا. غنى كبار السن قبلي على السفينة وكنت أتبعهم وأغني من بعدهم..ثم ارتقيت سلم العمل وحصلت أخيرًا على نصيب من تلك الأنصبة التي توزع وفقًا للأنظمة المعمول بها على سفن صيد اللؤلؤ - أي ما يعادل نصف حصة الغطاس. انا نهام.*

بول: ألم تفكر في أن تصبح غواصًا؟

أبو صالح: *بالتأكيد فكرت، لكن القبطان رفض وأخبرني أنني إذا غطست، فإن إحساسي سيتغير. قال لي أنه ضحى بآلاف النقود من أجل صوتي الجميل، لا من أجل الغوص. يترك الماء المملح على جسم الغواص بقعًا وجروحًا لا يمحوها الغسيل. على رأسه وعلى أذنيه وعينيه وصدره وحتى أصابعه.*

بول: ما هي المدة التي قضيتها في صيد اللؤلؤ؟

أبو صالح: *أكثر أو أقل من ٢٠ عامًا.*

بول: متى قمت بآخر رحلة لصيد اللؤلؤ؟

أبو صالح: *آخر مرة ذهبت في رحلة لصيد اللؤلؤ، كنت مع طاحوس بن شديد[2]، منذ ما يقرب من ٢٢ عامًا. بعد ذلك كرست نفسي للسفر (في الرحلات التجارية).*

بول: عندما سافرت في رحلات تجارية، هل عينت نهامًا أيضًا؟

أبو صالح: *بالتأكيد، حدث ذلك.*

image 65

بول مطر: هلا قدمت نفسك؟

أبو صالح:
راشد بن صالح الجماز.

بول:كم عمرك؟

أبو صالح: *٧٠ عامًا.*

بول: ما عملك؟
أبو صالح: *أنا مسؤول عن حراسة مخزن تابع لوزارة الإعلام.*

بول: ماذا كان يعمل والدك؟

أبو صالح: *لم يكن لديه عمل. كان بحاراً.*

بول: هل كان غواصًا؟

اللآلئ التي تغني: بول مطر يتحدث مع أبو صالح في الكويت ١٩٧٨

بول مطر

توفيق كرباج

يحمل توفيق كرباج، المولود في بيروت، لبنان، درجة الدكتوراة في علم الموسيقى من جامعة كوبنهاجن حصل عليها عن رسالة بعنوان «إيقاعات موسيقى صيد اللؤلؤ،» مما يحيل بشكل مباشر إلى اهتماماته الرئيسية. كرباج هو رئيس قسم النظرية الموسيقية الشرقية بالمعهد الوطني اللبناني العالي للموسيقى منذ عام ١٩٨٨. كأستاذ، درس كرباج النظرية الموسيقية الشرقية والغربية كما درس التحليل والتأليف الموسيقي والغناء الأوبرالي وهو مستمر في تدريس المواد المذكورة حتى اليوم. عمل كرباج كمتعاون مع العديد من المؤتمرات العالمية المهتمة بالموسيقى الحديثة والموسيقى التقليدية في أوروبا والشرق الأوسط، وقد كتب العديد من الكتب المدرسية لصالح العديد من المؤسسات وهو مؤلف ومحرر عدة كتب مهتمة بالتاريخ ونظرية الموسيقى في الشرق الأوسط مثل كتابه المعروف «الموسيقى في البحرين: الموسيقى التقليدية في الخليج العربي.» كعازف ومؤلف موسيقي، قاد كرباج العديد من المغنين المرموقين والفرق الموسيقية الشرق أوسطية في حفلات حول العالم، ويظل شغله الشاغل هو اسهامه في حفظ الموسيقى عبر البحث ودراسة التراث الكلاسيكي والفلكلوري في العالم العربي، قديمه وحديثه.

[١] الجن –وهي لفظة تشير في معناها الأعم إلى الأرواح أو الشياطين، على حسب المصدر الواردة فيه- هي كائنات خارقة في الميثولوجيا واللاهوت الإسلاميين.

[٢] الجانب الشرقي من العالم العربي والواقع في غرب آسيا وشمال شرق أفريقيا، ويتكون من البحرين ومصر والعراق والأردن والعراق والكويت ولبنان وعمان وفلسطين وقطر والسعودية والسودان وسوريا والإمارات واليمن.

[٣]اسم مستقى من اللغة الفارسية يستخدم في وصف قبطان سفن صيد اللؤلؤ وأحياناً في وصف مالك السفينة.

[٤] في عام ١٩٢٨، بعد اختراع زراعة اللؤلؤ في اليابان وفي الوقت الذي بدأ فيه أسطول مراكب صيد اللؤلؤ في الخليج في الانخفاض، قدرت الإحصائيات الرسمية أعداد مراكب الأسطول في البحرين وحدها بأربعمائة مركب.

[٥] حرفياً تعني «البومة»

[٦] سمعياً تعني كلمة جالبوت «ها قد جاء القارب. «

[٧] تعبير عام يستخدم لوصف أغاني وترانيم البحر ويمكن استخدامه بشكل أكثر دقة للإشارة إلى أغاني العمل اعتماداً على الصياغة.

[٨] تعبير عام يستخدم للإشارة إلى أغاني التسلية التي تؤدى في فترات الراحة وإلى كل الموسيقى التي حفظت من الجن (في إشارة للأسطورة المذكورة سابقاً).

[٩] الأحواض الجافة هو مصطلح يشير إلى ساحات الخدمة حيث تؤخذ السفن للإصلاح. أثناء الرسو الجاف تؤخذ السفينة إلى الأحواض الجافة لفحص وتنظيف الأجزاء المغمورة من هيكل السفينة.

[١٠] شراع صغير على هيئة مثلث، يوجد أمام الشراع الرئيسي على المركب.

[١١] طبلة اسطوانية كبيرة مزدوجة الوجه برق من جلد الحيوانات. كل وجه من أوجه الطبلة متصل بأوتار ممنوعة من أمعاء الحيوانات. تلعب باستخدام عصا على أحد الأوجه وبالكف المفتوحة على الوجه الآخر. تعلق في الرقبة باستخدام حبل يبلغ طوله حوالي ٦٠ سم.

[١٢] في الموسيقى العربية، الموال هو نوع تقليدي وشاعري وشعبي من الغناء الغربي، بطيء الإيقاع وعاطفي الطبيعة ويتصف بتطويل حروف المد والغناء المؤثر وعادة ما يتم استخدامه كافتتاحية قبل بدء الأغنية.

[١٣] الزهيري هي قصيدة من سبعة أبيات وقافيتين. ينظم هذا النوع من الشعر بصرامة شديدة ويمثل أحد أكثر الأشكال الشعرية إثارة للاحترام والحب في الخليج العربي.

image 66

الأشرعة الضخمة، إلى موسيقى الدواري المذهلة التي تصحب الأعمال المتغيرة أبداً حول المرساة مستعيرة بعض العناصر من نوع الفجيري المنمق. النطاق الموسيقي واسع وغامض في ذات الوقت مما يترك الإمكانية لأعضاء الطاقم إما للتصفيق بأكفهم وإما باللعب فوق أباريق المياه حينما لا يكون مطلوب منهم القيام بأعمال.

تراث الغناء العربي، الجدلي والكلاسيكي، يكشف رابطاً شديد القوة بين الشعر وبين النغمات غير الموقعة والتي تدعى الموال[١٢]. الزهيري[١٣] هي قصيدة صغيرة مقارنة بالقصيدة التقليدية بسبعة أبيات وقافيتين وتستخدم غالباً في منطقة الخليج. هذا الشكل الشعري مبني بصرامة باستخدام قافية تعتمد على استخدام كلمة كاملة في نهاية كل كلمة ولكن بمعاني مختلفة، وهو الأعز على أذهان وأرواح العرب. أصبح شكل الموال -البالغ من العمر ألفاً من الأعوام- هو الشكل الغالب على الموسيقى المغناة في المنطقة. في أثناء رحلة صيد اللؤلؤ، قد يتعين على الطاقم أحياناً انتظار الرياح لتعود إلى أشرعتهم وتدفعهم من موقع للصيد إلى آخر. في سبيل تسلية أنفسهم، يوظف النهام كل خبرته الارتجالية لغناء أغنيات وأشعار شديدة الحزن تدفع الكثير من البحارة اللامبالين إلى البكاء.

تتكرر كلمة «يا مال» أكثر من مرة بصوت المغني المنفرد وترددها الأصوات العميقة من الكورال والتي تستلهم أعماق البحر. حالما يعود المجدفون إلى عملهم الشاق، يصبح زفيرهم العنيف الموقع مرة أخرى صحبتهم الوحيدة، مردداً للأبد في الخليج العربي أغنيات ملاحيه.

عن السداد بعدة أشهر مع نهاية الموسم. تتكرر هذه الدورة من عام إلى عام بحيث يبقى الطاقم مقيدين إلى مالك السفينة طوال حياتهم في نمط يشبه القنانة.

في حالة موت أحد أعضاء الطاقم أثناء الرحلة، يقوم النوخذة بضم صبي من عائلة الرجل المتوفي -من عمر ٩ و١٠ أعوام- ليقوم بأداء المهام الأساسية على السفينة قبل أن يصبح مستقبلاً عضواً كامل العضوية في الطاقم أو، كما في بعض الأحوال، غواص. كان الانتقاء من بين أقارب أعضاء الطاقم المتوفين هو وسيلة التوظيف المفضلة للغواصين. أما الرجال الذين كانوا يقومون بالأعمال على ظهر المركب وأعمال سحب الغواصين من الماء فكانوا عادة عبيد أفارقة متيني البنيان تم شرائهم من سوق زنجبار أو أتوا من سواحل شرق أفريقيا التي سيطر عليها العرب في تلك الآونة.

في الوقت الذي كانوا يدفعون فيه إلى تعاقد يوقعهم في دين مؤبد للقبطان وطواقمهم، كان الرجال يتزوجون كذلك ليتمكنوا من عيش حياة مريحة بالنظر إلى أجورهم المنخفضة الأمر الذي سمح لهم بتنظيم عمل هادئ نوعاً بين أعضاء الطاقم وملاك السفن المسئولين عن الرحلات. كانت بداية الموسم وليمة للعيون مع استعراض عدد هائل من انطلاقات السفن [٤] من قوارب البوم [٥] وأسطول من قوارب الجالبوت ذات الحجم العادي. [٦]

كان يتم الاستعانة بمغن محترف واحد على الأقل للمركب. تشارك العرب مع الإغريق القدماء الاعتقاد القوي بوجود وحوش البحر والحوريات والكائنات الخرافية الأخرى التي سكنت أعماق البحر الغامضة، لذلك يطلق على المغني «نهام» في إشارة واضحة إلى «النهم» -وحش من وحوش البحر في العربية. كان المغنون مسئولون عن التغطية على كافة الأصوات الأخرى خلال الرحلة باستخدام أصواتهم؛ بالنظر إلى اندماج أصوات طاقم السفينة في الغناء الجماعي، يحتاج المغنون الفرديون إلى مجهود رهيب ليجعلوا أصواتهم مسموعة بين أصوات الكورال العالية والإيقاعات والتصفيقات الشرسة وغير المنتظمة المميزة لهذا النوع الموسيقي الجميل. في بعض السفن الأكبر كان يتم الاستعانة بعدد قد يبلغ أربعة مغنين للرحلة، لكن النهام لا يغني أبداً فوق صوت زميله، بدلاً من ذلك كانوا يتناوبون في إطلاق الأصوات.

يتناوب المغنون بحيث يحددوا إيقاع حياة الطاقم اليومية مؤدين في الأثناء أنواعاً فرعية مختلفة من الموسيقى مثل البحري [٧] المرتبطة بالعمل، والفجيري [٨] المرتبطة بأوقات الاسترخاء في البحر.

كانت المهام المختلفة في أثناء الرحلة مصحوبة دائماً بالغناء والإيقاع وموشاة بالابتهاج الصوتي القوي للطاقم في أعقاب أنشطة مثل اطلاق المجاديف الثقيلة في البحر. الفارق الرئيسي الذي يميز بين الموسيقى المرتبطة بالعمل (البحري) والمرتبطة بالراحة (الفجيري) هو أن في الوقت الذي ينشغل فيه الرجال بالتجديف والتحكم في الأشرعة أو بالمهام الأخرى المتطلبة بدنياً فإن البحري هو الأنسب بسبب افتقاره للأدوات الموسيقية في حين يوظف الفجيري مجموعة إيقاعية داخل وصلات غواصي اللؤلؤ حيث يتوفر عدد من أعضاء الطاقم للعب الآلات الإيقاعية. الاستثناء الوحيد لهذه الثنائية يحدث في نهاية رحلة الصيد حينما يعيد الرجال المراكب إلى الأحواض الجافة [٩]. في هذه الحالة تحمل الآلات إلى الشاطئ وقد يستخدمها بعض أعضاء الطاقم في أداء نوع موسيقي فرعي يسمى السنجني.

تختلف أنماط الغناء والأنغام والإيقاعات بشكل كبير بين كل نوع من الأنواع الموسيقية المتفرعة من موسيقى غواصي اللؤلؤ. لكن وعلى الرغم من اختلافهم موسيقياً، تتداخل بعض الأغنيات أحياناً طبقاً للغرض المقصود والسياق، الإقلاع بالمركب على سبيل المثال. مع مرور الزمن ظهرت استثناءات عديدة جعلت بعض أغاني البحري تستعين بآلات فيما خلت بعض أغاني الفجيري منها، مما يجعل تحديد الأنواع الموسيقية أصعب بالنسبة للأذن غير الخبيرة. عادة تصنف الأغنيات طبقاً لإيقاعها وأسلوب غنائها.

كنتيجة لأهمية الموسيقى في هذا السياق البحري، تمنح الدورة الإيقاعية المصاحبة لفرد شراع الجب [١٠] أحياناً مجموعة كاملة من أدوات الإيقاع المصاحبة، في حين تصحب في أحيان أخرى بطبلة وحيدة كبيرة تدعى طبل العود [١١] والصنج، الأمر الذي يوضح التنويعات المحتملة داخل ذات النوع الفرعي من أغنيات غواصي اللؤلؤ.

الوصلات الموسيقية لغواصي اللؤلؤ غنية بالأغاني؛ من أغاني العمل مثل «خطفة الشراع» والتي تشير إلى طي

كبر الأصدقاء الثلاثة في السن لكنهم استمروا في اللقاء للغناء وأداء الأغنيات التي تعلموها من الكائنات الخرافية. مع مرور الوقت مات أحدهم وتلاه ثانٍ وبقي الثالث وحيداً. منقطعاً عن أصدقاءه الذين غادروه للموت، فكر العجوز في مشاركة أغنيات الجن مع أسرته حيث كان قد بدأ بالفعل في فقدان بصره وسمعه.

مقتنعاً بأنه لم يبق له شيء ليخسره، قرر الثالث أن يشارك القصص والأسرار الموسيقية مع أحباءه. لكن بعد كسر قسمه مباشرة، فقد العجوز بصره كليةً ومات بسبب حنثه بيمينه للجن. غير أنه عن غير قصد كان قد بذر بالفعل بذرة الموسيقى التي سيشار إليها في بعد بموسيقى غواصي اللؤلؤ.

على مدار تاريخ المشرق تخبرنا حوليات الموسيقيين العرب عن أغاني استعيرت نغماتها من الأديرة وتحولت إلى أغانٍ علمانية.

على الرغم من أن أغلب أغاني غواصي اللؤلؤ وموسيقاهم قد تكون أقرب للأسطورة منها للحقيقة فإن أغلب التفاصيل حقيقية ويمكن التحقق منها، على الأقل بالمعنى الموسيقي.

إلى جوار الغوص والصيد، يعتمد تراث صيد اللؤلؤ على مجموعة محددة ومتطلبة من مهارات الملاحة والجلد على النقيض من المعتقد السائد من أن موسم الصيد يدين باستمراريته إلى الحظ وحده. في ذلك الزمن، حددت التقاليد والعمليات المستقرة إيقاع حياة طواقم غواصي اللؤلؤ حيث يتم توظيف طاقم الغواصين وبقية عمال الطاقم سنوياً بالنظر إلى الديون التي يدينون بها للنواخذة. عبر احتجاز دفعات أجور الغواصين الأفقر في بداية الموسم، حيث لم يتم بيع اللؤلؤ بعد، يراكم الغواصون الديون عند مالك السفينة ليتمكنوا من توفير المعاش لأسرهم خلال الوقت الذي يقضونه في البحر. يتم تأجيل الديون من شهر إلى شهر بحيث يبقى الغواصون وأعضاء الطاقم متأخرين

image 1

قصة غواصي اللؤلؤ في الخليج قديمة قدم الزمان ذاته، قصة تبدو وكأنها قصة جنيات فانتازية وساحرة مغزولة من عناصر طبيعية وخوارقية كمقطع ذو بريق لؤلؤي من ألف ليلة وليلة. لكن الواقع أكثر مشقة من ذلك بكثير، فقصص غواصي اللؤلؤ هي قصص رحلات لا تنتهي وجَلَد على مدار شهور من الإبحار بطول شواطئ بحر العرب.

تبدأ الرحلة بظهور نجوم برج الثور في المساء قرب نهاية شهر مايو وتستمر حتى نهاية شهر سبتمبر مع رؤية برج الميزان في الأفق عند الفجر. أحياناً قد يمتد موسم صيد اللؤلؤ إلى شهر أكتوبر أو حتى نوفمبر، اعتماداً على الجو واستمرار هبوب الريح.

يدعى موسم الغطس العادي الغوص الكبير، فيما يدعى امتداده في فصل الشتاء بالغوص الصغير.

أسطورة البيت المهجور – نشأة موسيقى غواصي اللؤلؤ

في في يوم من الأيام، وبينما يتجول ثلاثة أصدقاء سوياً بعيداً عن حيهم، صك مسامعهم أصوات غريبة وإنشاد يصعد من أحد البيوت المهجورة العديدة في المنطقة. توارى الخوف الذي شعروا به بدايةً وهم يقتربون من البيت وفتنوا بالموسيقى المميزة. سيعود الأصدقاء الثلاثة للمكان مراراً للاستماع إلى هذه الأغنيات الغريبة.

في أحد الأيام، قرر الأصدقاء دخول البيت المهجور. من الصعب تبين الحقيقي من الخيالي في هذه القصة حيث يؤمن البعض بأن الرجال الثلاثة قابلوا جن في هذا البيت وشاركوا في الرقص والاحتفالات عدة مرات حتى تمكنوا من إتقان جزء كبير من الأغاني والإيقاعات التي اجتذبتهم إلى البيت للمرة الأولى. لكن الجن حذروهم من إعادة انتاج هذه الموسيقى لأي شخصٍ كان أثناء حياتهم لكيلا يضربوا بالعمى.

image 2

قصص وأساطير في أناشيد غواصي اللؤلؤ

توفيق كرباج

فلي

تُعتبر فلي (FLEE) ، والتي أسسها آلان مارزو وأوليفييه دوبورت وكارل أونبرينك ، منصة هندسة ثقافية مستقلة تتخصص في توثيق الثقافات الهجينة وتعزيزها. تعمل هذه المنصة ذات التخصصات المتنوعة كعلامة تسجيل ودار نشر ومنتج معارض. تسلّط منصة فلي (FLEE) الضوء على الظواهر الثقافية المختارة ذاتيًا ، ذلك من خلال البحث والتركيز على خصال العولمة بشكل خلاق من منظور تاريخي ، ومع جعل كل الاستنتاجات تتفاعل مع الأساليب الفنية المعاصرة.

[١] الاسم العام لقوارب الإبحار التقليدية المستخدمة في البحر الأحمر ومنطقة الخليج الهندي.

[٢] كوخ صغير بجوار الشاطئ حيث يلتقي البحارة للثرثرة وشرب الشاي والقهوة وبالأساس للموسيقى والغناء.

[٣] محمية بريطانية سمحت بدرجات متنوعة من السيطرة السياسية والاقتصادية على عدة دول في الخليج العربي حتى ١٩٧٤، بما في ذلك ما يعرف اليوم بالإمارات العربية المتحدة وفي أوقات مختلفة أجزاء جنوبية من فارس والبحرين والكويت وعمان وقطر.

والأغاني لاحقاً إلى الاختيار الدقيق على يد فنانين كان عليهم تخيل مؤلفات موسيقية جديدة في هيئة رحلة صيد لؤلؤ صوتية جديدة.

تجعل السياقات التاريخية الاستقطابية الحوار الاشتمالي، العابر للثقافات والأجيال أكثر أهمية من أي وقت مضى. في ذات الوقت فإنها تخلق منصة للتبادل تلتقط روح منطقة الخليج وتاريخها كنقطة لقاء. باستخدام كلمات عالم اللاهوت تشارلز ستانج محللاً ما يعتقده تعددية دينية تاريخية في المنطقة، «هذا التاريخ من المفترض أن يرينا الرهبان والزهاد في الخليج كجزء من تاريخ أكبر للتنوع والتعددية في المنطقة، ليس مفاجئاً في الواقع، باعتبار أن الخليج، من بين العديد من الأشياء، هو سلسلة من الموانئ، تبودل فيها ليس فقط البضائع ولكن الأفكار كذلك...» بهذا الخصوص، وبوجود أفكار ووجهات نظر نظر متنوعة وأحياناً متضاربة، فإن هذا المشروع يسائل الديناميات المتعلقة بالتراث الثقافي وحمايته والترويج له إلى جانب عمليات «صنع التراث» المتنوعة. يسعى الكتاب إلى رسم صورة كبيرة لهذه الظاهرة وتاريخها وثقافتها و، في المقام الأول، موسيقاها. يتحقق ذلك عن طريق الابحار بين المناهج والوسائط المتنوعة وتفادي المقاربات المجمدة نحو ثقافة متعددة الأوجه.

«هل خاطروا جميعاً بحياتهم حقاً، ليل ونهار، من أجل لسحة من حاية صغيرة براقة؟ حتى يستطيع ملك ما في بلد بعيد أن يستعرضها على شخصه غير عالم كم شخص عاش وقضى في سبيل استخراجها من البحر؟ هل كان حقيقياً أنهم جميعاً كانوا عبيداً لسيد واحد، اللؤلؤ؟» هذه الأسئلة التي أثارتها الفنانة منيرة القديري أسئلة فاصلة، حيث أنهم في النهاية يستكشفون مفهوم الجمال؛ قدرته على إلهام طقوس وممارسات عميقة وساحرة، وقدرته على أن يكون مركزاً لديناميات سلطة مستغلة أحياناً، وتسليعه وتواجده في القلب من نظام اقتصادي عالمي. هناك، في قلب البحر، تصبح اللؤلؤة البراقة مرآة شديدة الوضوح، مرآة تعكس الطبيعة البشرية مصائرها وادماناتها:

«ياللصيادون البؤساء! سذج في البداية وكسح لاحقاً، تلك هي قسمتهم. أما بالنسبة لمالهم، فإنهم يغنونه بينما يأخذه آخرون.» آلبرت لوندرس، صيادون اللؤلؤ، ١٩٣١

الأيام. باعتباره صياد لؤلؤ تقليدي، فإن رحلته شديدة التفرد بين الاكتشافات العلمية والمقاربات المبدعة لصناعة اللؤلؤ تقدم منظوراً بديلاً لمستقبل صيد اللؤلؤ.

بعيداً عن اختلافاتهم، فإن الالتزام القوي لنقل هذا التراث إلى الجيل القادم يجمع هؤلاء الخبراء والفنانين والفاعلين المختلفين الذين شاركوا في هذا المشروع. في القلب من هذا المسعى نجد الرائد علي، عسكري سابق اهتزت حياته في حرب الخليج الأولى وهاله تأثيرها البشع على النظام البيئي الهش للمنطقة. بعد هذه التجربة الصادمة، أصبح الرائد رئيساً لمجموعة الإمارات للبيئة البحرية. من خلال هذا الدور، يسعى الرائد إلى توعية الأجيال الجديدة بثقافتهم الخاصة بينما يذكرهم بهشاشة البيئة وتحديداً مهاد المحار، في حوار استغراقي، يركز هذا الابن الروحي لجاك إيف كوستو على ما يعتبره تحديات مترابطة بحماية المحار ونظامهم البيئي في المنطقة.

حماية التراث الثقافي والمحافظة عليه موضوعٌ صعب وعادة ما يؤدي إلى مواقف قطبية. في البحرين تتحدث نورا السايح، مديرة برنامج مسار اللؤلؤ، عن رؤيتها واستراتيجيتها لتكريم والترويج لإرث صيد اللؤلؤ عبر الهندسة الحضرية وإعادة تنشيط المحرق باعتبارها مساراً حضرياً كان يقع في القلب من صناعة اللؤلؤ الخليجية في ذات يوم. المعمارية الموهوبة المكلفة بمهمة معقدة تشرح كيف تحاول حماية التراث الثقافي والمحافظة عليه موضوعٌ صعب وعادة ما يؤدي إلى مواقف قطبية. في البحرين تتحدث نورا السايح، مديرة برنامج مسار اللؤلؤ، عن رؤيتها واستراتيجيتها لتكريم والترويج لإرث صيد اللؤلؤ عبر الهندسة الحضرية وإعادة تنشيط المحرق باعتبارها مساراً حضرياً كان يقع في القلب من صناعة اللؤلؤ الخليجية في ذات يوم. المعمارية الموهوبة المكلفة بمهمة معقدة تشرح كيف تحاول انجاز مهمتها بينما تجد طريقها عبر تحديات متنوعة من بينها المجازفة بالإخلال بالتوازن الحيوي الخاص بالمجتمعات التي تعيش في المنطقة في مدن وبلدان أكثر تركيزاً على الحداثة والتكنولوجيا.

بينما توثق هذه المبادرة صيد اللؤلؤ والثقافة المرتبطة به من خلال منظور نفسي واجتماعي-تاريخي واقتصادي، فإنها تهدف أيضاً إلى إعطاء المساحة للفنانين المفاهميين والمشتغلين عبر الوسائط المعنيين بمنطقة الخليج. في هذا السياق تستكشف تالين هزبر في عملها تسرب اللآلئ قاع البحر وتطوره. تحاول هزبر عبر الهيكل الذي أبدعته وغطسته في الماء في محاكاة لرحلة محارة أن تستنطق مهاد المحار بينما تستخدم الزمن كأداة تشكيل رئيسية لمنحوتاتها البحرية.

منحوتات منيرة القديري كذلك يشكلها الزمن، رمزياً على الأقل. في الواقع، فإن القطع المنمقة والهشة التي صنعتها للمشروع تبدو وكأنها تمثل فراغ زمني خلالي بين فترتين رئيسيتين من النماذج الاقتصادية أثرتا في دول الخليج: تجارة اللؤلؤ وانفجار النفط. بمنحوتة تمثل نصف لؤلؤة ونصف من حفارات البترول وباستخدام مواد ملونة شديدة التهجين والإبداع، يبدو أن الفنانة الكويتية تقترح أنه سيكون على المنطقة التصالح مع ماضيها وتاريخها الحديث للمضي قدماً.

إنه نفس ذلك التاريخ، أو على الأقل الخطابات المتعلقة به، هو ما يسائله حسن الحجيري في مقاله العابر للوسائط وبرمجية الموسيقى التي يطورها ليتسامى عما يسميه «خيبات». تدعونا أعمال الحجيري لتحدي المقاربات شديدة البلاهة عادة تجاه الاحتفال بالفجيري وسردية صيد اللؤلؤ. داعياً القارئ إلى تفادي الفهم الرومانسي الساذج للموضوع، يذكر الحجيري الجميع بأن «بنيت صناعة اللؤلؤ بأكملها والثقافات المرتبطة بها على الاستغلال والعبودية، ومع ذلك يتم الاحتفال بهم علانية دون إقرار لتواريخها المظلمة.»

بالطبع يختلف أن تتحدث عن موضوع من خلال مناظير ومناهج متنوعة عن أن تختبره مباشر. في سبيل أن نتمكن من إدراك الأمر في كليته، يحتوي هذا المشروع أعمال مجمعة عن موسيقى صيد اللؤلؤ تتكون من تسجيلات غير مفصح عنها تنتمي إلى باحث الموسيقى الإثنية بول روفسينج أولسن، أول شخص يقوم بتسجيل هذا النوع الموسيقي. ضم هذه التسجيلات غير المحررة عن وعي إلى المجموعة يعيد تدوين حدة ومعنى هذه الموسيقى التي أداها رجال تركوا حيواتهم على الشاطئ لشهور دون التوقف بينما يبحثون عن تلك اللآلئ النادرة الثمينة في البحر. متأثرة بثقافات من حول العالم، خضعت الإيقاعات

مياه ضحلة

الشمس تصبغ الأفق بدرجة من الأصفر الذابل في تلك العصرية من شهر ديسمبر بينما ترسو عدة داوات[1] محطمة على شواطئ المحرق. بقايا هامدة لعهد مضى حينما كان الخليج العربي يزخر بالحركة اللاهبة في موسم صيد اللؤلؤ. اليوم، لا تثير هذه البقايا أي شيء سوى لامبالاة السيارات المارة على الطريق السريع المزدحم المؤدي إلى مطار المنامة. رمز مثالي لعالمين لم يتعايشا حقاً ضمن واقع إقليمي واحد: النفط واللآلئ.

لكن على بعد مئات الأمتار، يقبع داو فخيم في الرسو الجاف بانتظار الإصلاحات بينما ينتظر إرث صيد اللؤلؤ عودةً طال أمد استحقاقها. على الرغم من احتفاظه بمكانته الثقافية فإن صيد اللؤلؤ، الذي أصيب باختراع اللآلئ المزروعة علي يد كوكيتشي ميكيموتو ودمره اكتشاف النفط في المنطقة، لم يتمكن أبداً من التعافي بشكل كلي من هذه الضربات.

على الناحية الأخرى من، هناك طريق ضيق يقود إلى الشوارع القديمة المتعرجة لمركز تجارة اللؤلؤ القديم الذي كانته المحرق يوماً ما. في الليل، يتردد صدى الغناء متعدد النغمات والإيقاع المميز في تلك الشوارع. في أحد دور القهوة[2] المرممة، تجتمع أحد فرق موسيقى صيد اللؤلؤ القليلة الباقية ليحتفلوا بالإرث الموسيقي لأجدادهم.

يعرف الجميع حول الخليج عن هذه الأصوات. باعتبارها جزء رئيسي من هوية المنطقة، فموسيقى وأغاني صيادي اللؤلؤ هي إرث هذه الكتلة السكانية المليئة بالحياة والتي واجهت حياة من الشظف على ضفاف هذا البحر المتقلب. هذه الممارسات الموسيقية المحددة التي يشار إليها بفن البحري، أو الفجيري، ساهمت بشدة في موروث صيد اللؤلؤ المحلي.

بعد قرون من السبات، تتصاعد شعبية اللآلئ بانتظام مدفوعة بتقنيات الغوص والمسح المتقدمة والحاجة الماسة للتنويع في نموذج اقتصادي متحجر.

يحاول كتابنا هذا تتبع هذا الإرث ليصل إلى أصوله في سبيل فهم تطوره المعاصر والتحديات التي يواجهها في عمل عابر للتخصصات يحيل إلى عدد من الشخصيات ووجهات النظر شارحاً، وواصفاً ومشكلاً للظاهرة الاجتماعية والثقافية المعقدة التي هي صيد اللؤلؤ.

يقود هذه الرحلة المؤلف الموسيقي وخبير موسيقى صيد اللؤلؤ المعروف توفيق كرباج مخبراً إيانا القصص والأساطير التي مهدت الطريق للفجيري كما نعرفه اليوم. عبر تفكيك المعتقدات التي أدت إلى ظهورها وتحليل بنيتها، يقدم لنا كرباج جولة حقيقية في هذه الأغنيات. ومن قد يعطينا تصور مباشر عما تعنيه هذه الموسيقى خير من نهام؟ عمل أبو صالح كمغني رئيسي على قارب داو في منتصف القرن العشرين في الكويت والبحرين. في حوار يعود إلى عام ١٩٧٩، مستلهماً خبرته الخاصة كمغني في العديد من الرحلات، يشارك أبو صالح مع الباحث بول مطر وجهة نظره في الحقبة المنطوية.

باعتباره نقطة مرور رئيسية بالنسبة للعديد من التجار والمسافرين، شهد بحر الخليج على الإقبال العالمي على موارده الطبيعية، اللؤلؤ على وجه الخصوص. من العلاقات المعقدة مع الحكم البريطاني، إلى تدفق المهاجرين الهائل، يصور دكتور مارك هوبز كيف بنى اقتصاد معولم يتمحور حول النفط نفسه وازدهر بدرجة مهولة لرخاء البعض وشقاء البعض الآخر. عبر التدقيق وإعادة اكتشاف العديد من الأرشيفات من الإقامات السياسية السابقة في الخليج العربي[3] ، يحل هوبز شفرة التجارة العالمية بين الفاعلين من الشرق والغرب العالميين المتحدين جميعاً في الخليج. في مفترق الطرق بين هذه المبادلات، ظلت عائلة مطر، واحدة من أهم عائلات تجار اللؤلؤ في البحرين، تقدر وتتاجر في اللؤلؤ الطبيعي لقرون. يشارك طلال مطر، عازف متحمس لموسيقى صيد اللؤلؤ ومدير أعمال العائلة، أفكاره عن الثقافة الموسيقية المحلية بينما يتدبر انهيار صناعة صيد اللؤلؤ المحلية بأكملها خلال القرن العشرين.

إلى الشرق، وعلى أطراف مركز تجارة اللؤلؤ السابق الذي كانته رأس الخيمة، يقوم عبدالله السويدي على مزرعة اللؤلؤ خاصته في خليج الرمس المكلل بأشجار الأيكة الساحلية عند سفح جبال الهجر المهيبة. كان السويدي الوحيد الذي كسر الحاجز الرمزي لزراعة اللؤلؤ في الخليج، النشاط الذي يمثل نهاية صناعة كانت عظيمة في يوم من

مياه ضحلة

أوليفييه دوبورت
آلان مارزو

نهمة: بوليفونية خليجية